LEADERSHIP
FOR THE
VIOLENT
LAST
DAYS

LEADERSHIP

FOR THE

VIOLENT LAST DAYS

LDS GUIDE FOR SURVIVING THE DARK YEARS TO COME

GEORGE POTTER

ISBN 13: 978-1-4621-4102-9

Published by CFI, an imprint of Cedar Fort, Inc.
2373 W. 700 S., Springville, UT 84663
Distributed by Cedar Fort, Inc., www.cedarfort.com

Library of Congress Control Number: 2021946175

Cover design by Shawnda T. Craig
Cover design © 2021 Cedar Fort, Inc.
Edited and typeset by Valene Wood

Printed in the United States of America

10 9 8 7 6 5 4 3 2 1

Printed on acid-free paper

To my great-grandfather
Scipio A. Kenner

Other Books by George Potter
Available at cedarfort.com

Lehi in the Wilderness

Ten More Amazing Discoveries

Nephi in the Promised Land

The Wise Men of Bountiful

The White Bedouin

The Voyages of the Book of Mormon

Discovering the Amazing Jaredites

Acknowledgments

I am grateful to Richard Whaley, Dennis Jacobson, and Gary Roberts for sharing their thoughts on leadership and encouraging me during the creation of this guide. They are natural leaders, great friends, and very good souls.

Contents

Introduction: Welcome to the Dark Future 1

PART ONE
8 Principles for Leadership during the Great Tribulation **21**

Principle 1: Prayer Driven Leadership 23
Principle 2: Defeating Secret Combinations
            Through Patriarchal Leadership 33
Principle 3: Equality with Meritocracy 63
Principle 4: Take Action against Violence and Evil NOW! 85
Principle 5: Don't Be Afraid and Don't Back Down 103
Principle 6: Be Guided by a Higher Purpose 129
Principle 7: Next Man Up—Next Women Up 145
Principle 8: Be Humble but Be Excellent 159

PART TWO
Preparing to Lead in the End of Days **179**

Chapter 9: Physical Preparedness
            and Building a Zion Community 181
Chapter 10: Emotional Preparedness to
            Overcome Satan's Demons 195
Chapter 11: Spiritual Preparedness—
            Leading in Righteousness 219

Conclusion 239
About the Author 251

*You will hear of magnificent cities,
now idolized by the people, sinking in
the earth, entombing the inhabitants.
The sea will heave itself beyond its
bounds, engulfing mighty cities.
Famine will spread over the nations,
and nations will rise up against
nation, kingdom against kingdom,
and states against states, in our own
country and in foreign lands.*

—Brigham Young, *JD*, vol. 8, 123

*The greatest leader is not necessarily
the one who does the greatest things.
He is the one that gets the people to do
the greatest things.*

—Ronald Reagan

Introduction

Welcome to the Dark Future

PRESIDENT RUSSELL M. NELSON OPENED THE APRIL 2021 GENERAL Conference with these words, "I also understand better now what He meant when He said, 'Behold I will hasten my work in its time' (D&C 88:73). Over and over again I have rejoiced as He has directed and executed the hastening of His work."[1] While our beloved prophet explained "what" is happening in our day, the Lord explained "why" the work needs to be hastened: "Because iniquity shall abound, the love of many shall wax cold. But he that shall endure unto the end, the same shall be saved. . . . For then shall be great tribulation, such as was not since the beginning of the world to this time, no, nor ever shall be. And except those days should be shortened, there should no flesh be saved: but for the elect's sake those days shall be shortened" (Matthew 24:12–13, 21–22). Compounding the trials of the extremely difficult times ahead is an alarming void of effective leadership in today's families, communities and nations. We are entering stormy waters and except for our divinely inspired church leaders, there are few able captains at the helms to guide our communities to safe harbors.

As abysmal and challenging as the years will be preceding the great and dreadful day of the Second Coming, if one has faith in Jesus Christ and is prepared, he or she need not fear. Isaiah reassured

---

1. Russell M. Nelson, "Welcome Message," April 2021 general conference.

1

the righteous, "Say to them that are of a fearful heart, Be strong, fear not: behold, your God will come with vengeance, even God with a recompence; he will come and save you" (Isaiah 35:4). Indeed, if leaders can build Zion communities based on celestial principles, they shall rejoice for "it shall be said among the wicked: Let us not go up to battle against Zion, for the inhabitants of Zion are terrible; wherefore we cannot stand. And it shall come to pass that the righteous shall be gathered out from among all nations, and shall come to Zion, singing with songs of everlasting joy" (D&C 45:70–71).

Modern revelation tells us that the land of Zion will be called the New Jerusalem, "a land of peace, a city of refuge, a place of safety for the Saints of the Most High God; And the glory of the Lord shall be there, and the terror of the Lord also shall be there, insomuch that the wicked will not come unto it, and it shall be called Zion. And it shall come to pass among the wicked, that every man that will not take his sword against his neighbor must needs flee unto Zion for safety" (D&C 45:66–68). However, we know that the Saints will endure the violence of a wicked world before the New Jerusalem is built. Furthermore, during such conditions it is likely that not all the Saints who are now spread throughout the world will be able to gather to the safety of the New Jerusalem or even survive the violence (Revelation 6:9). If we are found outside Zion gates, President Russell M. Nelson has reminded us. "[W]hat is the Lord willing to *do* for Israel? The Lord has pledged that He will 'fight [our] battles, and [our] children's [battles] . . . to the third and fourth generation'! (see D&C 98:37; Psalm 31:23; Isaiah 49:25; D&C 105:14)."[2]

THE GREAT LEADERSHIP CHALLENGE

The safety and refuge of Zion is not made of brick and mortar. It is a community molded from the pure hearts of its people (D&C 97:12). It is a community that is based on the laws of the celestial kingdom (D&C 105:5, 32). The leadership challenge facing the Latter-day

---

2. Russell M. Nelson, "Let God Prevail," November 2020 general conference.

Saints is how can they help their people survive the bloody calamities in years to come and at the same time prepare to lead as righteous administers in the Kingdom of Heaven. Apostle James E. Talmage wrote:

> The Kingdom of Heaven is the divinely ordained system of government and dominion in all matters, temporal and spiritual; this will be established on earth only when its rightful Head, the King of kings, Jesus the Christ, comes to reign. His administration will be one of order, operated through the agency of His commissioned representatives invested with the Holy Priesthood. When Christ appears in His glory, and not before, will be realized a complete fulfillment of his supplication: "Thy kingdom come. They will be done in earth, as it is in heaven."[3]

President Henry B. Eyring has encouraged us:

> Every day, we are approaching closer to the glorious moment when the Savior Jesus Christ will come to earth again. We know something of the terrible events that will precede His coming, yet our hearts swell with joy and confidence also knowing of the glorious promises that will be fulfilled before He returns.
>
> . . . Here is the Lord's revealed description of what would happen in this last dispensation of the fullness of times:
>
> "And that day shall come that the earth shall rest, but before that day the heavens shall be darkened, and a veil of darkness shall cover the earth; and the heavens shall shake, and also the earth; and great tribulations shall be among the children of men, *but my people will I preserve*."[4]

While the primary focus of this book is to prepare leaders for overcoming the challenges of an ever more wicked and dangerous future, it should be remembered that these trials will help leaders prepare to

---

3. James E Talmage, *Jesus the Christ* (Salt Lake City: The Church of Jesus Christ of Latter-day Saints, 1981), 788–789.
4. Henry B. Eyring, "Sisters in Zion," October 2020 general conference.

administer in a glorious kingdom ruled over by our Lord. As you read on, remember the inspired text of William W. Phelps, "Come Let Us Rejoice" (3rd verse).

> In faith we'll rely on the arm of Jehovah
> To guide thru these last days of trouble and gloom,
> And after the scourges and harvest are over,
> We'll rise with the just when the Savior doth come.
>
> Then all that was promised the Saints will be given,
> And they will be crown'd with the angels of heav'n,
> And earth will appear as the Garden of Eden,
> And Christ and his people will ever be one.[5]

LEADERSHIP IN A DARK FUTURE

Whether the tremulous years of the prophesized Great Tribulation begin with lawless mobs taking over our cities, comets hitting the earth, nuclear wars, deadly plagues, solar bursts, massive earthquakes, global famines, unquenchable wildfires, or any other events, the reality is that you could wake up tomorrow in a very dangerous and very alien world. While the events portrayed in The Revelation of St. John and other scriptures depicted tangible calamities, the greater danger will be the underlying spiritual battle likened even to what unfolded in the preexistence. Joseph Smith declared in reference to The Revelation of St. John the Divine, "that which is temporal in the likeness of that which is spiritual" (D&C 77:2).

In reference to the book of Revelation, the Lord warned the Gentiles in the last days that if they did not repent, they would be "brought down into captivity, and also into destruction, both temporally and spiritually, according to the captivity of the devil" (1 Nephi 14:7; see also verses 26–27). Thus, we can be certain in the years prior to the Second Coming, Satan will fight with all his evil powers to try to impede the glorious coming of our Lord. Undoubtedly, it will take daily miracles and exceptional leadership to overcome the trials that

---

5. William W. Phelps, "Come Let Us Rejoice," *Hymns*, no. 3.

are soon to come. Are you prepared to lead in what will be a new and violent reality?

At 32 years old, I was already a Senior Vice President of a multinational corporation; then, at 36, the Managing Director of a European organization. For the last 27 years, I have served as an executive leadership consultant for one of the largest organizations in the world. On the one hand, I know the leadership competencies that are necessary to grow an organization in today's global market place. On the other hand, I also realize that today's leadership competencies will not suffice to tomorrow's dark future. Very distinctive leadership skills will be required if you expect to have your family and your community survive what is coming. The leadership principles found in this book have been proven to be effective in satanic situations similar to what can be expected to prevail at the end of the latter days.

Now is the time to prepare to lead. The good old days will soon be are gone, and gone for good. The Lord declared of the tribulation of the last day:

> And Jesus answered and said unto them, Take heed that no man deceive you.
>
> For many shall come in my name, saying, I am Christ; and shall deceive many.
>
> And ye shall hear of wars and rumors of wars: see that ye be not troubled: for all these things must come to pass, but the end is not yet.
>
> For nation shall rise against nation, and kingdom against kingdom: and there shall be famines, and pestilences, and earthquakes, in diverse places.
>
> All these are the beginning of sorrows.
>
> Then shall they deliver you up to be afflicted, and shall kill you: and ye shall be hated of all nations for my name's sake.
>
> And then shall many be offended, and shall betray one another, and shall hate one another.
>
> And many false prophets shall rise, and shall deceive many.
>
> And because iniquity shall abound, the love of many shall wax cold.

But he that shall endure unto the end, the same shall be saved. (Matthew 24:4–13)

The question that needs to be addressed is: "How can we endure to the end in such a violent, deceitful, and deranged world?" The principles taught in this book have been proven effective by people who actually led others through terrible situations and prevailed. Whether the initial cause of the violent years will be civil unrest, natural disasters, nuclear war, a killer plague, or a comet reaping worldwide destruction, the scriptures describe a dog-eat-dog world prior to the Second Coming of the Lord. President Ezra Taft Benson warned that among our enemies will be secret combinations:

> The Prophet Moroni described how the secret combinations would take over a country and then fight the work of God, persecute the righteous, and murder those who resisted. Moroni therefore proceeded to describe the workings of the ancient "secret combinations" so that modern man could recognize this great political conspiracy in the last days: "Wherefore, O ye Gentiles, it is wisdom in God that these things should be shown unto you, that thereby ye may repent of your sins, and suffer not that these murderous combinations shall get above you, which are built up to get power and gain—and the work, yea, even the work of destruction come upon you,
>
> "Wherefore, the Lord commandeth you, when ye shall see these things come among you that ye shall awake to a sense of your awful situation, because of this secret combination which shall be among you; . . .
>
> "For it cometh to pass that whoso buildeth it up seeketh to overthrow the freedom of *all* lands, nations and countries; and it bringeth to pass the destruction of *all* people, for it is built up by the devil, who is the father of all lies;[6]

A quick brainstorming session can identify numerous versions of today's Gadianton robbers. As the Lord's Second Coming draws closer and closer, Satan is attacking the children of God from every angle.

---

6. Ezra Taft Benson, in Conference Report, October 1961, 71–72.

Whether it is a communist government, street gangs controlling our neighborhood, anarchists, religious fanatics, drug and porn lords, corrupt police, or human traffickers, their objectives are the same—to destroy our families, communities, nations, and faith. In other words, Satan wants to create a hell on earth to hinder the glory of the coming of the Lord. How can you prevent him from winning? It will take smart leadership that understands how to defeat Satan's snares in a world filled with dark angels and evil powers.

WHAT CAN WE EXPECT FROM SATAN IN THE YEARS AHEAD?

As the Lord's Second Coming approaches, we can be certain Satan will use the same tactics he employed while trying to disrupt the Lord's First Coming in the flesh. Prior to the Lord's early ministry in Palestine, Satan planted the false doctrines and practices of the discriminatory Sadducees who even declared that there was no resurrection—*therefore no need for a redeemer*! He also nurtured the Pharisees whose very name denotes "separatists" or apart from others, instead of "being one" as Christ requires of His believers. In the New World, the Lamanite prophet Samuel warned the wicked Nephites six years before the birth of Jesus Christ:

> O that we had repented in the day that the word of the Lord came unto us; for behold the land is cursed, and all things are become slippery, and we cannot hold them. Behold, we are surrounded by demons, yea, we are encircled about by the angels of him who hath sought to destroy our souls. (Helaman 13:36–37)

Though there will be many signs and wonders observed before the Second Coming of Christ, these will do little to turn back the tide of wickedness and violence that will precede the glorious event. Within a few short years after the awe-inspiring sign of the Lord's birth, the night with no darkness, Satan had already regained the initiative in the war to impede the Lord's coming to the Nephites and Lamanites. We read:

And it came to pass that from this time forth there began to be lyings sent forth among the people, by Satan, to harden their hearts, to the intent that they might not believe in those signs and wonders which they had seen; . . .

. . . Gadianton robbers, who dwelt upon the mountains, who did infest the land; for so strong were their holds and their secret places that the people could not overpower them; therefore they did commit many murders, and did do much slaughter among the people.

. . . [T]here were many dissenters of the Nephites who did flee unto them [Gadianton robbers], which did cause much sorrow unto those Nephites who did remain in the land.

And there was also a cause of much sorrow among the Lamanites; for behold, they had many children who did grow up and began to wax strong in years, that they became for themselves, and were led away by some who were Zoramites, by their lyings and their flattering words, to join those Gadianton robbers.

And thus were the Lamanites afflicted also, and began to decrease as to their faith and righteousness, because of the wickedness of their rising generation. (3 Nephi 1:22, 27–30)

It is so disheartening to read how Satan attacked the "rising generation" of the Lamanites, and how seeing their children fall away the parents themselves became discouraged and their faith decreased. Can we expect no less from Satan as the Lord's Second Coming becomes eminent? As the Nephite civilization approached the coming of Jesus Christ to their land, the Book of Mormon record revealed the tactics Satan used to disrupt as much as possible the glorious visit of our Savior to the people of the Book of Mormon. To an alarming degree Lucifer was successful since, as a whole, the Nephites turned increasingly wicked during the decades prior to the Lord's visitation and as a result all the unrepentant Nephites were destroyed at the Lord's coming to the New World (3 Nephi 9:1–2). For the same evil objective, we should expect Satan to employ similar tactics against us as we approach the years of the Great Tribulation and the Lord's Second Coming. The question begs to be asked: Do the tactics used by Satan against the ancient Book of Mormon people provide us an indication of how close we are to the Second Coming of Christ? Here is a check list of what happened to the Nephites and Lamanites in the years prior to the Lord's visit to the promised land. Can you find parallels to what is happening in our time?

90–52 BC—Period of the great wars between the Nephites and the Lamanites, from Alma to Moroni and Helaman (Alma 2–Helaman 1).

73 BC—Amalickiah and lower government officials tried to kill Helaman and take control of the government. Captain Moroni raises the title of liberty (Alma 46).

72 BC—Nephite dissenters are more wicked and ferocious than the Lamanites (Alma 47).

72 BC—Amalickiah, a Nephite dissenter, incites the Lamanites to violence against the Nephites (Alma 48).

67 BC—King-men seek to change the laws and set up a king (Alma 51).

62 BC—Insurrection and rebellion against the Nephite government (Alma 61).

51 BC—Elected chief judge Paharon (the second) is murdered as he "sat upon the judgment-seat" (Helaman 1).

38 BC—The Church dwindles and the people become weak (Helaman 4, see preface).

29 BC—Lucifer, the author of sin, guides the Gadianton robbers in their murders and wickedness. The robbers take over the Nephite government (Helaman 6).

27 BC—Chief Judge Cezoram and son murdered while in the judgment-seat (Helaman 6:19). Secret Combinations grow stronger (Helaman 6:17–35).

25 BC—Nephites join secret combinations so they can plunder, steal, and commit whoredoms and all manner of wickedness, contrary to the laws of their country and the laws of God (Helaman 6:21–23).

23 BC—Criminals allowed to go free because of their money, and are even allowed to hold high offices in government (Helaman 7:4–5).

23–20 BC—Corrupt judges deny their religion, the scriptures, the prophets, the Messiah, and even God (Helaman 8:13:25).

23–20 BC—Chief Judge assassinated while sitting upon the judgments-eat. Innocent Nephi and others imprisoned, but later released (Helaman 9).

17 BC—Great drought that caused famine throughout the land (Helaman 11).

17 BC—Pestilence (plague, epidemic, disease) in the land so that some might repent (Helaman 11:15).

6 BC—Nephites remain in "great wickedness" while Lamanites strictly obey the commandments. Samuel the Lamanite testifies of the coming of the Lord (Helaman 13:1–6).

6 BC—Nephites are full of pride "unto boasting" and do not thank the Lord for their riches. Nephites are full of iniquities (Helaman 13:21–22).

6 BC—Nephites surrounded by demons and Satan's angels (Helaman 13:37).

2 BC—Unbelievers taught that it is unreasonable that such a being as a Christ shall come (Helaman 16:18).

1 BC—Day set apart by unbelievers that all those who believed in the sign of the Lord's coming would be put to death if the sign was not fulfilled (3 Nephi 1:8–9).

AD 1—Lord is born, no darkness during all the night (3 Nephi 1:19).

AD 3—Youth of the faithful are led astray by dissenters (3 Nephi 1:28–29).

AD 3–9—Despite the great signs, wickedness and abominations increase (3 Nephi 2).

AD 17—The righteous need to gather together for protection from the Gadianton robbers (3 Nephi 3).

AD 26—Nephites prosper—Pride, wealth, and class distinctions arise—The Church is rent with dissensions—Satan leads the people in open rebellion—Many prophets cry repentance and are slain—Their murderers conspire to take over the government (3 Nephi 6, see preface).

AD 29–30—Chief Judge murdered, government overthrown, an antichrist appears. To survive, people establish family tribes (3 Nephi 7).

AD 34—Darkness covers the land, tempests, earthquakes, etc. Many people are destroyed (3 Nephi 8).

AD 34—Lord comes and only the repentant are not killed (3 Nephi 9:1–2), the Lord declares of Satan's efforts:

> Wo, wo, wo unto this people; wo unto the inhabitants of the whole earth except they shall repent; for the devil laugheth, and his angles rejoice, because of the slain of the fair sons and daughters of my people; and it is because of their iniquity and abominations that they are fallen! (3 Nephi 9:2)

What does the above checklist tell us about Satan's tactics? And what does this short 124-year timeline tell us about how near we are to the Lord's Second Coming?

From the great Nephite/Lamanite wars to the coming of Christ is approximately 124 years. From World War 1 to our time is roughly 107 years.

From the assassination of President John Kennedy to the present has been 48 years, while the time between the assassination of the Chief Judge announced by Nephi to the coming of the Lord was 47 years.

The new plagues that have crippled our world started 45 years ago with the discovery of Ebola in 1976, followed by SARS (Severe Acute Respiratory Syndrome) in 2003, and most recently Covid-19. The pestilence, which means plagues and diseases, started among the Nephites 51 years prior to the coming of the Lord to the New World.

55 years ago, the cover on the April 1966 edition of *Time Magazine* asked the question "Is God Dead?" It was only 36 years before the coming of Christ to the New World that Satan had influenced the unbelievers to teach that it was unreasonable to believe in Christ.

57 years before the Lord's coming to the Nephites and Lamanites, corrupt Nephi judges started denying religion, the scriptures, the prophets and even God. 55 years ago in a landmark case the US Supreme Court banned prayers in school (370 U.S. 421, 1962); 41 years ago the same court prohibited posting the Ten Commandments in public schools (449 U.S. 39, 1980); and 32 years ago in *County of Allegheny v. American Civil Liberties Union* (1989), the US Supreme Court banned Christmas decorations in public buildings if they promoted Christianity.

Just 8 years before the Lord's appearance in the promised land, murderers conspired to take over the Nephite government. Recently far-left anarchist took over parts of the city of Seattle and rioted in Portland for 100 days, while a few months later far-right extremists took over the US Capitol Building and threatened the lives of US senators, congressmen, and congresswomen.

If the disintegrating Nephite timeline is relevant to our day, can the Lord's Second Coming be that far off?

SATAN'S ALL-OUT WAR AGAINST THE SECOND COMING IN OUR DAY

Within our generation, Satan's attack on faith in Christ and His Second Coming have been highly effective and hard to stomach. The prevailing world culture has decayed from Christian-based to casual to crude to disgusting to vulgar to abominable to glorifying violence—especially in regard to women. If you hope events will be any less hellish on earth before the Lord's Second Coming, you're wrong. In fact, things will become much worse. In the October 2020 general conference, Elder Neil L. Andersen related:

> Interestingly, while this spiritual conviction is increasing
> within us, there are many on the earth who know very little
> of Jesus Christ, and in some parts of the world where His

name has been proclaimed for centuries, faith in Jesus Christ is diminishing. The valiant Saints in Europe have seen belief decline in their countries through the decades. Sadly, here in the United States faith is also receding. A recent study revealed that in the last 10 years, 30 million people in the United States have stepped away from believing in the divinity of Jesus Christ. Looking worldwide, another study predicts that in the decades ahead, more than twice as many will leave Christianity as well embrace it.[7]

People are ever more ashamed to admit that they believe in Jesus Christ. This is not surprising, for the Lord declared of those in the last days: "Whosoever therefore shall be ashamed of me and of my words in this adulterous and sinful generation; of him also shall the Son of man be ashamed, when he cometh in glory of his Father with his holy angels" (Mark 8:38). As of 2019, twenty-six percent of Americans consider themselves as either atheist, agnostic, or "nothing in particular" up from seventeen percent in 2009.[8] If the exponential rate of increase continues, by 2039, two thirds of all Americans will be nonbelievers. Sadly, the current trend of rejecting Christ was also prophesied in the Book of Mormon:

> And thus commandeth the Father that I [Christ] should say unto you: At that day when the Gentiles shall sin against my gospel, and shall reject the fullness of my gospel, and shall be lifted up in the pride of their hearts above all nations, and above all the people of the whole earth, and shall be filled with all manner of lyings, and of deceits, and of mischiefs, and all manner of hypocrisy, and murders, and priestcrafts, and whoredoms, and of secret abominations; and if they shall do all those things, and shall reject the fulness of my gospel, behold, saith the Father, I will bring the fulness of my gospel from among them. (3 Nephi 16:10)

7. Neil L. Andersen, "We Talk of Christ," October 2020 general conference.
8. Pew Research Center, "In U.S., Decline of Christianity Continues at Rapid Pace," October 17, 2019, pewforum.org.

THE ALARMING LEADERSHIP CRISIS

For humanity as a whole, it seems Satan has the world just where he wants it—spiritually weak and with most of God's children living without hope in Christ. Nowhere is this more evident than in the lack of righteous leadership. In 2015, the World Economic Forum conducted a Survey of Global Agenda in which 86% of the respondents agreed that there is a leadership crisis in the world today.[9] Leadership consultant Chris Pearse states of this crisis, "There is an alarmingly weak correspondence between power and competency. Those in power are not necessarily up to the job of discharging their responsibilities to the benefit of those they lead."[10] Of the five roots causes Pearse cites for the current leadership crisis, the source that stood out most to me was what he classifies as "Ego, Vanity and Arrogance" in today's leaders. He notes:

> Ego can be considered as the identification of the 'I' with an idea; 'I am successful', for example. The nature of our egos is determined by the particular ideas we identify with and the strength of the identification.
>
> The energy invested in the egos of some leaders can be very much more intense than the general population. When that is the case, the individual can exhibit very low levels of empathy and compassion accompanied by more extreme displays of arrogance and vanity.[11]

Practically leaderless and without hope in Christ, the world is grossly unprepared for what is about to befall it. Things might seem bad now, but they will only get worse. It might seem impossible that things could be worse in the last days than during the final Nephite genocide when "they did not come unto Jesus with broken hearts and contrite spirits, but they did curse God, and wish to die. Nevertheless they would struggle with the sword for their lives" (Mormon 2:14). Consider for a moment the dire conditions described by John in

---

9. Chris Pearse, "5 Reasons Why Leadership is in Crisis," *Forbes*, 7 November 2018, https://www.forbes.com/sites/chrispearse/2018/11/07/5-reasons-why-leadership-is-in-crisis/?sh=13e09d273aca, accessed 12 December 2020.
10. Ibid.
11. Ibid.

the book of Revelation. Picture yourself trying to live, let alone lead others, during these calamities:

Rev. 6:1–2	Beast released to conquer
Rev. 6:3–4	Peace taken, people are killing one another
Rev. 6:5–6	Worldwide famine
Rev. 6:7–8	A quarter of the people die by sword and hunger
Rev. 6:9–11	Righteous are martyred and seek revenge
Rev. 6:12	Earthquake, sun blacked out, moon turned to blood
Rev. 6:13	Stars in heaven fall to the earth
Rev. 6:14	Heaven departs, mountains and islands moved from their place
Rev. 6:15	Kings, rich men, and all others who can, hide in caves
Rev. 6:16	People wish to die rather than see the face of the Lord
Rev. 8:7	Third of all vegetation is burned up
Rev. 8:8–9	Third of the seas turn to blood
Rev. 8:10–11	Third of fresh water will be contaminated
Rev. 8:12–13	Third of the sun, moon, and stars darkened
Rev. 9:1–11	Locust torment people with bitter pain for 5 months
Rev. 9:13–21	Army of 200 million destroy the remaining third of mankind
Rev. 13:16–18	People forced to wear the sign of the beast (666)
Rev. 16:1–2	Terrible sores plague the followers of the anti-Christ
Rev. 16:3	All seas turn to blood, killing everything in them
Rev. 16:4–7	All fresh water turns to blood

Rev. 16:8–9	People scorched by intense light and heat
Rev. 16:12	Euphrates River dries up
Rev. 16:14	Unclean spirits come out of dragons and beasts
Rev. 16:18	Greatest earthquake ever, Babylon destroyed
Rev. 16:20	Earth pounded by 100-pound hailstones
Rev. 16:16	Final conflict between God and forces of evil
Rev. 16:19	Armageddon!

HOW FAST THINGS CAN DEGENERATE

If the above events are not daunting enough, it is not certain that John's list even includes the great Abomination of Desolation that will befall mankind in the last days (Daniel 9:27, Matthew 24:15–16, Thessalonians 2:4, D&C 45:19–21). Further, while the book of Revelation describes an unrighteous world, it does not detail the social blight that will result from increasing moral decay. Editorial Board of the Latter-day Saint Church owned newspaper, the Deseret News, described the mob violence the day before Congress certified the 2020 US presidential elections as follows:

> The United States has withstood many perils in its history, from British soldiers sacking the White House to civil war, to even an armed attack on the Capitol by Puerto Rican nationalists in 1954.
>
> But it has never seen the Capitol stormed by an angry mob egged on by a president of the United States.
>
> The passions that fueled Wednesday's disgraceful moment in U.S. history have been building among the ideological fringes for years. They are strong on the left, as well, as evidenced by Trump administration officials who were accosted and harassed in various public places and by mob rule that has recently occupied portions of Seattle and Portland.

. . . It was a shameful moment, one every American must work to overcome through a renewed commitment to the systems the Founding Fathers established.[12]

NEED FOR CATACLYSMIC LEADERSHIP COMPETENCIES

We are not expected to simply endure social violence and natural catastrophes, but while being severely persecuted (Revelation 12:13–17) we must gather Israel on both sides of the veil and prepare the Church, the bridegroom of Christ, for His Second Coming.

How urgent is the need to prepare to lead in the end of times? The Book of Revelation describes the opening of the seventh seal with such devastating events as angels taking "the censer, and filled it with fire of the altar, and cast it into the earth: and there were voices, and thunderings, and lightnings, and an earthquake" (Rev. 8:5). In a 72–96-hour period in August 2020, 12,000 lightning strikes hit the San Francisco Bay Area causing 585 separate fires that burned 2,100,000 square acres in northern California. A day earlier, California experienced fire tornadoes, fire clouds, and running crown fires.[13] The state was completely overwhelmed and begged for resources from other states.

Of course, these lightning and fires and earthquakes are only indicators that the hour of greater tribulations is near. Furthermore, they are only a taste of the natural events you will need to overcome just to survive. However, we should be even more concerned and prepared for the spiritual battle that will be raged by Satan to deceive the survivors of these natural events (Revelation 13). The Lord has warned the latter-day gentiles:

And thus commandeth the Father that I should say unto you: At that day when the Gentiles shall sin against my gospel, and

---

12. The Deseret News Editorial Board, "America's day of disgrace," *Deseret News*, January 6, 2021, https://www.deseret.com/opinion/2021/1/6/22217718/capitol-riot-protest-trump-electoral-college-vote, accessed 7 January 2021.
13. "August 2020 California lighting wildfires," *https://en.wikipedia.org/wiki/August_2020_California_lightning_wildfires*, accessed August 11, 2021.

shall be lifted up in the pride of their hearts above all nations, and above all the people of the whole earth, and shall be filled with all manner of lyings and of deceits, and of mischiefs, and all manner of hypocrisy, and murders, and priestcrafts, and whoredoms, and of secret abominations; and if they shall do all those things, and shall reject the fulness of my gospel, behold, saith the Father, I will bring the fulness of my gospel from among them. (3 Nephi 16:10)

To understand the consequences that can happen to a once righteous people that reject the Savior, consider what happened to the Nephites when they turned away from Jesus Christ. When He appeared to the unbelieving Nephites, everyone was killed who received not the prophets (3 Nephi 10:12), great tempests came with whirlwinds, thunderings, and lightnings, earthquakes changed the geography of the land, cities burned, and other wicked communities were sunk into the deep or covered with earth (3 Nephi 8).

The Lord specifically warned the Gentiles in the latter days that if they did not repent, He would "cut off the cities of thy land, and throw down all thy strongholds; . . . For it shall come to pass, saith the Father, that at that day whosoever will not repent and come unto my Beloved Son, them will I cut off from among my people, O house of Israel; and I will execute vengeance and fury upon them, even as upon the heathen, such as they have not heard" (3 Nephi 21:15, 20–21).

Don't be caught as by a thief in the night. The prophet Mormon pondered how quickly a righteous people could become so spiritually void that they committed cruel murders, tortured then raped women, and finally ate the flesh of their victims (Moroni 9:9–10). He wrote to Moroni:

Oh my beloved son, how can a people like this, that are without civilization—

(And only a few years have passed away, and they were a civil and a delightsome people)

But O my son, how can a people like this, whose delight is in so much abomination—

How can we expect that God will stay his hand in judgment against us? (Moroni 9:11–14)

Of course, God did not stay His hand. The Nephites were destroyed. You can serve as your own judge. How long do you believe God will stay His hand against the Gentile nations of our day? How does our Father in Heaven look upon the whoredoms and abominations of our civilizations? And finally, do you know and practice the leadership principles necessary to inspire and direct your family and community so they can survive what is about to happen?

THE PURPOSE OF THIS BOOK

This book does not provide a detailed description of the events of the last days or theorize when these traumatic times might happen. Rather, it is to provide the leadership context in which you will find yourself in the coming years, begin a discussion of the leadership competencies that will be required to survive and to still fulfill your missions during the tribulations to come, warn that these leadership competencies will require training and time to master, and convince the reader that today is the time to prepare by practicing righteous leadership.

Whether you are a police chief trying to restore order in your town that is being burned and looted by rioters, a sergeant trying to hold the line against a dark and invisible enemy, a business leader whose company is facing a killer app from a deceitful competitor, a hospital administer in a third world country trying to fight a pandemic without the necessary resources, a fire chief attempting to save cities from a forest fire that won't give in, or a Church leader trying to save the youth in his or her congregation from the grip of drug gangs and porn pushers, you will find this book helpful.

> Blessed are they that do his commandments, that they may have the right to the tree of life, and may enter in through the gates into the city.
>
> For without are dogs, and sorcerers, and whoremongers, and murderers, and idolaters, and whosoever loveth and maketh a lie. (Revelation 22:14–15)

PART ONE

8 Principles for Leadership during the Great Tribulation

Therefore be ye also ready: for in such an hour as ye think not the Son of man cometh.

Who then is a faithful and wise servant, whom his lord hath made ruler over his household, to give them meat in due season?

Blessed is that servant, whom his lord when he cometh shall find so doing.

Verily I say unto you, That he shall make him ruler over all his goods.

—Matthew 24:44–47

Get on your knees and ask
for blessings of the Lord;
Then stand on your feet and
do what you are asked to do.

—Gordon B. Hinckley

Principle 1

Prayer Driven Leadership

Seeking the hand of the Lord in our battles is ingrained in the fabric of American history. President Ronald Reagan stated, "One of the most inspiring portrayals of American history is that of George Washington on his knees in the snow at Valley Forge. That moving image personifies and testifies to our Founders' dependence upon Divine Providence during the darkest hours of the Revolutionary struggle."[1] The following excerpt was taken from Nathaniel Randolph Snowden's (1770–1851) "Diary and Remembrances," who was with the Quaker Isaac Potts when he recounted the day he found General George Washington praying alone in the woods at Valley Forge.

---

1. Ronald Reagan, "Proclamation 5551—Thanksgiving Day, 1986," Online by Gerhard Peters and John T. Woolley, *The American Presidency Project*, https://www.presidency.ucsb.edu/node/254029, accessed 23 July 2021.

In that woods, pointing to a close in view, I heard a plaintive sound as, of a man at prayer. I tied my horse to a sapling & went quietly into the woods & to my astonishment I saw the great George Washington on his knees alone, with his sword on one side and his cocked hat on the other. He was at Prayer to the God of the Armies, beseeching to interpose with his Divine aid, as it was ye Crisis, & the cause of the country, of humanity & of the world. 'Such a prayer I never heard from the lips of man. I left him alone praying.

Someday soon you might find yourself needing to lead your family to safety from a violent enemy, a killer plague, the grips of a famine, or the eye of a destructive storm. Will you and your family survive? Henry B. Eyring advises, "The first, the middle, and the last thing to do is to pray."[2] As the leader of your family, community, or church, the most essential thing to do to survive the violent and wicked years to come is to pray constantly.

Immaculée Ilibagiza has already lived through an indescribable horror that no daughter of our Heavenly Father should have endured. She survived only through constant praying and in so doing developed a deep, powerful, and enduring relationship with God.

Immaculée Ilibagiza had a blessed childhood growing up in Rwanda. She had a loving family and a religious upbringing. However, her idyllic world suddenly turned into a bloody horror in 1994. Rwanda descended into a gory genocide that killed nearly a million Rwandans in three months. Immaculée is a Tutsi, the tribe that was the target of the slaughter. Unfortunately, the Tutsi genocide echoes a revolting and recurring Satanic behavior that will undoubtedly raise its ugly head in the last days. Living memory still reeks of the Jewish slaughter at the hands of the Nazis, the killings fields of Cambodia, the Christian purge in Iraq, and the Muslim ethic cleaning in China. The list goes on and on. It is the familiar human killing disease of the soul that finished off the unrepentant Nephites. "And behold, the Lamanites have hunted my people, the Nephites, down from city to city and from place to place, even until they are no more"

---

2. Henry B. Eyring, "In the Strength of the Lord," April 2004 general conference.

(Mormon 8:7). Are you prepared to navigate your family and community through such a horror?

For 91 days, Immaculée Ilibagiza and seven other women survived in the cramped bathroom of Pastor Murinzi, a Hutu. The pastor hid the women in tiny small bathroom with only a closet covering the door. Time and time again, killing gangs entered the pastor's home searching for any Tutsis who might still be alive. At times hundreds of people dressed like devils surrounded the house and chanting a song of genocide while doing a dance of death: "Kill them, kill them, kill them all; kill them big and kill them small! Kill the old and kill the young . . . a baby snake is still a snake, kill it, too, let none escape! Kill them, kill them, kill them all." To compound the horror, the killing gangs were none other than her neighbors. The lesson Immaculée learned during this hellish experience just might save your family when the mob is pounding on your front door. Immaculée relates in her book, *Left to Tell*, how her desperate prayers led her to God.

> "Dear God, save us . . ." I whispered in my ear. *Why are you calling of God? Look at all of them out there . . . hundreds of them looking for you. They are legion, and you are one. You can't possibly survive—you* **won't** *survive. They're inside the house, and they're moving through the rooms. They're close, almost here . . . they're going to find you, rape you, cut you, kill you!*
>
> My heart was pounding. What was this voice? I squeezed my eyes shut as tightly as I could to resist the negative thoughts. I grasped the red and white rosary my father had given me, and silently prayed with all my might: *God, in the Bible You said that You can do anything for anybody, Well, I am one of those anybodies, and I need You to do something for me now. Please, God, blind the killers when they reach the pastor's bedroom—don't let them find the bathroom door, and don't let them see us! You saved Daniel in the lions' den, God, You stopped the lions from ripping him apart . . . stop these killers from ripping us apart, God! Save us, like You saved Daniel!*
>
> I prayed more intensely than I'd ever prayed before, but still the negative energy wracked my spirit. The voice of doubt was in my ear again as surely as if Satan himself were sitting

on my shoulder. I literally felt the fear pumping through my veins, and my blood was on fire. *You're going to die, Immaculée!* the voice taunted. *You compare yourself to Daniel? How conceited you are . . . Daniel was pure of heart and loved by God—he was a prophet, a saint! What are you? You are nothing . . . you deserve suffering and pain . . . you deserve to die!*

I clutched my rosary as though it were a lifeline to God. In my mind and heart I cried out to Him for help: *Yes, I am nothing, but you are forgiving. I am human and I am weak, but please, God give me Your forgiveness. Forgive me my trespasses . . . and please send these killers away before they find us.*

My temples pounded. The dark voice was in my head, filling it with fear, unthinkable images. *Dead bodies are everywhere. Mothers have seen their babies chopped in half, their fetuses ripped from wombs . . . and you think you should be spared? Mothers prayed for God to spare their babies and He ignored them—why should He save you when innocent babies are being murdered? You are selfish, and you have no shame. Listen, Immaculée . . . do you hear them? The killers are outside your door—they're here for you.*

My head was burning, but I did hear the killers in the hall, screaming, "Kill Them! Kill them all."

No! God is love, I told the voice. He loves me and wouldn't fill me with fear. He will not abandon me. He will not let me die cowering on the bathroom floor. He will not let me die in shame!

One might ask, "Was Immaculée a leader?" All she did was to pray for God's help. Of course, the answer is yes. Her action saved the lives of the seven other women. In the same manner, the greatest of all leaders, Jesus Christ took the leadership action in the garden of Gethsemane to console with His father. His triumph had the potential for exalting every person who ever lived. "And he went a little further, and fell on his face, and prayed, saying, O my Father, if it be possible, let this cup pass from me: nevertheless not as I will, but as thou wilt" (Matthew 26:39).

If you want to be a leader in the last days, one who can save his or her family, friends, community, or nation, you must start leading on your knees. You will need God's help, and be assured your Father in Heaven will not fail you. To outwit the forces of Satan as the Second Coming approaches, one must walk in the paths of the Lord and receive daily inspiration to know the problems that are coming your way. When Alma inquired of the Lord as to where their enemy's army would attack, the Lord told him that they were headed to Manti (Alma 43:23–24). This inspired knowledge helped save the Nephite nation in the hour of their need.

One of America's greatest military leaders, General George S. Patton, understood the direct relationship between victory over evil forces and the power of prayer. Msgr. James H. O'Neill provides his personal account of his famous Third Army Prayer:

> The incident of the now famous Patton Prayer commenced with a telephone call to the Third Army Chaplain on the morning of December 8, 1944, when the Third Army Headquarters were located in the Caserne Molifor in Nancy, France: "This is General Patton; do you have a good prayer for weather? We must do something about those rains if we are to win the war." My reply was that I know where to look for such a prayer, that I would locate, and report within the hour. As I hung up the telephone receiver, about eleven in the morning, I looked out on the steadily falling rain, "immoderate" I would call it — the same rain that had plagued Patton's Army throughout the Moselle and Saar Campaigns from September until now, December 8. The few prayer books at hand contained no formal prayer on weather that might prove acceptable to the Army Commander. Keeping his immediate objective in mind, I typed an original and an improved copy on a 5" x 3" filing card:
>
> "Almighty and most merciful Father, we humbly beseech Thee, of Thy great goodness, to restrain these immoderate rains with which we have had to contend. Grant us fair weather for Battle. Graciously hearken to us as soldiers who call upon Thee that, armed with Thy power, we may advance from victory to victory, and crush the oppression and wickedness of our enemies and establish Thy justice among men and nations."

He [Patton] took his place at his desk, signed the card, returned it to me and then Said: "Chaplain, sit down for a moment; I want to talk to you about this business of prayer." He rubbed his face in his hands, was silent for a moment, then rose and walked over to the high window, and stood there with his back toward me as he looked out on the falling rain. As usual, he was dressed stunningly, and his six-foot-two powerfully built physique made an unforgettable silhouette against the great window. The General Patton I saw there was the Army Commander to whom the welfare of the men under him was a matter of Personal responsibility. Even in the heat of combat he could take time out to direct new methods to prevent trench feet, to see to it that dry socks went forward daily with the rations to troops on the line, to kneel in the mud administering morphine and caring for a wounded soldier until the ambulance came. What was coming now?

The General left the window, and again seated himself at his desk, leaned back in his swivel chair, toying with a long lead pencil between his index fingers.

"Chaplain, I am a strong believer in Prayer. There are three ways that men get what they want; by planning, by working, and by Praying. Any great military operation takes careful planning, or thinking. Then you must have well-trained troops to carry it out: that's working. But between the plan and the operation there is always an unknown. That unknown spells defeat or victory, success or failure. It is the reaction of the actors to the ordeal when it actually comes. Some people call that getting the breaks; I call it God. God has His part, or margin in everything, That's where prayer comes in. Up to now, in the Third Army, God has been very good to us. We have never retreated; we have suffered no defeats, no famine, no epidemics. This is because a lot of people back home are praying for us. We were lucky in Africa, in Sicily, and in Italy. Simply because people prayed. But we have to pray for ourselves, too. [3]

---

3. James H. O'Neill, "The True Story of The Patton Prayer," from the Review of the News, 6 October 1971.

It is human nature to expect the Lord to bring us victory over our enemies. To seek injury to the forces that align to destroy us. However, our enemies, while under the influence of Satan, are Heavenly Father's children. Rather than hope for harm for our enemies, we should pray that the Lord will soften their hearts. Elder M. Russell Ballard has taught:

> The Savior taught us to not limit who we pray for. He said, "Love your enemies, bless them that curse you, do good to them that hate you, and pray for them which despitefully use you, and persecute you."
>
> On the cross of Calvary, where Jesus died for our sins, He practiced what He taught when He prayed, "Father, forgive them; for they know not what they do."
>
> Sincerely praying for those who may be considered our enemies demonstrates our belief that God can change our hearts and the hearts of others. Such prayers should strengthen our resolve to make whatever changes are necessary in our own lives, families, and communities.[4]

Prayer opens the door to direct revelation. When Lehi prayed for his people, he was told Jerusalem would be destroyed (1 Nephi 1:5, 13). Later in a dream he was told to take his family and flee into the wilderness (1 Nephi 2:1–2). In the Book of Joel, we are promised:

> And ye shall know that I am in the midst of Israel, and that I am the Lord your God, and none else: and my people shall never be ashamed.
>
> And it shall come to pass afterward, that I will pour out my spirit upon all flesh, and your sons and your daughters shall prophesy, your old men shall dream dreams, your young men shall see visions:
>
> And also upon the servants and upon the handmaids in those days will I pour out my spirit.
>
> And I will show wonders in heavens and in the earth, blood, and fire, and pillars of smoke.

---

4. M. Russell Ballard, "Watch Ye Therefore, and Pray Always," October 2020 general conference.

The sun shall be turned into darkness, and the moon into blood, before the great and terrible day of the Lord come.

And it shall come to pass, that *whosoever shall call on the name of the Lord shall be delivered:* for in mount Zion and in Jerusalem shall be deliverance, as the Lord hath said, and in the remnant whom the Lord shall call. (Joel 2:27–32, emphasis added)

Elder Ballard has counseled in our day, "The world's current chaotic situation may seem daunting as we consider the multitude of issues and challenges. But it is my fervent testimony that if we will pray and ask Heavenly Father for needed blessings and guidance, we will come to know how we can bless our families, neighbors, communities, and even the countries in which we live."[5] If prayer is so vital today, it will be even more so during the calamities leaders will face during the Great Tribulation.

---

5. Ibid.

Pray always, that you may come off conqueror; yea, that you may conquer Satan, and that you may escape the hands of the servants of Satan that do uphold his work. (D&C 10:5)

And in that day shall be heard of wars and rumors of wars, and the whole earth shall be in commotion, and men's hearts shall fail them, and they shall say the Christ delayeth his coming until the end of the earth. And the love of men shall wax cold, and iniquity shall abound.

(D&C 45:26–27)

Principle 2

Defeating Secret Combinations Through Patriarchal Leadership

In our time, President Ezra Taft Benson warned against the evil designs of secret combinations, the ancient orders that destroyed both the once righteous Jaredite and Nephite civilizations. Secret combinations started with Cain and are the "most abominable and wicked above all, in the sight of God" (Ether 8:18). The Book of Mormon warns the righteous in our dispensation that it is the devil who "stirreth up the children of men unto secret combinations of murder and all manner of secret works of darkness" (2 Nephi 9:9).

Many horrible calamites will befall men and women before the Second Coming. These conditions can be attributed to the impact of natural forces, i.e. plagues, earthquakes, comets, droughts, etc. On second thought, it seems even more likely that acts of God will not be the primary causes of human miseries at the end of time. Rather, mankind's pride and greed will cause them to form combinations that will be the root cause of most of the trauma and deprivation experienced during the years of tribulation. The Book of Mormon proclaims that in the last days "It shall come in a day when the blood of saints shall cry unto the Lord, because of secret combinations and the works of darkness" (Mormon 8:27).

Consider what befell prior nations. In the New World, the Jaredites rejected the words of prophets because of a secret society (Ether 11:22). As the Jaredite nation came to an end, many Jaredites were slain by the sword of secret combinations (Ether 13:18). After two centuries of righteous living, the Nephites became wicked and started secret combinations after the order of Gadianton (4 Nephi 1:42); thus, their days became numbered. President Benson taught that in the Eastern Hemisphere, "a world so wicked that it killed the Son of God soon began killing the apostles and prophets and so plunged itself into a spiritual dark age. (See 2 Thes. 2:2–7.) Scripture ended, apostasy spread, and the church that Christ established during His earthly ministry ceased to exist. (See 2 Ne. 27:4–5.)"[1]

President Benson alerts us, "I testify that wickedness is rapidly expanding in every segment of our society. (See D&C 1:14–16; D&C 84:49–53.) It is more highly organized, more cleverly disguised, and more powerfully promoted than ever before. Secret combinations lusting for power, gain, and glory are flourishing. A secret combination that seeks to overthrow the freedom of all lands, nations, and countries is increasing its evil influence and control over America and the entire world. (See Ether 8:18–25.)"[2]

Secret combinations will likely be the root cause for failed governments in the last days. From Afghanistan to Angola, central governments have already failed throughout the world, resulting in chaos and unthinkable violence. For example, think of beheadings, rapes, and mass murders committed by the so-called Islamic State in Iraq. The Islamic terrorist society was only given birth and allowed to grow because of the lack of a true central government in post-Desert Storm Iraq. Another example is in Book of Mormon times when secret combinations destroyed the Nephite government (3 Nephi 7:6, 9).

The Prophet Joseph Smith declared of the United States government, "Even this nation will be on the verge of crumbling to pieces and tumbling to the ground and when the Constitution is upon the brink of ruin this people will be the staff upon which the nation shall lean and they shall bear the Constitution away from the very verge

---

1. Ezra Taft Benson, "I Testify," October 1988 general conference.
2. Ibid.

of destruction."[3] Eliza R. Snow indicated that Joseph Smith prophesied that "[t]he time will come when the government of these United States will be so nearly overthrown through its corruption, that the Constitution will hang as it were by a single hair."[4]

Once secret combinations gain power, they rewrite the scriptural and historical narratives by the power of the devil "to keep them [God's children] in darkness" (Ether 8:16). Street gangs turn children against parents; Nazis burn books; communists outlaw religion and free speech; anarchists degrade national heroes and institutions; and social media bends values and blackmail reputations. What was once good is seen as evil; and what is universally evil becomes generally accepted as good. Stated simply, the devil's strategy is to change his victim's mindset unto the point where God's children become blinded to the light of the Christ. The great Jaredite prophet Ether taught "great and marvelous" truths (Ether 12:5). He even tried to enlighten the Jaredites about the coming of the Savior (Ether 13:4) and "all things, from the beginning of man" (Ether 13:2). Unfortunately, the Jaredites believed not, "because they saw them not" (Ether 12:5).

THE SECRET COMBINATIONS IN THE LAST DAYS

Bruce R. McConkie, then of the Council of the Seventy, taught this about secret combinations: "Reliable modern reports describe their existence among gangsters, as part of the governments of communist countries, in some labor organizations, and even in some religious groups."[5] These combinations are numerous and variant. As the Second Coming approaches, here are just a few members of Satan's secret family.

---

3. D. Michael Stewart, "What do we know about the purported statement of Joseph Smith that the Constitution would hang by a thread and that the elders would save it?" *Ensign*, June 1976.

4. Ibid.

5. Bruce R. McConkie, "Secret Combinations," *Mormon Doctrine*, 2d ed., (United States: Bookcraft, 1966).

GANGS

M. Russell Ballard, then an apostle, declared that secret combinations include "gangs, drug cartels, and organized crime families. . . . They have secret signs and code words. They participate in secret rites and initiation ceremonies. Among their purposes are to 'murder, and plunder, and steal, and commit whoredoms and all manner of wickedness, contrary to the laws of their country and also the laws of their God.' (see Helaman 6:23)"[6] Throughout the world there are members of The Church of Jesus Christ of Latter-day Saints and other faithful families suffering the scourge of street gangs. Fearful parents live the nightmare that their children will be forced into violent gangs or killed because they do not comply with the gangs' evil demands.

In the United States, gangs became prominent about the time of the Industrial Revolution. During that period, rural families moved from their farms into the cities and poor immigrants settled in ethnic neighborhoods. There was inadequate housing and few jobs available, so some of the unemployed turned to crime to survive. Eventually, gangs became well-disciplined and fought in groups and covered large territories. Similar circumstances allowed criminal gangs to form and grow throughout the developed and lesser developed nations.

Today, the majority of street gangs are comprised of young people seeking attention and interaction not found within their immediate family. Street gangs are usually loosely organized, not crime specific, goalless, and have informal initiations and leadership. However, if allowed to mature, gangs increase their ability to torment communities and nations. With time, gangs evolve into mafias, cartels, and juntas and become highly organized, crime specific (i.e. human trafficking, drugs, arms dealing, prostitution, etc.), profit-making, goal oriented, and extend their reach internationally. Their membership is for life and requires detailed oaths and initiations. Today their treasuries are counted in the trillions of dollars and the lives they alarmed total in the billions.

---

6. M. Russell Ballard, "Standing for Truth and Right," October 1997 general conference.

HATE GROUPS

A joke claiming to help people save money goes like this, "To save money, talk politics at your family's Thanksgiving dinner and you won't have to buy so many Christmas presents this year." Joking aside, hate is a spiritual cancer that if not checked, grows into uncontrolled violence. Having grown up in the United States, it is hard to witness groups on all sides of the political spectrum threatening violence in the streets if their candidate is defeated in the 2020 national elections. Such threats are a form of domestic terrorism. President Gordon B. Hinckley compared modern terrorists to "Gadianton robbers, a vicious, oath-bound, and secret organization bent on evil and destruction."[7]

The US Federal Bureau of Investigation (FBI) classifies most US domestic secret hate societies into four groups: eco-terrorist/animal rights extremist, lone offenders, sovereign citizen movements, and anarchist extremism. To simplify the discussion, all these groups tend to fall on either the furthest left or furthest right of the political spectrum—if on the spectrum at all.

Let's consider the evils of just two forms of secret hate societies: anarchist extremist and white supremacy groups. Anarchism is a movement that rejects all involuntary forms of hierarchy and calls for the abolition of the state. A recent example would be the 100 nights of violent rioting in Portland, Oregon in 2020. Anarchism is a gullible philosophy that is in direct opposition to the Twelfth Article of Faith—"We believe in being subject to kings, presidents, rulers, and magistrates, in obeying, honoring, and sustaining the law." It is a naïve viewpoint which, as Bertrand Russell argued, could never provide the essential services that a government can.[8] After reviewing hundreds of "Me To" generation job performance reviews and psychological assessments, I believe that so-called anarchist groups in our day are no more than a band of over-indulged youth who have never been taught to work or even to be responsible for taking care of themselves. An

---

7. Gordon B. Hinckley, "The Times in Which We Live," October 2001 general conference.

8. Steven A. Peterson, "Moral Development and Critiques of Anarchism," *Journal of Libertarian* Studies (1987), 8 (2): 238.

image I have witnessed while visiting the home of an elderly relative reinforced my conclusion. Entering into the kitchen was a 35-year-old grandson with tattoos and blue-dyed hair cut into a mohawk. The grandson was living entirely off his grandfather. Waking up around 12:00 noon, the grandson walked into his grandfather's kitchen, rudely said nothing to his grandfather or the family guest, opened the refrigeration and ate standing before the open appliance. The back of his T-shirt read, "I want it. Give it to me NOW!"

White supremacist groups are also in direct opposition to the teaching of Jesus Christ. In 2017, the Church of Jesus Christ of Latter-day Saints issued a statement condemning "white supremacist attitudes":

> Two days after decrying racism and calling for peace and compassion, The Church of Jesus Christ of Latter-day Saints offered a stronger statement condemning white supremacist attitudes, saying they "are morally wrong and sinful."
>
> "It has been called to our attention that there are some among the various pro-white and white supremacy communities who assert that the church is neutral toward or in support of their views. Nothing could be further from the truth," Tuesday's church statement begins.
>
> "In the New Testament, Jesus said, 'Thou shalt love the Lord thy God with all thy heart, and with all thy soul, and with all thy mind. This is the first and great commandment. And the second is like unto it, Thou shalt love thy neighbour as thyself.' (Matthew 22:37-39) The Book of Mormon teaches 'all are alike unto God' (2 Nephi 26:33).
>
> "White supremacist attitudes are morally wrong and sinful, and we condemn them. Church members who promote or pursue a 'white culture' or white supremacy agenda are not in harmony with the teachings of the church."[9]

9. Scott Taylor, "LDS Church issues statement condemning 'white supremacist attitudes,'" *Deseret News*, Aug 15, 2017, 1:05pm MDT,

It is embarrassing that the state of Utah appears to be "exporting" white supremacist gangs.[10] Of course, such hate groups do not originate in chapels of any faith, rather in prisons. Not only are these violent gangs a danger to non-whites, the hate groups actively recruit the confused white youth while funding their sick goals selling drugs and guns.[11]

WARLORDS

A warlord is an agent of Satan who exercises military, economic, and political control over a subnational territory within a weakened sovereign state. These armed militias are loyal to the chief warlord rather than to the legitimate government. Warlords have existed throughout much of history, in a variety of different capacities. Today, such brutal chiefs rule in many parts of the world. Without their approval, people within their territories have little freedom. The word "warlord" dates to 1856 when used by poet Ralph Waldo Emerson. During WWI, Chinese warlords were called Junfa (軍閥), derived from the Japanese gunbatsu, which was taken in turn from German.

Although the term describing these illegitimate organizations has changed with time, these feudal tyrants have existed throughout history. Giddianhi, the chief of the Gadianton robbers, was a warlord who sought to steal lands and resources from the Nephites (3 Nephi 3:9; 10–12). Warlords come to power when legitimate governments become "weak state" societies or "failed states." As central governments begin to fail more and more, Latter-day Saints could find that they are involuntarily living under the control of warlords, even within the borders of a broken United States. Under such conditions, freedom will be limited to the whim of the warlord and his cronies.

10. Dennis Romboy, "Feds crack down on 'very unfortunate' Utah export: white supremacist gangs." *KSL*, October 16, 2020. https://www.ksl.com/article/50032731/feds-crack-down-on-very-unfortunate-utah-export-white-supremacist-gangs.
11. Ibid.

THE SECRET COMBINATION OF THE INTERNET

The marvelous blessings of the internet and other advanced technology seem to ever flow to improve our lives. Evermore, we use our electronic devices without thinking. Often we check our emails and social media accounts before getting out of bed. Many believe these technologies as inspired of God. Yet, how often do we consider how the father of all lies can use these same technologies to drag our families down to destruction? Do we associate these technologies with the increased rates of loneliness, depression, anxiety, and even suicides among our youth? Do we understand how these sophisticated technologies can be used by secret combinations? Their influence in the lives of our families will only increase. Already researchers are developing brain insert chips that can be used through thought waves to access the internet. Will such devices be numbered 666? Here are just four examples of internet secret combinations that are impacting our communities.

One: The Big Brother of Big Data

Whether you authorize it or not, every time you type in a letter on your computer keyboard or click on an internet advertisement or download a picture, your data is being collected by internet servers, social media sites, and other digital organizations. They mine *your* information and make it *their* secrets. Even if the organization declares that it will not share *your* data with other organizations, there are numerous incidents of contract developers or hackers extracting Your Data and selling it. *Your* data is then used for target advertising and to build a personality profile on *you* and the members of *your* family. The profiles are then used to influence your behavior. Although the collected data is mined from *your* past behavior and the personality profiles become *your* hidden internet identity, *you* have no property rights to them. *Your* profiles can be sold and used for whatever innocent or malicious purpose possible and without *your* permission.

Take for example the case of Cambridge Analytica. The scandal involved personal data on more than 50 million American Facebook users and their Facebook friends without their consent.[12] Cambridge Analytica claimed to have over 5,000 data points on every American voter.[13] The company then hired Cambridge academic Dr. Aleksandr Spectre to build psychological profiles on each voter.[14] The end product was Cambridge Analytica selling its services to US political campaigns to influence voters. Using their psychological profiles, Cambridge Analytica targeted voters based on voters two most influential emotions, *hate* and *fear*, to pursue them to select candidates based on their hate and fear of the alternative candidate. These hate and fear campaigns included millions of fake news articles (lies) about the opposing candidate.[15] Lies, hate and fear are some of Satan's better-known tools. Can there be any doubt that Satan is behind the civil hatred and political polarization that is spinning out of control in the United States?

Two: Big Data and Free Agency

Satan and his army of evil angels have been keeping tags on your behaviors since you were born. Big Data and customized targeted advertising are now at his aid. Again, thousands of data points on your past behavior have already been mined and are available to marketing organizations that don't have your best interest in mind. For example, just click once on an advertisement for wine. Within minutes you will be bombarded with ads that expound the pleasures of drinking a certain brand of wine. The following week, you might even receive brochures for collector's wines in the mail. While this might seem harmless, consider its impact on a person who is recovering from the grips of alcoholism. It could be life threatening. In essence, whatever you have done in your past, you will be constantly exposed to do

---

12. Issie Lapowsky, "Facebook Exposed 87 Million Users to Cambridge Analytica," *Wired*, ISSN 1059-1028, 4 April 2018. Retrieved March 23, 2020.

13. *The Great Hack*, Netflix, directed by Karim Amer and Jehane Noujaim, 2019, documentary film.

14. Allan Smith, "There's an open secret about Cambridge Analytica in the political world: It doesn't have the 'secret sauce' it claims," *Business Insider*, 21 March 2018. Retrieved May 8, 2020.

15. *The Great Hack*, Netflix, directed by Karim Amer and Jehane Noujaim, 2019, documentary film.

it in your future. Efforts to repent from past addictive behaviors—i.e. video games, pornography, conspicuous shopping, gambling—will be jeopardized. Indeed, Big Data is a secret tool Satan can use to try to degrade our ability to exercise our free agency. As apostle Ulisses Soares teaches, such enticing to do evil is the exact opposite of "the Savior Jesus Christ [who] exemplified the importance of constantly resisting everything that might dissuade us from realizing our eternal purpose."[16]

Three: Your Sins Will Never Be Forgotten

Big Data mines data on whatever past records exist that pertain to your personal history; be it police convictions, nasty divorces, bankruptcies, social media posting bulling you, etc. Yes, Big Data can and will show to the world even false allegations against you and without your ability to fight back. And yes, Big Data does make mistakes—exposing your personal and financial information to criminal organizations or erroneously attaching other people's bad behavior to your name. You can be sure, the internet can damage your reputation without the least degree of guilt. It never forgets, and seldom makes amends. For example, what if a faithful bishop had a driving under the influence (DUI) conviction when he was 18 years old? At the time he fully repented and never tasted alcohol again. Still, the internet doesn't forget—just type in his name in your internet browser and you will find several sites willing, for a price that is, to share the dirt. Repentance is hard enough in the privacy of prayer and behavior change. Anyone who has ever repented knows that Satan loves to torment you with your past mistakes. The internet has the power to expose your past mistakes to everyone—even your spouse and children. Discouragement is a powerful ally of the adversary, and he can now use the secret domains of the internet to discourage you and your family members.

---

16. Ulisses Soares, "Seek Christ in Every Thought," October 2020 general conference.

Four: Dark Web

In the 1990s, the US Department of Defense tried to develop an anonymized and encrypted network that would protect US intelligent agents. The clandestine tool was never fully developed, yet the researchers launched a nonprofit service to protect human rights and privacy activists. The service technology is called "The Onion Router" and is now available free by downloading the *Tor* browser. While the service protects individuals living under suppressive government, medical records, and other sensitive data, it didn't take Satan's legions long to discover how to use the Dark Web for trafficking drugs, stealing identities, child pornography, arms sales, and other illicit activities. Criminals use the Dark Web to conduct their "untraceable" financial transactions using crypto currencies, i.e., Bitcoin. The Dark Web is also the domain of left-wing and right-wing hate groups and is an undetectable platform for sexual perverts baiting their next victim.

Over a two-and-a-half-year period, one website alone, "Silk Road 2.0," hosted several thousand drug dealers with well over 100,000 buyers. The site laundered hundreds of millions of Bitcoins worth approximately $1.2 billion dollars.[17] If you believe your family and community are safe from Satan's use of the Dark Web, you are naïve.

COMMUNIST DICTATORSHIPS

By far the most destructive form of Satan's secret combinations is communist dictatorships. While masking themselves in the faulty virtues of philosophers like Karl Marx, they are draconian syndicates that serve only the greed of a few leaders while spiritually and fiscally breeding their victims. In 1988, President Ezra Taft Benson taught, "A secret combination that seeks to overthrow the freedom of all lands, nations, and countries is increasing its evil influence and control over America and the entire world."[18]

---

17. Aditi Kumar and Eric Rosenbach, "The Truth about the Dark Web," *International Monetary Fund—Finance & Development*, September 2019, Vol. 56, No. 3, https://www.imf.org/external/pubs/ft/fandd/2019/09/the-truth-about-the-dark-web-kumar.htm#author, accessed 30 November 2020.
18. Ezra Taft Benson, "I Testify," October 1988 general conference.

Nine years earlier, in a general conference address entitled "A Witness and a Warning," as President of the Quorum of Twelve Apostles, President Benson declared:

It is well to ask, what system established secret works of darkness to overthrow nations by violent revolution? Who blasphemously proclaimed the atheistic doctrine that God made us not? Satan works through human agents. We need only look to some of the ignoble characters in human history who were contemporary to the restoration of the gospel to discover fulfillment of Isaiah's prophecy. I refer to the infamous founders of Communism and others who follow in their tradition.

Communism introduced into the world a substitute for true religion. It is a counterfeit of the gospel plan. The false prophets of Communism predict a utopian society. This, they proclaim, will only be brought about as capitalism and free enterprise are overthrown, private property abolished, the family as a social unit eliminated, all classes abolished, all governments overthrown, and a communal ownership of property in a classless, stateless society established.

Since 1917 this godless counterfeit to the gospel has made tremendous progress toward its objective of world domination.

Today, we are in a battle for the bodies and souls of man. It is a battle between two opposing systems: freedom and slavery, Christ and anti-Christ. The struggle is more momentous than a decade ago, yet today the conventional wisdom says, "You must learn to live with Communism and to give up your ideas about national sovereignty." Tell that to the millions—yes, the scores of millions—who have met death or imprisonment under the tyranny of Communism! *Such would be the death knell of freedom and all we hold dear.* God must ever have a free people to prosper His work and bring about Zion.[19]

---

19. Ezra Taft Benson, "A Witness and a Warning," October 1979 general conference.

Despite the raise of these powerful secret combinations in the last days, the Lord has promised that "whatsoever nation shall uphold such secret combinations, to get power and gain, until they shall spread over the nation, behold, they shall be destroyed; for the Lord will not suffer that the blood of his saints, which shall be shed by them, shall always cry unto him from the ground for vengeance upon them and yet he avenge them not" (Ether 8:22).

ALL FORMS OF SECRET COMBINATIONS ARE ON THE RISE

One might pretend that secret combinations are cyclical. Unfortunately, the truth is they are here to stay until the Lord's Second Coming and are increasing in both their numbers and influence. Satan is not about to let his foot off the gas pedal. Hate and animosity is growing within families, communities, and nations. Wars and rumors of war abound. Circumstances are so bad that on November 20, 2020, President Russell M. Nelson included in his prayer for gratitude these words: "We pray for relief from political strife. Wilt Thou bless us with a healing spirit that unites us despite our differences."[20] Communist nations have become so rich that they no longer need to fight surrogate wars. They simply payoff political and business leaders in democratic and non-democratic nations to implement their secret and cancerous agendas. The question must be answered: How can righteous leaders defeat the influence of secret combination, the most abominable and wicked above all, in the sight of God? The answer is Patriarchal Order Leadership.

---

20. Russell M. Nelson, "The Healing Power of Gratitude," posted by The Church of Jesus Christ of Latter-day Saints on YouTube, 20 November 2020, https://www. youtube.com/watch?v=i51gcWCs-Ho. Transcript accessed 28 November 2020 at https://assets.ldscdn.org/ac/ce/acce1d6a5b114c8c6eb33605830000a4176eb859/ prayer_of_gratitude_video_and_awareness_materials.pdf.

PATRIARCHAL LEADERSHIP

To ward off the growing evils of secret combinations in the last days, each Latter-day Saint man and women must be a leader. By stewardship they are the guardians of Heavenly Father's children and His most sacred organization, the family. Indeed, it is "a law unto the inhabitants of Zion, or in any of her stakes which are organized" that they teach their children the gospel and "also teach their children to pray, and to walk uprightly before the Lord" (D&C 68:25–28). To support parents in their family leadership callings, prophets of The Church of Jesus Christ of Latter-day Saints have continuously revealed programs to fight off Satan's increasing attacks on the family. In 1915, the Church leaders recommended that church members arrange monthly (and later, weekly) "home evenings" to strengthen family ties. President David O. McKay taught that "[n]o other success can compensate for failure in the home."[21] In 1995, under the divine inspiration of President Gordon B. Hinckley, the First Presidency revealed "The Family: A Proclamation to the World." The Proclamation included the following duties associated with family leadership:

> We, the First Presidency and the Council of the Twelve Apostles of The Church of Jesus Christ of Latter-day Saints, solemnly proclaim that marriage between a man and a woman is ordained of God and that the family is central to the Creator's plan for the eternal destiny of His children.
>
> . . . Husband and wife have a solemn responsibility to love and care for each other and for their children. "Children are an heritage of the Lord" (Psalm 127:3). Parents have a sacred duty to rear their children in love and righteousness, to provide for their physical and spiritual needs, and to teach them to love and serve one another, observe the commandments of God, and be law-abiding citizens wherever they live. Husbands and wives—mothers and fathers— will be held accountable before God for the discharge of these obligations.[22]

---

21. David O. McKay, in Conference Report, April 1964, 5.
22. "The Family: A Proclamation to the World," October 1995 general conference.

Righteous leadership starts and ends in the home. The family is the core unit of the kingdom of God. Satan knows this and is attacking the core with every means available to him. As the leaders in their home, fathers and mothers must protect the heart of the kingdom. Otherwise, if men and women do not fulfill their leadership responsibilities at home, their children will be prey to gangs, hate societies, drug cartels, the dark side of the internet, and even human traffickers. If families are destroyed, communities fail and governments fall victim to warlords and communist dictatorships. As an apostle, Russell M. Nelson stated: "No other work transcends that of righteous, intentional parenting!"[23] Recently, the prophet has reemphasized the leadership role of parents in the home by introducing the *Come Follow Me* curriculum. In his closing remarks at general conference in October 2018, President Nelson stated:

> The new home-centered, Church-supported integrated curriculum has the potential to unleash the power of families, as each family follows through conscientiously and carefully to transform their home into a sanctuary of faith. I promise that as you diligently work to remodel your home into a center of gospel learning, over time *your* Sabbath days will truly be a delight. *Your* children will be excited to learn and to live the Savior's teachings, and the influence of the adversary in *your* life and in *your* home will decrease. Changes in your family will be dramatic and sustaining.[24]

Obviously, the Lord, through His prophets, is calling upon each father and mother to lead in the fight against the increasing influences of Satan's secret combinations. The question is, how can we win the battle? The answer is straightforward; men and women must lead through the Patriarchal Order.

---

23. Russell M. Nelson, "The Sabbath is a Delight," April 2015 general conference.
24. Russell M. Nelson, "Becoming Exemplary Latter-day Saints," October 2018 general conference.

WHAT IS THE PATRIARCHAL ORDER?

Elder Dean L. Larsen, then of the Presidency of the Seventy, taught:

> The patriarchal system provides a basis for government in the kingdom of God. It places parents in a position of accountability for their own direct family, and it links these family kingdoms in a patriarchal order that lends cohesiveness to the greater kingdom of God of which they are a part. The patriarchal order has no relevance in the eternal worlds except for those husbands and wives and families who have entered into the covenant of eternal marriage.[25]

The patriarchal authority is the highest level of the Melchizedek Priesthood. In this world it was first given to Adam and Eve. Elder James E. Talmage taught it is the authority when "woman shares with man the blessing of the Priesthood" and where husband and wife minister "seeing and understanding alike, and co-operating to the full in the government of their family kingdom."[26]

Patriarchal leadership exists in the home where the parents live up to the covenants they made when they were sealed together in temple marriage and then work in harmony as a perfect leadership team to bring priesthood power to their family. The Prophet Joseph Smith taught: "Go to and finish the [Nauvoo] temple, and God will fill it with power, and you will then receive more knowledge concerning this priesthood."[27]

HONORING PARENTS—THE POWER OF EXAMPLE, THE POWER OF LOVE

The foundational principle that empowers patriarchal leadership is "honoring" and "loving" our parents and ancestors as far back to Father Adam and Mother Eve. In essence, the principle extends

---

25. Dean L. Larsen, "Marriage and the Patriarchal Order," *Ensign*, September 1982.
26. James E. Talmage, "The Eternity of Sex," *Young Woman's Journal*, October 1914, 602–603.
27. *Teachings of the Prophet Joseph Smith*, (Salt Lake City: The Church of Jesus Christ of Latter-day Saints, 2007), 323.

even further to a pure love and worshipping of our heavenly parents. In ancient times the finger of God wrote from Mount Sinai, "Thou shalt have no other gods before me;" and "Honour thy father and thy mother: that thy days may be long upon the land which the Lord thy God giveth thee" (Exodus 20:3, 12). God is our supreme Father, the giver of all, and His righteous, mercy, and glory are the reasons why we should unconditionally love Him "with all your might, mind and strength" (Moroni 10:32).

For each family unit, the patriarchal order begins with temple marriage and expands through temple service. Achieving its endless blessings is accomplished by sealing one set of our ancestral parents to their parents all the way back to Adam and Eve. Patriarchal leadership could not have been achieved without Elijah's return before the dreadful day of the Lord. He carried with him the keys to the temple sealing powers to "turn the hearts of the fathers to the children, and the heart of the children to their fathers, lest I come and smite the earth with a curse" (Malachi 4:5–6). As conditions deteriorate before the dreadful day that precedes the Lord's Second Coming, it is interesting to consider the possibility that one of the reasons why the need to honor our parents has been reemphasized in the last days is that it will be necessary for fathers and mothers to lead by its principles to protect their families from the secret combinations of the last days. Author and Hebrew scholar Avraham Gileadi writes:

> Scriptural prophecies about the last days tell of worldwide calamities that will precede Jesus's Second Coming to the earth. That time of calamity, worse than any other for destructiveness and human misery, will leave only a tithe of the earth's population alive. And yet, in spite of the prophecies, the great day of the earth's judgment will catch most people unawares. World conditions may look promising to those who do not understand the prophecies of the last days. Others will not be deceived by appearances of peace. . . .
>
> But how, we may ask, can we truly prepare for that day? How can we make sure we will be on the Lord's side, and not on the side of those destined to die? . . .

A simple answer to these questions may be that if we honor our father and mother, our days will be long upon the land (compare Ex. 20:12; Deut. 5:16). Lest the iniquity of the fathers come on the children, however (see Ex. 20:5; Deut. 5:9), God has ordained a higher law. This law requires that in addition to honoring our father and mother we honor God (compare 1 Sam. 2:30, John 5:23). As far as it concerns our salvation, temporal or spiritual, the Lord is bound when we do what he says, but when we do not what he says, we have no promise (D&C 82:9–10).[28]

Honoring our parents seems like a straightforward commandment. During their lifetime, I respected my parents' council and loved them. However, during most of my adult life I lived far from them in Switzerland and Arabia. I called my parents a couple of times a month and tried to visit them when on vacation. It was not until I lived in Saudi Arabia that I realized that there was a culture that truly understood what it means to honor a father and a mother. A traditional Arab house is made from sunbaked mud bricks. While visiting with an Arab friend, Fahad, I noticed the decaying ruins of a house next to his modern luxurious villa. To me the crumbling building was simply an ugly eye sore. I asked my friend why he didn't tear down the decaying old structure next to his beautiful mansion. He said, "That is the house of my deceased father and mother. It is our tradition to let our parents' house slowly melt away so that when we see it, our hearts will remember our parents."

Another Arab friend of mine, Saleh, a self-made billionaire who owns companies throughout the Gulf nations and Great Britain, drives each week an hour and a half to spend time visiting his elderly parents. If he was in Saudi Arabia, he never missed a weekend visit to his parents. I had met his humble father. At the time, Saleh's father was in his nineties. Both of Saleh's parents grew up poor and uneducated. Certainly, his parents were clueless as to the complex business and financial affairs of their son. I asked Saleh one day, "What do you

---

28. Avraham Gileadi, *The Last Days: Types and Shadows from the Bible and the Book of Mormon* (Utah: Covenant Communications, 1991), 167–168.

do when you visit your parents each week?" He replied, "I sit with each one for several hours and 'listen' to their advice."

Each day before going to the office of the large company he owns, my Arab friend Faisal visits his blind mother to hand-feed her breakfast. After work and before going to his own family, he returns to his mother to feed her dinner. I asked why his mother's maid didn't feed her. Faisal replied, "I am her son." On another occasion I asked Faisal if he had considered putting his mother into a nursing home. He was shocked and replied, "Who would do such a thing to their mother? There are no nursing homes in Arabia."

While teaching a leadership program on assertiveness, an Arab manager raised his hand and explained to me. "It is hard to say 'no' to a boss in our culture. They are a father figure to us. We are taught to never say no to our parents. I am fifty years old. At times my father makes me so irritated I could scream. But to this day, I have never disagreed to my father. Whatever he says, I do."

Undoubtedly, the deep level of honor my Arab friends have for their parents is rooted in the principles of their religion. The Qur'an teaches: "Thy Lord hath decreed that ye worship none but Him [God] and that ye be kind to parents. Whether one or both of them attain old age in thy life, say not to them a word of contempt, nor repel them, but address them in terms of honour" (Qur'an 17:23).

Paul taught that "in the last days perilous times shall come. For men [children] shall be . . . disobedient to parents, unthankful, unholy" (2 Tim. 3:1–2). However, by being faithful to covenants made in the temple—the initiation to the Patriarchal Order—and by honoring our parents, perilous times do not have to destroy our families. Leadership begins with followship. If you honor, love, and respect your earthly and heavenly parents when hard times arrive, your children will more than likely follow your leadership. Your gospel home-centered teaching will be impactful, the core will be strengthened, and your children will develop immunity against street gangs, drug dealers, internet hidden bullies, and predators and Satan's other secret combinations.

FATHER'S ESSENTIAL ROLE AS THE LEADER OF THE FAMILY

Satan has spared no efforts in trying to degrade the father's responsibility to presided over his family. Ultimately, each priesthood holder will be held responsible by the Lord for the welfare of his family. Ezra Taft Benson has declared, "Each father in the Church is establishing, or should be establishing, his patriarchal order—an order that will extend into the eternities."[29] In 1902, shortly after becoming sixth president of the Church, President Joseph F. Smith stated:

> There is no higher authority in matters relating to the family organization, and especially when that organization is presided over by one holding the higher Priesthood, than that of the father. The authority is time honored, and among the people of God in all dispensations it has been highly respected and often emphasized by the teachings of the prophets who were inspired of God. The patriarchal order is of divine origin and will continue throughout time and eternity. There is, then, a particular reason why men, women and children should understand this order and this authority in the households of the people of God, and seek to make it what God intended it to be, a qualification and preparation for the highest exaltation of his children. In the home the presiding authority is always vested in the father, and in all home affairs and family matters there is no other authority paramount.[30]

Hebrew scholar, John A. Tvedtnes explains: "The term 'patriarch' literally means 'father-ruler' and denotes the relationship of a priesthood holder to his posterity. As we have seen in D&C 107, this priesthood passed from father to son in antiquity."[31] Unfortunately today, a family being led by a righteous patriarch, in partnership with a devoted wife, is rare indeed. As far back as 1968, Dr. Edward J.

---

29. Ezra Taft Benson, *The Teachings of Ezra Taft Benson* (Salt Lake City: Deseret Book, 1981), 138.

30. Joseph F. Smith, *Gospel Doctrine* (Utah: Deseret Book Company, 1968), 286–287.

31. John A. Tvedtnes, "The Patriarchal Order of the Priesthood," *Meridian Magazine*, 19 April 2005. https://latterdaysaintmag.com/article-1-201/.

Rydman, executive director of the American Association of Marriage and Family Counselors, noted:

> . . . [T]here has been a profound shift from the authoritarian family in which the husband-father had the major control over his wife and children. Most of the family power, decision-making responsibility, and authority rested upon him, as did the responsibility for supporting the family economically. The shift from the authoritarian to a more equalitarian family has profoundly affected the position of the head of the family as women have entered the economic marketplace in ever-increasing numbers and especially as even larger numbers of mothers take their place in offices, assembly lines, and other occupations and professions. As women assume more important roles outside the home, so stresses, strains, and problems within the family relationships proliferate.[32]

Again, that was 1968 when Dr. Rydman wrote these words. Since then family leadership has only gotten worse throughout the world. The family, the core and sacred unit of the kingdom, is becoming leaderless. Joseph F. Smith taught:

> In the home the presiding authority is always vested in the father, and in all home affairs and family matters there is no other authority paramount. Wives and children should be taught to feel that the patriarchal order in the kingdom of God has been established for a wise and beneficent purpose, and should sustain the head of the household and encourage him in the discharge of his duties, and do all in their power to aid him in the exercise of the rights and privileges which God has bestowed upon the head of the home. This patriarchal order has its divine spirit and purpose, and those who disregard it under one pretext or another are out of harmony with the spirit of God's laws as they are ordained for recognition in the home. It is not merely a question of who is perhaps the best qualified. Neither is it wholly a question of who is living the

---

32. Edward J. Rydman, in the foreword of *Handbook of Marriage Counseling*, Ben N. Ard, Jr., and Constance Ard, ed. (Science and Behavior Books, Inc., 1969), vii.

most worthy life. It is a question largely of law and order, and its importance is seen often from the fact that the authority remains and is respected long after a man is really unworthy to exercise it.[33]

Ramona Whaley simplified Patriarchal Order leadership the day she married Captain Whaley. She told her new husband, "It is your responsibility to the Lord to provide everything spiritually and temporally for our new family; and it is my responsibility as your wife to support you and raise the kids."[34] A priesthood holder does not have the option of not being the leader of his family. The Patriarchal Order is not one of several good forms of family governance. As John Taylor taught, it is "the only true basis of good domestic and popular government, the ancient and honored patriarchal order, the only one ever sanctioned by heaven."[35] Nothing pleases Satan more than to attack families where there is no patriarch presiding. Again, leadership for the last days starts at home.

TRIBAL GOVERNMENT AND TRIBAL LEADERSHIP

Have you ever wondered why your patriarchal blessing assigns you to a tribe? While it might seem like merely a nice discussion piece around Latter-day Saint friends, in reality the placement into tribes will take on significant importance for those living in the days prior to the Lord's Second Coming. From the little we know about the Lord's government, it appears that it will be organized into tribes. We believe in the "*literal* gathering of Israel and the restoration of the Ten *Tribes*; that Zion (the New Jerusalem) will be built upon the American continent; that Christ will reign personally upon the earth" (Tenth Article of Faith, emphasis added). According to *Encyclopedia of*

33. Joseph F. Smith, *Gospel Doctrine: Selections from the Sermons and Writings of Joseph F. Smith* (Salt Lake City: Deseret Book, 1971), 286.
34. Richard Whaley, "Vietnam Experiences 1971–1972," email to author May 29, 2020.
35. John Taylor, The Gospel Kingdom: Selections from the Writings and Discourses of John Taylor Third President of the Church of Jesus Christ of Latter-day Saints, G. Homer Durham, ed. (Salt Lake City: Deseret Book Company, 2002), 303.

Mormonism, "the patriarchal order of the priesthood is the organizing power and principle of celestial family life. It is the ultimate and ideal form of government."[36] With Christ reigning as king, the patriarchal order will be the incorruptible form of government that will eliminate all secret combinations and will rule during a thousand years of peace and righteousness.

It appears that prior to Lord's Second Coming, tribes will have been at least partially restored. Christ taught: "And then shall appear the sign of the Son of man in heaven: and then shall all the tribes of the earth mourn, and they shall see the Son of man coming in the clouds of heaven with power and great glory" (Matthew 24:30). Specifically, the Lord has instructed:

> For behold, the Lord God hath sent forth the angel crying through the midst of heaven, saying: Prepare ye the way of the Lord, and make his paths straight, for the hour of his coming is nigh—
>
> When the Lamb shall stand upon Mount Zion, with him a hundred and forty-four thousand [12,000 from each tribe] having his Father's name written on their foreheads. (D&C 133:17–18)

The 133rd section of the Doctrine and Covenants describes those who will return from the northern countries (the Lost Tribes) and "there they shall fall down and be crowned with glory, even in Zion, by the hands of the servants of the Lord, even the children of Ephraim" (D&C 133:32). We can only wonder what it means that the tribes will be "crowned" by the leaders of the Church. A crown could imply some form of governing authority. What we are told is that "this is the blessing of the everlasting God upon the tribes" (D&C 133:34).

It would appear that in the days of the tribulation, and in preparation for establishing New Jerusalem, your membership in a tribe of Israel through your patriarchal blessing will be of great importance to you. You will be members and family leaders of an actual tribe. Perhaps you will even experience the same feelings that will be

---

36. Lynn A. Mckinlay, "Patriarchal Order of the Priesthood," *Encyclopedia of Mormonism* (New York: MacMillan Publishing Company, 1992), 1067.

experienced by the Lost Tribes when they returned and realized their true identities: "And they shall be filled with songs of everlasting joy" (D&C 133:33).

THE NEED FOR TRIBAL (PATRIARCHAL) LEADERSHIP DURING THE YEARS OF TRIBULATION

The organizing of the Lord's people into tribes in the last days is probably the result of the restoration of the Patriarch Order but might also be necessitated by living conditions as more and more legitimate governments fail due to the general wickedness of the people and the evil forces' secret combinations. Even amidst the rule of gangs, warlords, communist governments, and other forms of secret combinations, if family tribes and their leaders are strong enough, they will be able to resist the destructive power of Satan's secret combinations. We read in the Book of Mormon how tribalism protected even the unrighteous Nephites from the Gadianton robbers at a time, which shadows in many ways the wicked conditions prophesized of the last days:

> Now behold, I will show unto you that they [the Gadianton robbers] did not establish a king over the land; but in the same year, yea, the thirtieth year, they did destroy upon the judgment-seat, yea, did murder the chief judge of the land.
>
> And the people were divided one against another; and they did separate one from another into tribes, every man according to his family and his kindred and friends; and thus they did destroy the government of the land.
>
> And every tribe did appoint a chief or a leader over them; and thus they became tribes and leaders of tribes.
>
> Now behold, there was no man among them save he had much family and many kindreds and friends; therefore their tribes became exceedingly great.
>
> . . . Now this secret combination, which had brought so great iniquity upon the people, did gather themselves together, and did place at their head a man whom they did call Jacob;

And they did call him their king; therefore he became a king over this wicked band; and he was one of the chiefest who had given his voice against the prophets who testified of Jesus.

And it come to pass that they were not so strong in number as the tribes of the people, who were united together save it were their leaders did establish their laws, every one according to his tribes; nevertheless they were enemies; notwithstanding they were not a righteous people, yet they were united in the hatred of those who had entered into a covenant to destroy the government. (3 Nephi 7:1–4, 9–11)

There are several important lessons we can learn from the sad situation the unrighteous Nephites had to endure. First, like then, most of the world will be wicked before the Lord's Second Coming. To defeat the powerful secret combinations, righteous leaders will probably need to bond together with unrighteous family members and neighbors into tribal alliances. Second, the Nephite tribes only became exceeding great because its members had "much family and many kindreds and friends." The message seems clear to leaders who want to resist the secret combinations—you must cement family bonds and create and maintain a strong and vast network of kindreds and friends. Third, even though the Nephite tribes were enemies to one another, there were no wars among them (3 Nephi 7:5) because they were united in their hatred of the Gadianton robbers. If the chaotic conditions that precede the Second Coming of Christ mirror what the Nephites experienced before the first coming of Christ to them, then leaders will need to be alliance builders among opposing tribes in order to overcome the power of the secret combinations. In other words, leaders will need to agree with opposing tribes to shared visions and commitment to common goals and objectives.

Finally, without a central government, the Nephites, through their individual tribes, were able to maintain a level of civil order by establishing their own laws. While living in Arabia, I would often ask Arabs, "What would happen if the Saudi Royal Family decided to pack up and leave Saudi Arabia?" The common answer was, "Nothing much, the nation would just revert back to seven main tribes and everyone would just continue on with their lives." By having an established line of patriarchal order (father to son), tribes can quickly establish order since there is a common sense of who rules the tribe and each of its units— the senior elder or patriarch. The question that begs to be answered is, "What would be the nature of the laws your tribe would adopt?" If the elders of Zion are to save the Constitution of the United States, hopefully righteous leaders will study the Constitution and will have the leadership skills necessary to influence their tribes to establish such a divinely inspired order.

WHAT IS TRIBAL LEADERSHIP?

There have been many dispensations since a righteous form of the Patriarchal Order ruled the faithful. I know of no modern inspired example to study. The Patriarchal Order is the most ancient of all forms of government, dating back to Father Adam and Mother Eve. While living in the Middle East, I witnessed how the Arabs still practice their traditional form of the family rule. The Arab father is ultimately responsible for the family and for the education of his children after the age of eight years. Before the child reaches the age of eight, the mother is responsible for nurturing the children. The oldest son of the family is responsible for the family when the father is absent. The eldest son will receive a "second portion" of the father's will or estate. He is to use the second portion to care for his mother and unmarried sisters.

Every father of the Arab family is accountable to his oldest brother for the welfare, education, and conduct of his family. In turn, that elder brother is then responsible to the senior uncle in the family for the welfare, education, and conduct of all the families under his care, and so forth all the way up the line to the chief elder of the tribe. Through each level of the Arab tribe, the fathers or elders meet together to council with one another and to discuss the needs of the tribe at their level. For example, if one member of the tribe needs a medical operation but does not have the funds, the tribal leaders at that level will request support from all the families so that the person can receive their operation. An Arab tribe can consist of over 100,000 members and is a powerful force for protection and mutual welfare. It also can serve as a means of civil order. If a member of the tribe does anything to dishonor the tribe's name, they must account to the tribal chiefs for what they have done. The ultimate punishment for an Arab is not a death sentence; it is banishment from his or her tribe.

Being born into an Arab tribe, one becomes a member of a great family, each individual a cousin to each member of the entire tribe. An Arab friend gave me this example of how leadership functions in his tribe, the Al Naim tribe in eastern Saudi Arabia. One of its members married an American wife while he was attending a university in the United States. Of course, before being permitted to marry her, the student needed the permission of his father and the senior members of the Al Naim tribe. Why? Because she would become a member of the tribe and the tribe would be responsible for her care and welfare. After completing his studies, the student returned to Saudi Arabia and began a career as an engineer for Saudi Aramco. Soon the couple was blessed with two children. Unfortunately, one night while driving home, the father's car hit a camel and he was killed. The entire tribe grieved at his death.

Following her husband's death, the American mother decided to return to her family in the United States. The tribe was devastated at her decision. They insisted that she and the children should stay in Saudi Arabia. The tribe promised to take care of all her needs and those of her children. She understood their love for her and the children but resolved to return to the United States. The grandfather of the children then met with his senior uncle (elder) to request that the senior uncle meet with his senior patriarch and to request him to meet with the Al Naim tribal chief. The grandfather requested that the Al Naim tribal chief meet with the governor of the East Providence of Saudi Arabia to ask him to prohibit the children, Saudi citizens, from moving to the United States. Their entire legal ground for making the request was "that the tribe could not bear the loss of two of their cherished children." The governor acknowledged the pain the family would experience by losing the children, however he ruled that the mother had the right to return to the United States with her children.

Of course, the Arab form of patriarch order cannot be compared to the order practiced by Adam and Eve. For example, the Arab husbands and wives do not share the leadership responsibilities equally. Still, I believe my Arab friends can provide some hierarchal insights as to how leadership functioned in ancient times. In their commentary on the Doctrine and Covenants, gospel scholars Leaun Otten and Max Caldwell discuss the attributes of the Patriarchal Order in ancient times including a review by President Spencer W. Kimball of the practices of patriarch Abraham. President Kimball taught that every father (patriarch) should emulate the example of Abraham in his leadership position in his home.[37]

1. He followed Jesus Christ.

2. He sought for priesthood and priesthood blessings. (Patriarchal Power)

3. He gave prompt obedience.

4. He received revelation for his family.

5. He presided over his family in righteousness.

6. He taught his family the gospel by example and precept.

7. He gave missionary service.

8. He acted as a peacemaker.

9. He possessed integrity—he kept his covenants at all costs.

10. He was honest with others.

11. He paid a full tithe—he put God first.

12. He exercised faith.[38]

Encyclopedia of Mormonism, "Gospel of Abraham" reads: "The gospel dispensation of Abraham includes the patriarchal order of the priesthood and the eternal marriage covenant (D&C 131:1–4; 132:28–30), by which the Abrahamic Covenant is perpetuated from generation to generation among the faithful. . . . The restoration of all things included the restoration of the keys to Joseph Smith to make

---

37. Leaun G. Otten & C. Max Caldwell, *Sacred Truths of the Doctrine and Covenants*, Vol. 2 (Salt Lake City, Deseret Book Company, 1993), 361.
38. See also Spencer W. Kimball, "The Example of Abraham," *Ensign*, June 1975, 3–7.

it possible in modern times for all who do the works of Abraham to inherit the covenant and blessings of Abraham."[39]

I personally believe that the need for the restoration of the patriarchal order in the last days is to help establish the Lord's form of government and to develop righteous leaders for that government who can ward off the secret combinations of Satan and provide the legal foundations for the Millennium. If you want to be a patriarch leader in this cause, following Abraham's example is a good starting point.

Spring Hill is named by the Lord Adam-ondi-Ahman, because, said he, it is the place where Adam shall come to visit his people, or the Ancient of Days shall sit, as spoken of by Daniel the prophet. (D&C 116:1)

---

39. Joel A. Flake, "Gospel of Abraham," *Encyclopedia of Mormonism* (New York: Macmillan Publishing, 1992), 555–556.

A people unused to restraint must be led, they will not be drove.

—George Washington to Major General Stirling,
19 January 1777

Principle 3

Equality with Meritocracy

ASSUME YOU ARE FACED BY AN ANGRY MOB THAT IS LOOTING, BURN-
ing, and attacking innocent citizens in your community. Maybe they
have no food because of a plague or natural disaster. Perhaps they
believe they have been unfairly treated their entire lives. When the
mob is raging, how does a leader stop the violence and restore order?
The solution starts by understanding what is the root cause of Blacks,
the urban poor, white supremacy groups, and other disassociated
groups in America demonstrating their anger? Whether these groups
are justified or not in their behavior, how would you feel if you believed
you were treated your entire life as a second-class citizen and under
privileged in your own homeland. If the leader believes they can gain
the mob's co-operation by just arresting its members or hitting them
over the head with billy clubs, their leadership won't succeed.

As always, the best cure for the problem is prevention. A recent
study on prison violence revealed that over 200 riots have occurred
between 1900 and 1970. A Select Committee on Crime listed the following problems as contributing to prison riots: poorly trained staff,
rural prison location, inmate overcrowding, lack of inmate educational programs, and insufficient vocational training. Three theories
have been proposed to explain riotous behavior. These include the
conflict theory, spontaneous behavior theory, and collective behavior
theory. Research into rioting reveals three important procedures that

can assist in preventing riots: inmate grievance mechanisms to hear and resolve inmate complaints, use of inmate councils to communicate with prison officials, and use of attitudinal survey instruments for inmates to communicate their concerns.[1]

In today's reality, many urban poor, regardless of race, have the notion, whether false or true, that they are being unfairly suppressed by a privileged class. Their resentment seems real to them since traditional income opportunities in high-paying production jobs have vanished through automated technologies or have been exported. House and rental costs have skyrocketed in the "hood." Their children watch internet and television ads that flaunt the happiness that seems to follow the purchase of new cars, expensive vacations, and stately homes. Gangs rule their communities and at times individual policemen have abused their positions or misused their weapons. As gaps continue to widen in the wealth, educational opportunities, and wage earning between social classes, the world is becoming ever riper for civil disobedience—a polite word for rioting.

What can leaders do to prevent mob rioting? Again, three tools were found effective in preventing prison riots: 1) a grievance mechanism; 2) councils to communicate these complaints; and 3) surveys of those involved to understand their needs. I would add two more tools: 4) effective programs through your community, government, and/or church to help those through aid, education, and jobs; and 5) interaction and education programs to eliminate racism and help create social inclusiveness.

As a leader, President Russell M. Nelson is an excellent example of fostering a positive approach to solving the root cause of civil disobedience. He made the following statement with regard to the tragic murder of George Floyd.

President Nelson's Facebook post said:

> We join with many throughout this nation and around the world who are deeply saddened at recent evidences of racism and a blatant disregard for human life. We abhor the reality

---

1. S. D. Dillingham and R. H. Montgomery, "Can Riots Be Prevented?" *Corrections Today*, Vol. 44, Issue 5 (October 1982) 50,52,54–56. https://www.ojp. gov/ncjrs/virtual-library/abstracts/can-riots-be-prevented, accessed 24 July 2021.

that some would deny others respect and the most basic of freedoms because of the color of his or her skin.

We are also saddened when these assaults on human dignity lead to escalating violence and unrest.

The Creator of us all calls on each of us to abandon attitudes of prejudice against any group of God's children. Any of us who has prejudice toward another race needs to repent!

During the Savior's earthly mission, He constantly ministered to those who were excluded, marginalized, judged, overlooked, abused, and discounted. As his followers, can we do anything less? The answer is no! We believe in freedom, kindness, and fairness for all of God's children![2]

In a Brigham Young University devotional, President Dallin H. Oaks explained the need for respecting all human life, but not using this truth as an excuse to justify wrong actions. Two wrongs never equal a right.

Of course Black lives matter! That is an eternal truth all reasonable people should support. Unfortunately, that persuasive banner was sometimes used or understood to stand for other things that do not command universal support. Examples include abolishing the police or seriously reducing their effectiveness or changing our constitutional government. All these are appropriate subjects for advocacy, but not under what we hope to be the universally accepted message: Black lives matter.

Now I speak of the subject that commands our attention—racism. Dictionaries typically define *racism* as "involving the idea that one's own race is superior [to others] and has the right to rule [over them]." This idea has led to many racist laws and administrative policies.

2. Russell M. Nelson, "President Nelson Shares Social Post about Racism and Calls for Respect for Human Dignity," *Newsroom.churchofjesuschrist.org*, 1 June 2020.

Some religious people have sought to justify practices of racism by references to the Bible, as I will discuss later. Nevertheless, the proper understanding of scriptures—ancient and modern—and recent prophetic statements help us to see that racism, as defined, is not consistent with the revealed word of God. [3]

The key is for a righteous leader to earn the angry mob's trust by treating the mob's leaders as equals and to recruit them into solving society's problems through positive engagement. The righteous leader needs to convince the mob that by joining together on the same team, things will get better and with time wrongs will be corrected. Dr. Hugh Nibley explained:

> The leader, for example, has a passion for *equality*. We think of great generals from David and Alexander on down, sharing their beans or *maza* with their men, calling them by their first names, marching along with them in the heat, sleeping on the ground, and first over the wall. A famous ode by a long-suffering Greek soldier, Archilochus, reminds us that the men in the ranks are not fooled for an instant by the executive type who thinks he is a leader.[4]

A policeman pushing people back with his riot gear and badge, or a Church leader demanding compliance based solely on his position, can think of themselves as "managers" of situations, but certainly not "leaders" in building a better world. They will never gain true cooperation, just movement. Nibley continues:

> For the manager, on the other hand, the idea of equality is repugnant and indeed counterproductive. Where promotion, perks, privilege, and power are the name of the game, awe and reverence for *rank* is everything, the inspiration and motivation of all good men. Where would management

---

3. Dallin H. Oaks, "Racism and Other Challenges," Brigham Young University devotional, 27 October 2020, speeches.byu.edu.
4. Hugh Nibley, "Leaders and Managers," Brigham Young University commencement address, 19 August 1983, speeches.byu.edu.

be without the inflexible paper processing, dress standards, attention to proper social, political, and religious affiliation, vigilant watch over habits and attitudes, and so forth, that gratify the stockholders and satisfy security?

"If you love me," said the Greatest of all leaders, "you will keep my commandments." "If you know what is good for me," says the manager, "you will keep *my* commandments, and not make waves." That is why the rise of management always marks the decline of culture.[5]

Treating people as equals will not cure all society's ills, but it just might save your community, your congregation, or your city from the violence and chaos that is sure to escalate in the latter days. Nephi, the son of Helaman, identified inequality as the root cause of the doomed Nephite society:

> Condemning the righteous because of their righteousness; letting the guilty and the wicked go unpunished because of their money; and moreover to be held in office at the head of government, to rule and do according to their wills, that they might get gain and glory of the world, and, moreover, that they might the more easily commit adultery, and steal, and kill, and do according to their own wills— (Helaman 7:5)

We are all children of God, and our Father, the Supreme Leader, is no respecter of men. This is not a cliché; it is a principle that might keep your city from burning. It is the principle that helped Captain Whaley put an end to the race riots during his command in Vietnam. Army LTC Richard Whaley retired as the Assistant Director of Military Affairs for The Church of Jesus Christ of Latter-day Saints. He led a company during the darkest days of the Vietnam War. Whaley inherited the company where on a daily basis Army officers were being threatened or mugged by their own soldiers. Drug gangs controlled the barracks and racial riots ignited on a regular basis. When the enemy attacked the base, many soldiers were so stoned on juicy fruit (Thai pot) or heroin that they could not man their post.

---

5. Ibid.

Prostitutes frequented the barracks and many soldiers spent more time looking for whores than the enemy. Richard's situation was not uncommon—it was Vietnam. What was different is that Whaley succeeded in making a difference. He earned a Bronze Star for stopping a riot. He recalls:

My NCOIC, a MSG was a big, highly competent African American NCO. I mention this because one must remember that the early 1970s saw a lot of racial discord in the military

Richard Whaley in Vietnam

and we were not exempt in my unit in Vietnam as I shall explain later. He knew his job and, best of all: he knew mine, too! It gave me time to learn some of the stuff; but I was decidedly out-of-my league as Transportation was NOT my branch.

I arrived at the 5th Trans around the 20th of March, 1971. On the 29th, my second wedding anniversary was spent in a foxhole watching the war. We were hit with a rocket attack that night which lasted a couple hours. (I did not go into the bunker that had been constructed because I had been told that there were cobra snakes in it. I do not know if that was true as I never went in there.) This was also the day the Marines pulled out of Monkey Mountain to redeploy Stateside (the Marines had conducted nightly patrols around the area and Charlie laid low. Now that they were gone, Charlie sent his "welcome" to us.) No one was injured (seldom did they hit anyone although they did hit the Officer's Club one night which upset everyone!) but I do remember saying to myself: "What am I doing here?" One thing that gave me comfort that night was knowing that I was blessed with a competent black non-commissioned officer. With his help I just might survive.[6]

ENDING RACISM ONCE AND FOR ALL

Ending racism and the violence it produces starts at home. The article entitled "President of Church of Jesus Christ and NAACP leaders call for changes to root out racism" was published in the Church owned *Deseret News* on June 8, 2020. It reads in part:

> In a joint op-ed published Monday by Medium, the president of The Church of Jesus Christ of Latter-day Saints and the senior national leaders of the NAACP called for racial reform in America's homes, schools, businesses and political bodies.
>
> "We share deep sorrow for the senseless, heinous act of violence that needlessly took the life of George Floyd. We mourn with his family, friends and community," the four co-authors wrote in an 844-word piece that is the latest product of an unexpected partnership that began two years ago.
>
> The piece was signed by the presidents of both organizations — Russell M. Nelson, president of The Church of Jesus Christ of Latter-day Saints since 2018, and Derrick Johnson, the president and CEO of the NAACP [National Association for the Advancement of Colored People] since 2017. The other signers are Leon Russell, chairman of the NAACP's national board of directors, and the Rev. Amos C. Brown, the emeritus chairman of religious affairs and former student of Martin Luther King Jr.
>
> They called on parents and families to be the first line of defense because "prejudice, hate and discrimination are learned."
>
> They also called for changes to end systemic racism.

---

6. Richard, Whaley, "Vietnam Experiences 1971–1972, " email to author, May 29, 2020.

"We likewise call on government, business and educational leaders at every level to review processes, laws and organizational attitudes regarding racism and root them out once and for all," they added. "It is past time for every one of us to elevate our conversations above divisive and polarizing rhetoric. Treating others with respect matters. Treating each other as sons and daughters of God matters."[7]

On the same day as the above article, the Church emailed its members the following social media message from the prophet issued on June 1, 2020:

We join with many throughout this nation and around the world who are deeply saddened at recent evidences of racism and a blatant disregard for human life. We abhor the reality that some would deny others respect and the most basic of freedoms because of the color of his or her skin.

We are also saddened when these assaults on human dignity lead to escalating violence and unrest.

The Creator of us all calls on each of us to abandon attitudes of prejudice against any group of God's children. Any of us who has prejudice toward another race needs to repent!

During the Savior's earthly mission, He constantly ministered to those who were excluded, marginalized, judged, overlooked, abused, and discounted. As His followers, can we do anything less? The answer is no! We believe in freedom, kindness, and fairness for all of God's children!

Let us be clear. We are brothers and sisters, each of us the child of a loving Father in Heaven. His Son, the Lord Jesus Christ, invites all to come unto Him—"black and white, bond and free, male and female," (2 Nephi 26:33). It behooves each of us to do whatever we can in our spheres of influence to preserve the dignity and respect every son and daughter of God deserves.

---

7. Tad Walch, "President of Church of Jesus Christ and NAACP leaders call for changes to root out racism," *Deseret News*, 8 June 2020.

Any nation can only be as great as its people. That requires citizens to cultivate a moral compass that helps them distinguish between right and wrong.

Illegal acts such as looting, defacing, or destroying public or private property cannot be tolerated. Never has one wrong been corrected by a second wrong. Evil has never been resolved by more evil.

We need to foster our faith in the Fatherhood of God and the brotherhood of man.

We need to foster a fundamental respect for the human dignity of every human soul, regardless of their color, creed, or cause.

And we need to work tirelessly to build bridges of understanding rather than creating walls of segregation.

I plead with us to work together for peace, for mutual respect, and for an outpouring of love for all of God's children.[8]

The same Church email provided these recommendations:

In an op-ed by President Russell M. Nelson and leaders of the National Association for the Advancement of Colored People—Derrick Johnson, Leon Russell, and Amos C. Brown—they describe how their unlikely collaborations can serve as an example of how we can open our hearts to build bonds of respect, reconciliation, and love.

To be part of the solution, they invite all to:
- Pray that we will all abandon attitudes of prejudice.
- Look for ways to reach out and serve someone of a different background or race.
- Teach children in the home to love all and to find the good in others.
- Learn to value the differences in others.

"Arm in arm and shoulder to shoulder, may we strive to lift our brothers and sisters everywhere, in every way we can."

---

8. Russell M. Nelson, quoted in "President Nelson Shares Social Post about Racism and Calls for Respect for Human Dignity," *Newsroom.churchofjesuschrist. org*, 1 June 2020.

In the last days, Satan will try to turn the hearts of the children of men against one another, Christian against Muslim, black against white, legal residents against refugees, police against criminals, gang against gang, the poor against the rich, spouse against spouse, son against father; his tactics for brewing hatred are everywhere. President Ezra Taft Benson declared, "The central feature of pride is enmity— enmity toward God and enmity toward our fellowmen. *Enmity* means 'hatred toward, hostility to, or a state of opposition.' It is the power by which Satan wishes to reign over us."[9] Even the word "race" is a Satanic lie to divide people. Scientists now hold that race is a myth noting that 99.9% of all human DNA is the same regardless of where one was born in the world.[10] We are all descendants of our first earthly parents and are all members of the family of our Heavenly Parents.

I spent 26 years in Saudi Arabia. While there I traveled extensively in some of the country's most remote areas retracing the migrations of the Jaredite and Lehite families. I slept in Bedouin tents and often dined at the invitation of Arab tribesmen. I know that in my world travels of over eighty countries, I have never met a more hospitable and caring people than the Muslim Arabs. Yet, after 9/11, I became so disgusted by the hate mail I received about the Arabs from my Latter-day Saint friends, I decided to write the novel *The White Bedouin* in an effort to show the world just how much the Latter-day Saints and our Muslim brothers have in common. To illustrate just how fearful and prejudiced people can be, I recall this experience I had:

> Many of the Americans who work in Saudi Arabia only seldom leave their guarded residential housing compounds to meet everyday Arabs. They are even more reluctant to venture into the outback desert in fear of the native Bedouin or are worried they might stumble upon a terrorist camp—which odds are less than being hit by lighting. At times, Latter-day Saints living in Saudi Arabia would ask me to take them to

---

9. Ezra Taft Benson, "Beware of Pride," April 1989 general conference.
10. "Genetics vs. Genomics: Why are genetics and genomics important to my health?" *National Human Genome Research Institute*, last updated 7 September 2018. https://www.genome.gov/about-genomics/fact-sheets/Genetics-vs-Genomics, accessed July 16, 2020.

see some of the interesting sights in the desert. On one such occasion I planned an outing that included a traditional Bedouin market, an abandoned adobe city, an ancient hilltop fortress, and a remote cave where huge mastodon bones and tusk are exposed.

On route to the mastodon cave, I was being followed by five 4X4 vehicles full of my guests. We were driving slowly to avoid getting stuck in soft sand. Suddenly, seemly out of nowhere, an old Toyota pickup came roaring up to the side my truck. A young Bedouin was wildly waving his headdress out the window of his truck as he approached me. I stopped. The Bedouin stuck his head out the window of his truck and made extended gestures at me with his hands. He spoke no English but seemed determine to get his message across.

I knew what the young man wanted. But what do you think the people in the cars behind me were thinking? In fear, they stopped a good hundred yards behind me, not wanting to get involved. Later I learned that each group in the five cars that followed were thinking something different was occurring. Some thought I was being robbed. Others thought the young man was the age of a terrorist and that we were in danger of attack. One truckload thought we had trespassed on some tribal land and were being told to get out. And so on.

The incident became even more confusing when the young man got out of his truck, reached back into the cab, brought out an infant baby, walked over to me and handed me the newborn baby.

Here's what actually was happening. In the Bedouin tradition, if you see a stranger in the desert you are obliged to invite him to your tent and host him for three days. The young Bedouin wanted me and my entire group to come to his tent. He gestured that he wanted to feed us by slaughtering some of his sheep and have us meet his extended family. When I let him know in my limited Arabic that we didn't have time that day for a long visit, his wife, who was sitting in the car, must have been disappointed, probably thinking that we did not trust them. She gave her infant child to her husband to give to me as a sign of trust and love. The infant was such a sweet soul.

It was just another one of the hundreds of wonderful experiences I had with the Arab Bedouin. Yet, all of my guests showed their prejudice (pre-judging) by assuming the young man was a person bent on doing us harm. They were so quick to judge people who were different from them. They didn't understand the saying, "A friend is a stranger I have not yet met."

Repeating, President Nelson has declared that "any of us who has prejudice toward another race needs to repent!" While Blacks might be the most vocal in expressing the need to eliminate racism, and justly so, the Gentiles will face the wrath of a much broader group of people if they don't repent of their prejudice in the last days:

And then, O ye Gentiles, how can ye stand before the power of God, except ye shall repent and turn from your evil ways?

Know ye not that ye are in the hands of God? Know ye not that he hath all power, and at his great command the earth shall be rolled together as a scroll?

Therefore, repent ye, and humble yourselves before him, lest he shall come out in justice against you—lest a remnant of the seed of Jacob shall go forth among you as a lion, and tear you in pieces, and there is none to deliver. (Mormon 5:22–24)

What is certain is that good people can win the war against inequality and racism if we follow the example of the Savior. It is essential to understand that when Jesus taught us to be perfect like our Father in Heaven, it wasn't about the Word of Wisdom or tithing, it was in reference to how we treat others. In His own words: "And if ye love them which love you, what reward have ye? Do not even the publicans the same? And if ye salute your brethren only, what do ye more than others? Do not even the publicans so? Be ye therefore perfect, even as your Father which is in heaven is perfect" (Matthew 5:46-48).

On December 18, 2020, the Church of Jesus Christ of Latter-day Saints announced:

All people are children of God. All are brothers and sisters who are part of His divine family. Prejudice is not consistent with the revealed word of God. Favor or disfavor with God depends on devotion to Him and His commandments, not on the color of a person's skin or other attributes. The Church calls on all people to abandon attitudes and actions of prejudice toward any group or individual.[11]

Could the Lord be any more clear? If a leader does not love his followers, regardless of their race, he or she is not qualified to lead in the kingdom of God—either before or during the Millennium.

REWARD PEOPLE FAIRLY AND BASED ON MERITOCRACY

As much as we admire the faith of Prophet Israel, his biased treatment of his son Joseph got his other children so angry that his favorite son was nearly killed by his own brothers and subsequently sold off as a slave to a caravan bound for Egypt. Indeed, it is a gross case of hypocrisy if you tell someone they are equal in your eyes, and then you pay them less than their labor is worth. Regardless of race, gender, or any other excuse, if a leader treats people unfairly, they will be subject to God. It is equally unjust for a man or women to demand more pay than they merit.

Lest we forget, the everlasting principle for income distribution is the United Order where people of the Church are to be treated "every man equal according to his family, according to his circumstances and his wants and needs" (D&C 51:3) and "let every man deal honestly, and be alike among this people, and receive alike, that ye may be one even as I have commanded you" (D&C 51:9). The United Order is eternal and is presently only in abeyance (D&C 105:34) probably due to our inability to merit equal blessings or to share our blessings

---

11. Newsroom of The Church of Jesus Christ of Latter-day Saints, "Church handbook update: Prejudice, policies for members with disabilities, and more topics included," *LDSLiving*, 18 December 2020.

equally. Regardless, today we are not living the United Order and are missing out of a "multiplicity of blessings" (D&C 104:2). As described in the book of Revelation, the day will come when people will be in dire need for food, water, shelter, and medical services. To survive as a community, leaders will need to inspire their followers to share their resources, and to do so based on merit and need.

Unfortunately, incomes are becoming less and less equal. Today's greedy world is rotten to the core in favoritism and materialism. Today's favorite sons are lavished in the modern idols of gold, silicon, and easy invitations to a carnal lifestyle. On the one hand, we have greedy politicians who enter public service with moderate wealth and retire as billionaires; corporate CEOs grabbing salaries and bonuses hundreds of times more than their average hardworking employees; abusive oil sheiks flying in gold-plated private jumbo jets; medical providers who bankrupt their patients with outrageous fees; greedy moneylenders who charge usurious rates; and even corrupt heads of charities and religious organizations. On the opposing side are social-ists preaching that everyone's desires for the material benefits of the society should be a right from birth rather than earned through merit; greedy attorneys burdening misery on people wherever they believe they can land the big settlement; and state-run lotteries preying on desperate victims. The worship of the material by both the haves and have nots has the world sitting on a loaded powder keg and don't expect things will get better until the Lord comes and ends man's thirst for idolatry, hedonism, and self-gratification.

For example, the May 2020 unfortunate death of George Floyd by abusive police officers in Minneapolis was followed by peaceful Black Lives Matter protests. However, as nightfall came, the justified protests were hijacked by greedy looters wanting what they believe is their share of those good things in life, à la wide-screen TVs, the latest I-phones, designer clothes, or controlled drugs in pharmacy safes. Materialism fueled the lootings, not the concern for police abuse on Blacks.

On a global scale, we saw a similar pattern with the failed Arabia Spring movement. Impoverished citizens of oil rich countries rose up against their exploiting rulers just to fight among themselves over how large a share of the oil booty their tribe should receive. It was this same downward spiral of materialism that doomed the Nephites and will only get worse as the world returns to Babylon. As one venture capitalist billionaire Nick Hanauer warned his fellow billionaires.

I see pitchforks.

At the same time that people like you and me are thriving beyond the dreams of any plutocrats in history, the rest of the country—the 99.99 percent—is lagging far behind. The divide between the haves and have-nots is getting worse really, really fast. In 1980, the top 1 percent controlled about 8 percent of U.S. national income. The bottom 50 percent shared about 18 percent. Today the top 1 percent share about 20 percent; the bottom 50 percent, just 12 percent.

But the problem isn't that we have inequality. Some inequality is intrinsic to any high-functioning capitalist economy. The problem is that inequality is at historically high levels and getting worse every day. Our country is rapidly becoming less a capitalist society and more a feudal society. Unless our policies change dramatically, the middle class will disappear, and we will be back to late 18th-century France. Before the revolution.

And so I have a message for my fellow filthy rich, for all of us who live in our gated bubble worlds: Wake up, people. It won't last.

If we don't do something to fix the glaring inequities in this economy, the pitchforks are going to come for us. No society can sustain this kind of rising inequality. In fact, there is no example in human history where wealth accumulated like this and the pitchforks didn't eventually come out. You show me a highly unequal society, and I will show you a police state. Or an uprising. There are no counterexamples. None. It's not if, it's when.[12]

Just three short years before the Lord appeared to the Nephites and Lamanites, Satan used pride and financial inequality to completely

---

12. Nick Hanauer, "The Pitchforks Are Coming . . . For Us Plutocrats," *Politico Magazine*, July/August 2014. https://www.politico.com/magazine/story/2014/06/the-pitchforks-are-coming-for-us-plutocrats-108014, accessed 1 June 2020.

break up the Church among the Nephites. Satan was successful in keeping the Nephites from having the Church ready for the Lord's coming unto them. As a result, there was great destruction and sorrow at His coming.

> But it came to pass in the twenty and ninth year there began to be some disputings among the people; and some were lifted up unto pride and boastings because of their exceedingly great riches, yea, even unto great persecutions;
>
> For there were many merchants in the land, and also many lawyers, and many officers.
>
> And the people began to be distinguished by ranks, according to their riches and their chances for learning; yea, some were ignorant because of their poverty, and others did receive great learning because of their riches,
>
> Some were lifted up in pride, and others were exceeding humble; some did return railing for railing, while others would receive railing and persecution and all manner of afflictions, and would not turn and revile again, but were humble and penitent before God.
>
> And thus there became a great inequality in all the land, insomuch that the church began to be broken up; yea, insomuch that in the thirtieth year the church was broken up in all the land save it were among a few of the Lamanites who were converted unto the true faith; and they would not depart from it, for they were firm, and steadfast, and immovable, willing with all diligence to keep the commandments of the Lord.
>
> Now the cause of this iniquity of the people was this— Satan had great power, unto the stirring up of the people to do all manner of iniquity, and to the puffing them up with pride, tempting them to seek for power, and authority, and riches, and the vain things of the world. (3 Nephi 6:10–15)

The question begs to be answered, as materialism takes an even greater grip on the children of men, where human life matters little and greed reigns unrestrained, what can a leader do to maintain a degree of safety and order? Equality will help. Apply the principle by treating everyone, regardless of wealth, education, rank, race, beliefs, or income level, as equals. Hugh Nibley wrote:

> To Parkinson's Law, which shows how management gobbles up everything else, he added what he calls the "Law of Injelitance": Managers do not promote individuals whose competence might threaten their own position; and so as the power of management spreads ever wider, the quality deteriorates, if that is possible. In short, while management shuns *equality*, it feeds on *mediocrity*.[13]

Captain Whaley wrote about racial tension in Vietnam:

> Racial tension was high—Blacks felt they were being overlooked in promotion decisions. I was called into the CO's office and asked why I promoted a white soldier over a black soldier. "This will cause more riots," the CO complained. I replied, "I would have promoted the African American soldier but he would have failed. He did not have the proper training. Instead, I promoted the other soldier who knew how to do the job and would not have decreased the war-time readiness of our company. However, I insisted that the promoted soldier train the Black soldier over the next two months so that he would get the next promotion if ready." The solution was fair, understood by each party as appropriate and in their best interest, and there was no racial tension over the decision. Two months later the Black soldier was ready, trained, received his promotion and succeeded in his new position.[14]

This story might seem antidotal, however, it pinpoints an important prophecy for those who live in the Americas, the land of promise, and the people who consider themselves Gentiles. They must treat everyone in a Christ-like manner—fairly and based on merit. If you are an American Gentile, it is best to stop complaining about illegal

---

13. Hugh Nibley, "Leaders and Managers," Brigham Young University commencement address, 19 August 1983, speeches.byu.edu.
14. Richard Whaley, "Vietnam Experiences 1971–1972," email to author May 29, 2020.

aliens, street gangs, and Latino drug cartels and consider this question: How do I treat those who are descendants of original inhabitants of the promised land? Do you practice any form, and in any degree, economic slavery or social bigotry? If so, have you repented? The Lord Himself has warned the Gentiles in the Americas as to how they must treat Lehi's seed. As noted earlier, the same warning to the Gentiles was repeated by the Lord through Mormon:

> And the Father hath commanded me that I should give unto you this land, for your inheritance.
>
> And I say unto you, that if the Gentiles do not repent after the blessing which they shall receive, after they have scattered my people—
>
> Then shall ye, who are a remnant of the house of Jacob, go forth among them; and ye shall be in the midst of them who shall be many; and ye shall be among them as a young lion among the flocks of sheep, who, if he goeth through both treadeth down and teareth down and teareth in pieces, and none can deliver. (3 Nephi 20:14–16)

The Lord did not provide exemptions to the Golden Rule. Leaders in the latter days must apply the rule's wisdom to all people regardless of skin color, heritage, religion, etc. Be fair to everyone; promote people based on performance and pay based on merit. Poverty, ignorance, disenfranchisement, and greed will nurture gangs, drugs, human trafficking, and eventually mob violence. Treating people fairly won't eliminate all of our society's problems; however, it might keep your home from being torn apart by mobs behaving like young lions.

Ghandi faced a very difficult situation in India. As the British started pulling out of India, Hindu and Muslim extremists started what seemed to be an endless cycle of genocide, including the Great Calcutta Killings. Muslims had been unfairly treated for centuries in Hindu areas. Muslims had forever treated Hindus with disrespect in their regions. In his article "What Did Gandhi Do During Communal Riots in India?", Maneesha Chaturvedi relates:

> March 5, 1947: In a speech at Prayer Meeting in Patna Gandhi said, "If Muslims believe that they would annihilate

the Hindus or if Hindus believe that they would annihilate the Muslims, I should like to ask them what they would gain thereby? Muslims will not serve Islam if they annihilate the Hindus; rather they would thereby destroy Islam. And if the Hindus believe that they would be able to annihilate Islam it means that they would be annihilating Hindu dharma . . . "

"The Hindus in Bihar . . . should do their duty by contributing to a fund for the relief of Muslims by way of repentance. No one should think that he need not lift his little finger since there is already a Congress ministry with a Congress majority here, which will do everything that needs to be done . . . I did not beg for money in Noakhali because I received unsought about three lakh rupees. Today I thought I should hold out the begging bowl here and awaken the conscience of the people . . . I can only remind you of your duty. I cannot perform your duty. Hence you must contribute generously to the Bihar fund."

Gandhi boldly states that it is not Hinduism but 'Satanism.'

Gandhi not only delivered speeches but also encouraged and raised fund for victims of the violence and responded to letters regarding the issues and addressed meetings personally, all to curb the series of riots.

Even then, the Hindu and Muslim extremists had spread the communal hatred in the name of religion and Gandhi went places to normalize the situation. While he failed in a lot of places due to vulnerable time as British were leaving India and the uncertainty of partition, Indian leaders can still use his ways to bring peace because India is in a much better place today.[15]

Indeed, the way people mistreat each other appears to be a social cancer in the latter days, one which will significantly diminish one's ability to lead others. President Benson warned.

---

15. Maneesha Chaturvedi, "What Did Gandhi Do During Communal Riots in India?", *HW English*, 26 February 2020, https://hwnews.in/uncategorized/what-did-gandhi-do-during-communal-riots-in-india/126462, accessed 25 July 2020.

Another major portion of this very prevalent sin of pride is enmity toward our fellowmen. We are tempted daily to elevate ourselves above others and diminish them. (See Hel. 6:17; D&C 58:41.)

The proud make every man their adversary by pitting their intellects, opinions, works, wealth, talents, or any other worldly measuring device against others. In the words of C. S. Lewis: "Pride gets no pleasure out of having something, only out of having more of it than the next man. . . . It is the comparison that makes you proud: the pleasure of being above the rest. Once the element of competition has gone, pride has gone." (Mere Christianity, New York: Macmillan, 1952, pp. 109–10.)[16]

---

16. Ezra Taft Benson, "Beware of Pride," April 1989 general conference.

*Blessed are the peacemakers; for they shall be
called the children of God. (Matthew 5:9)*

"We went west willingly—because we had to."

—Brigham Young

Principle 4

Take Action against Violence and Evil NOW!

WHETHER IT IS A GLOBAL PANDEMIC, DEGENERATING CURRICULUM in public schools, or mobs burning the cities, how often have you watched and wondered where your elected leaders are? What becomes quickly apparent is that they are leaders in name only. When a crisis arrives, these managers hide behind their titles and offices. Hugh Nibley explains:

> "A ship in port is safe," says Captain Hopper, speaking of management; "but that is not what ships were built for" . . .
>
> Above all, Moroni was the charismatic leader, personally going about to rally the people, who came running together spontaneously to his "title of liberty," the banner of the poor and downtrodden of Israel (Alma 46:12–13, 19–21). He had little patience with management and let himself get carried away and wrote tactless and angry letters to the big men sitting on their thrones "in a state of thoughtless stupor" back in the capital. And when it was necessary, he bypassed the whole system; he "altered the management of affairs among the Nephites," to counter Amalickiah's managerial skill (Alma 49:11; emphasis added). Yet he could apologize handsomely when he learned that he had been wrong, led by his generous

impulses to an exaggerated contempt for management, and he gladly shared with Pahoran the glory of the final victory—the one thing that ambitious generals jealously reserve for themselves.[1]

Effective leaders will do things they naturally might not want to do, but have to. Can you imagine having to disobey orders because you had to? This problem was faced by leaders in Vietnam who were commanded not to fire back at the enemy unless they first received explicit permission to do so from senior commanders in Saigon. Captain Whaley would have nothing to do with that. He would refuse orders rather than wait until his base was overrun and his soldiers killed. As soon as the enemy attacked, he fired his weapon and ordered his soldiers to take the same action. You can't ask forgiveness when you are dead.[2]

When looters start robbing business owners and burning the evidence, leaders need to take action before the entire community is destroyed and innocent people's dream are left in ashes. The leader must take control first and then earnestly resolve the issues at hand.

HOW TO CONTROL THE MOB

Why do Latter-day Saints fight? Only when they have to—a last resort in order to protect their family and homes. So, what does a community leader do when an angry mob with guns and torches is entering their community and the police and the National Guard have fled? The leader must mobilize the resources in his or her community and take control. Here are sixteen rules of engagement to help control a riot. They are scripted by Lt. Dan Marcou, an internationally-recognized police trainer who was a highly-decorated police officer with 33 years of full-time law enforcement experience. Marcou's awards include Police Officer of the Year, SWAT Officer of the Year, Humanitarian of the Year, and Domestic Violence Officer of the Year.

---

1. Hugh Nibley, "Leaders and Managers," Brigham Young University commencement address, 19 August 1983, speeches.byu.edu.
2. Richard Whaley, "Vietnam Experiences 1971–1972," email to author May 29, 2020.

Upon retiring, Lt. Marcou began writing. He is a co-author of *Street Survival II, Tactics for Deadly Encounters*. His tactics are meant for police officers but can be adapted for community militia.

> It should be disconcerting to all police officers that violence—or the threat of violence—by contemporary demonstrators have caused the cancellation of speeches, political rallies, and concerts over the last two years. It is the sworn duty of American law enforcement to thwart through righteous action the efforts of masked or unmasked hooligans who would violently suppress the freedoms of others.

> Modern demonstrators are sometimes paid, and often trained. Through scripted behaviors—called "conflict engagement"—they hope to trigger violence in the crowd, or an over-reaction by police officers.

Marcou and the other authors then give crowd control tactics they believe every police agency in the nation should consider deploying. Here are my interpretations for applying it to the leadership settings we are discussing:

1. Communication Skills—Find ways to communicate with the mob that your intentions are good and that you will not back down from your righteous cause.

2. Team Arrest Skills—Know how to make a citizen's arrest and avoid harming those arrested.

3. Crowd Dynamics 101—"Officers [leaders] present must recognize the dynamics that exist in every crowd. For example, many good people—who are followers—will engage in a violent disturbance if malevolent leaders take control without being deterred or arrested."

4. Classic Crowd Control Team Tactics—Leaders should have a trusted team to assist them, and they should all receive training from a crowd control expert.

5. Miami Field Force Tactics—Leaders should receive training from a crowd control expert on how to "immediately diffuse disturbances and disperse small groups of problem individuals."

6. Dynamic Los Angeles Cross-Bow Techniques—Leaders should receive training from a crowd control expert on how to pick out individuals or groups who will turn a peaceful demonstration into a riot.

7. Grenadiers—Leaders should acquire the resources they need to project their communities against violence and receive training from a crowd control expert.

8. SWAT—Be prepared if it becomes violent—only a last resort to protect your families.

9. Mutual Aid Contingencies—"Have a plan for mutual aid in advance, which includes protocols for personnel call-in, command and control, major event communication, transportation and mass arrest procedures."

10. Plainclothes Observers—Be sure to document every incident and be sure all actions taken to protect the community are within the law—if the mob doesn't get you, the courts might.

11. Cameras—"Police cameras should be well placed, documenting crowd and police actions. Video recordings will not only be evidence in court, but they will also be able to counter edited truth-bending recordings put out by both professional protestors and the 'legitimate media.' Be timely in release of truth-telling footage. Rumors trigger more riots."

12. Protective Equipment—"Some crowds warrant eight point hats and white gloves and others require protective equipment. Commanders must have the wisdom to know the difference and the courage to realistically prepare your officers for the challenges they face."

13. Know the Recipe for Failure—"Take one highly trained (or especially untrained) crowd control team, garnish it with

untrained leadership calling the shots (like micro-managing mayors) and you will cook up a memorable failure."

14. Detours and Designated Areas—Protect uninformed innocents from wandering into dangerous situations.

15. Report Writing Skills—Enough said.

16. KNOW THE LAW!—"Do what is right and do what is legal. You will notice that a trained response will look like a restrained response."

In conclusion, the authors say:

Neo-communists, neo-fascists, neo-Nazis, anarchists and Antifa thrive in violence and chaos. Nothing ensures their failure in achieving their violent ends like a well-equipped, highly-trained team of honorable professionals standing on that thin blue line between order and chaos saying, "Not in the land of the free . . . at least, not on our watch."[3]

THE NEED FOR THE TRUSTED COMMUNITY LEADER

Police Brigadier General Sotero DG. Ramos, Jr., Police Attaché to the United States from the Philippines, has been the commander over many hostage situations, including shootouts with the terrorist group Abu Sayyaf. He understands well that a key to successfully ending an emotionally fragile and violent hostage situation is to maintain a network of trusted local leaders and to use them to immediately help substitute out of control emotions of desperation and anger with empathy and trust. As an example, he shared with me an incident where a deranged mother held her two small children with knife blades resting on their throats. The woman's husband had left her without any means of supporting her young family. She was at her wit's end and threatening to kill her children and to end her own life. Action had to

---

3. Lt. James Glennon, Lt. Dan Marcou, and Chuck Remsburg, *Street Survival II: Tactics for Deadly Force Encounters* (United States: Calibre Press, 2018).

be taken, and now! Fortunately, the general had, over time, developed a close relationship with local leaders. He knew which leaders were trusted in the cities he was responsible for. In this crisis, he called upon a trusted local leader in the desperate mother's community to talk with her and to try to calm her down through kind words of understanding, concern, and love. However, before proceeding, he ordered one of his police officers to accompany the local leader, and to first have the police officer remove his police uniform and put on casual civilian clothes. The uniform was a sign of authority and possible punishment which could have triggered the woman to panic and cut her children's throats. By the time the trusted local leader and the officer were ready to negotiate with the woman, blood was already starting to dip down the small children's necks. Slowly the leader was able to calm the woman to the point where the leader and the plain clothes police officer could draw nearer and nearer to her. When they reached the point where the officer could jump the woman, in one motion he sprang on her, forcing his arms from under her shoulder to push the knife blades away from the children's throats. The general has witnessed this tactic work successfully time and time again. The key is taking action, but first employing the calming effect of a trusted and concerned community leader.[4]

You might ask, "That is an admirable example of how law enforcement should handle domestic violence, but what does that have to do with me?" Perhaps very little today, but what will your community be like during the extremely trying conditions that will precede the Second Coming of Christ? Families will be broken, plagues will ravage communities, neighbors will be hungry, sick, and feeling desperate and hopeless. In most communities, there will probably be no functioning police force. The prophet Isaiah spoke of seven desperate women taking hold of one man in the last days (Isaiah 4:1). What kind of living hell will you and your neighbors be facing in the coming years? Who will be the trusting and concerned leaders that will come to the aid of your neighbors who are at wit's end? Hopefully, the trusted leader will be you, a righteous priesthood holder or Relief Society sister who through

---

4. Sotero DG. Ramos, Jr., Police Attaché, Embassy of the Philippines, Washington, D.C., conversation with author in Elk Ridge, UT, 4 December 2020.

the years have loved and ministered to your community members and have the Christ-like mannerisms to calm the bewildered.

TAKING ACTION NOW!

I remember well a letter my bishop read to our ward while I was living in Florida in 1992. It was a gracious letter of appreciation that had been written by a stake president in the Florida Homestead area and sent to the units of the Church who had provided aid to Homestead. In August 1992, the city of Homestead had been devastated by Hurricane Andrew. Wind gusts of 175 miles per hour ripped apart tens of thousands of homes. Church leaders throughout the US Southeast mobilized the priesthood and Relief Society members to provide labor, materials, and food to aid the victims—both members and non-members alike. Within hours of the eye of the storm passing, hundreds of Latter-day Saints from many states were on the ground providing aid in Homestead.

What I remember most about the stake president's letter was what the members of his stake were most grateful for. Not to discount the amazing amount of actual material and labor that was provided, what mattered most to the members of Homestead was that at their darkest moment— when the morning light revealed the horrible extent of the damage—the members of the Church took comfort and strength in knowing that Church members from afar off would come to their aid. They had complete faith that their brothers and sisters would take action, come to provide relief, and do so as soon as possible. On the one hand, their non-member neighbors had no support system, no leadership, and nowhere to turn. Their houses were gone, local stores destroyed, and the streets were impassable. Homestead members found their neighbors wondering the streets, dazed and in shock. On the other hand, Latter-day Saints had a sure faith that help was on the way. Because of that sure knowledge, Latter-day Saints told their stake president how they were most grateful that at that dire moment, they could put their arms around their neighbors, embrace them in love and say, "All is well, you'll be okay, help is coming, help is coming." As promised, through the power of loving and action-oriented Church members and their action-oriented leaders, Latter-day Saint aid groups were the first to reach the victims of Hurricane Andrew. When even greater devastations occur during the years of the Great Tribulation, will you be ready to fulfill your role as the trusting, loving, and action-oriented community leader?

General Moroni is a prime example of not sitting around and letting things deteriorate. Over and over again this outstanding general chose to take action. Here is just one example:

> Yea, we see that Amalickiah, because he was a man of cunning device and a man of many flattering words, that he led away the hearts of many people to do wickedly; yea, and to seek to destroy the church of God, and to destroy the foundation of liberty which God had granted unto them, or which blessing God had sent upon the face of the land for the righteous' sake.
>
> And now it came to pass that when Moroni, who was the chief commander of the armies of the Nephites, had heard of these dissensions, he was angry with Amalickiah.
>
> And it came to pass that he rent his coat; and he took a piece thereof, and wrote upon it—In memory of our God, our religion, and freedom, and our peace, our wives and our children—and he fastened it upon the end of a pole.
>
> And he fastened on his head-plate, and his breastplate, and his shields, and girded on his armor about his loins; and he took the pole, which had on the end thereof his rent coat, (and he called it the title of liberty) and he bowed himself to the earth, and he prayed mightily unto his God for the blessings of liberty to rest upon his brethren, so long as there should a band of Christians remain to possess the land—
>
> For thus were all the true believers of Christ, who belonged to the church of God, called by those who did not belong to the church.
>
> And those who did belong to the church were faithful; yea, all those who were true believers in Christ took upon them, gladly, the name of Christ, or Christians as they were called, because of their belief in Christ who should come.

And therefore, at this time, Moroni prayed that the cause of the Christians, and the freedom of the land might be favored.

And it came to pass that when he had poured out his soul to God, he named all the land which was south of the land Desolation, yea, in fine, all the land both on the north and on the south—A chosen land, and the land of liberty.

And he said: Surely God shall not suffer that we, who are despised because we take upon us the name of Christ, shall be trodden down and destroyed until we bring it upon us by our own transgressions.

And when Moroni had side these words, he went forth among the people, waving the rent part of his garment in the air, that all might see the writing which he had written upon the rent part, and crying with a loud voice, saying:

Behold, whosoever will maintain this title upon the land, let them come forth in the strength of the Lord, and enter into a covenant that they will maintain their rights, and their religion, that the Lord God may bless them.

And it came to pass that when Moroni had proclaimed these words, behold, the people came running together with their armor girded about their loins, rending their garments in token, or as a covenant, that they would not forsake the Lord their God; or, in other words, if they should transgress the commandments of God, or fall into transgression, and be ashamed to take upon them the name of Christ, the Lord should rend them even as they had rent their garments. (Alma 46:10–21)

Captain Whaley had his own moment of truth and took immediate action to correct his officers:

The Viet Cong hit us around midnight. As soon as the rockets started coming in, our machine guns opened up and the sirens went off. The troops came tearing out of their bunks, grabbing their weapons and getting in their fighting positions. Normally, my position was in the Company TOC with the First Sergeant and the XO would check the positions. One look at my XO and I knew he would instill nothing but fear in the troops if he didn't get killed, so I told him to stay in the TOC and watch things. I also quietly told the First Sergeant, he was in charge and to take no orders from the XO. He understood.

I crawled from position to position giving orders, making sure everyone was where they should be and that they were ok. I immediately noticed that several foxholes only had one soldier when they should have had two. (I later learned that perhaps 1/3 of the unit was strung out on drugs and incapacitated.) I came upon a position where a newly arrived kid was crouched.

He looked like the guy from Mad Magazine: big ears, freckles, etc. He was shaking like a leaf and scared out of his wits. I rolled into the position and chatted with him for a few moments. I kidded him a little and then told him I was really glad he was here protecting me. He said, "Really?" I told him, yes, and my wife was counting on him to do his job so she wouldn't be a widow. He sort of calmed down, smiled and said he'd be okay and she wouldn't have to worry. So, with a pat on the shoulder, I took off to the next spot.

The rockets didn't last too long (they usually didn't) and they didn't hit anything of importance, which was also normal, but it was still scary. I got back to the TOC and, shortly thereafter, the all-clear signal was sounded. Now began the job of accounting for all the weapons. That took about an hour before it was concluded.

My XO and I began walking back to our hooch when, suddenly, six mortars landed about 50 meters from us with a huge explosion, dirt, shrapnel, etc. We hit the ground, got up and headed back to the TOC on a dead-run. The troops were really moving fast this time because THIS was flat-out CLOSE! The next hour was intense but no injuries, however, the company were believers now.

The next morning, I held a Company formation and informed everyone that I was not happy that so many had not gone to their fighting positions (I discovered that most were strung out on drugs a major problem at that time and one which took considerable effort to get a handle on). I told them that this was not only unacceptable to me, but also dangerous, and would not be tolerated. At our Commander's Call, I ordered all the Platoon Leaders, Section Leaders, and Sergeants to ensure everyone was out and in their positions in the future whether it was a practice alert or a real one and that I was holding them personally accountable. I was pleased that we had no further problems during the remainder of my command time.[5]

TAKING CHRIST-LIKE ACTION

Are you a bystander or do you take action when needed? Do you allow injustice and violence to rule your community or do you do something about it so matters don't get worse? Are you a Jesse Owens or a Carl 'Luz' Long? In 1936, the International Olympic Committee had awarded the Olympic Games to Nazi Germany. The games became a stage for Hitler to try to display the repulsive notion of the superiority of the fictitious Aryan race. Hitler had tried to ban Blacks and Jews from the games. The African American Jesse Owens stood up, participated, and won four gold medals in front of the deranged dictator.

Owens chief rival in the games was Carl Long, a German, who held the European long jump record. During the long jump competition, Owens stepped past the takeoff board on his first two attempts. One more foot fault and Jesse would be eliminated from the competition. At this point, Long took action. He chose the right and acted upon it. He suggested to Owens that he jump from a spot behind the takeoff board. Jesse Owens won the gold medal with a jump of 8.06 meters with Long taking second. Long embraced Owens and then put his arm around him as they left the field. Hitler was furious at his countryman who stood up to the violent Nazi agenda.

Taking action now, often referred to as being proactive, seldom requires arresting someone or entering a raging battle. Remember, the real battles of the Tribulation will be more spiritual than physical.

---

5. Richard, Whaley, "Vietnam Experiences 1971–1972, " email to author, May 29, 2020.

More often our leadership will be measured by how we proactively follow the example of Jesus Christ. As a leader you must act as Christ would when the Spirit directs. To remind us, we have the second verse of the Prophet Joseph Smith's favorite song, "A Poor Wayfaring Man of Grief":

> Once, when my scanty meal was spread
> He entered; not a word he spake,
> Just perishing for want of bread.
> I gave him all, he blessed it, brake,
>
> And ate, but gave me part again.
> Mine was an angel's portion then,
> For while I fed with eager haste,
> The crust was manna to my taste.[6]

One example of taking Christ-like action was provided by perhaps the richest man in the world and a devote Muslim. In his personal history of World War II, Russell Harland Rock, a Latter-day Saint Navy combat medic assigned to Marines, tells of his experience meeting the King of Saudi Arabia. During the invasion of Guadalcanal, Rock lost his leg during the battle. While recovering at the Navy hospital in Vallejo, California, he and a fellow wounded sailor decided to ask two young women from the University of California at Berkeley to dinner and a concert by the Russ Morgan Band at the Claremont Hotel. The girls had a midnight curfew. After the concert, the two couples stood in a line outside the entrance of the hotel. Both men were on crutches, and the taxis were being grabbed by "top brass" who commanded away each taxi from the wounded men. Rock states in his own words:

> Standing under the canopy of the hotel, we wondered how we were going to get our dates home by their midnight curfew. Just then a limousine pulled up. The United Nations was being organized in San Francisco, and the Claremont Hotel was headquarters for King Ibn Saud of Arabia. When the limousine door opened, King Saud got out. We recognized

---

6. "A Poor Wayfaring Man of Grief," *Hymns*, no. 29.

him from pictures in the newspapers. He was a huge man, perhaps six-foot-six. He appeared to have only one eye, and his face bore several noticeable scars. He walked past us with a nod and a smile. He really was *something* to see.

He paused as he entered the hotel and looked back at us. He then turned to one of his aides, who approached us and said that the king wished to place his limousine at your disposal. We couldn't believe it. We looked to the king, he nodded affirmatively.

We got into his luxurious car and the chauffeur asked where we want to go. We directed him to the Gamma Phi Beta house and pulled up just at midnight. A lot of the other girls were also returning from dates. When they went inside, they peeked out the windows at us and the limousine. We escorted our girls to the door and said goodnight. After that we could date any girl in the sorority house.

When we got back inside the car, the driver asked us where we wanted to go. "Take us back to the bus station, and we'll catch a bus out to Vallejo." He said, "I'll drive you to Vallejo." We told him it was 25 miles away. "That's all right. This limousine is at your disposal, and I am authorized to take you." Glen and I relaxed and enjoyed the ride.

A couple of days later, King Ibn Saud sent Glen and me each a Bulova watch. I still have mine, and it runs perfectly.[7]

Seventy years after his death, King Abdulaziz ibn Saud is revered as the founder of Saudi Arabia and the kingdom's finished example of leadership. He was brave in the many battles he led, but also kind and sensitive to those around him. He was a king and very rich, but respected these two young American warriors and treated these strangers as equals. Arriving at the hotel at nearly midnight, the aging king must have been exhausted, yet he nodded and smiled at the young Americans, sensed their need and acted upon it. In so doing, the Arab leader made two admirers for life and friends for his nation. As a leader, have you mastered that level of Christ-like leadership competency?

---

7. Paul H. Kelly and Lin H. Johnson, *Courage in a Season of War: Latter-day Saints Experience World War II*, (Self-published, 2002), 401–402.

LITTLE ACTS OF KINDNESS MATTER THE MOST

How often have you sat discussing terrible world events and said to yourself, "There is nothing I can do to stop the killing or solve world hunger." A righteous leader is always asking: "What can I do to help?" and then takes an *action* regardless of how insignificant it might seem at the time. Political and international business consultant Gary Roberts leads by action. He relates how by just "doing the right thing" he not only helped save thousands of lives, but also received a marvelous blessing by so doing. He relates:

Gary Clay Roberts

I first met Willy Mishiki at the Washington D.C. Temple Visitors' Center. I was there to meet Elder Don Christensen who was the center's director and the man who had baptized and ordained me to both priesthoods six months prior. Elder Christensen wanted me to meet a delegation of foreign dignitaries who were visiting the center. Mr. Mishiki was the head of the delegation.

Mr. Mishiki, a short, stocky, and erect man, greeted me with a warm smile and asked, "What do you do?" I told him that I was a political consultant. After the delegation finished their tour of the center, Mr. Mishiki asked if we could meet. He had an urgent matter he wanted to discuss. So we set an appointment to meet the next day, 30 April 1997.

We met at DC Delegate Walter Fauntroy's offices on Connecticut Avenue at 10 a.m. Mr. Mishiki began by explaining that he was the Secretary General of the Union for Democracy and Social Progress (UDPS), the largest political opposition party in Zaire. His mission was to meet with the US Secretary of State to request United States protection from the President of Zaire, Mobutu Sese Seku. The urgency was that President

Mobutu was returning from cancer treatment in France to Zaire, and it was rumored that he had ordered his elite guard to kill all the UDPS leaders and their families before he returned to vacate the capital city of Kinshasa. President Mobutu was also worried about facing the imminent attack on Kinshasa which was led by the rebel leader, Laurent Kabila.

I told Mr. Mishiki that I thought getting a meeting with Secretary of State, Madeline Albright, would be difficult considering the timing constraints of the current situation. However, I believed contacting the South African government might be more constructive. He agreed. My secretary placed a call to the South African Embassy and requested an urgent meeting with the South African Ambassador. A meeting was arranged for 4:00 p.m. that afternoon.

Before leaving for the meeting, I told Mr. Mishiki that he and I needed to sign a consultancy agreement with a retainer of $1.00 to be paid as consideration. I wrote the agreement; we signed it and shook hands.

The same day we were greeted by the Ambassador of South Africa, Mr. Franklin Sonn. Mr. Mishiki and I explained the situation, and the ambassador asked if he could get confirmation of these events from the President of the UDPS, Mr. Frederic Kibassa Maliba. Mr. Mishiki said, "Yes." The ambassador said, "Get the confirmation to me and I will forward it to Pretoria for action."

Mr. Mishiki sent a cable out that evening to Kinshasa, and the ambassador received confirmation the next morning.

On May 2nd we received confirmation that President Mandela was meeting with President Mobutu and Laurent Kabila off the west coast of Africa.

On Monday morning, May 5, I met with Mr. Mishiki, and he said that President Kibassa was very pleased and happy with what we had accomplished; an impending bloodbath was avoided and not one UDPS member or any of their family members were harmed or hurt!

Then Mr. Mishiki said, "President Kibassa was very pleased with what you did for the DRC. He said that you should get paid for your work because we owe you our lives. Then he told me that we would give you some land as a payment, and you cannot say no."

President Kibassa of the UDPS offered me 800,000 acres of land in the Northern Kivu region of the country. Mr. Mishiki, as the authorized UDPS representative, went with me to set up the agreement with my lawyers. I agreed to the terms offered me and signed an agreement of ownership. A few months later, the CIA estimated the land value to be—much to my surprise—100 billion dollars.

Footnote: Willy Mishiki was baptized and became a faithful member of the church. Mobutu died in exile. Laurent Kabila became Zaire's Head of State and was later assassinated by one of his security guards. His son, Joseph Kabila, replaced him as President. Zaire was renamed the Democratic Republic of Congo (DRC). President Russell M. Nelson announced at the April 2020 General Conference that a second temple was to be constructed in Lumbumbashi, Democratic Republic of Congo.

I learned some very important lessons during that time. One, our Heavenly Father has a place and time for everything. It is important for us not to be deterred from doing what we believe is the correct path. Second, the Holy Ghost will not leave us stranded. We should obey his promptings. Third, we must follow through until the end.[8]

In the turbulent days ahead, taking action might require a tremendous amount of faith in God. When the six hundred chariots of Egypt overtook the children of Israel, many complained against Moses, seeking to return to Egypt as slaves rather than be slaughtered next to the waters of the Red Sea. Moses replied to their murmuring:

Fear ye not, stand still, and see the salvation of the Lord, which he will shew to you to day: for the Egyptians whom ye have seen to day, ye shall see them again no more for ever.

The Lord shall fight for you, and ye shall hold your peace.

8. Gary Clay Roberts, "Two stories for your consideration in the book," email to author, July 18, 2020.

And the Lord said unto Moses, Wherefore criest thou unto me? Speak unto the children of Israel, that they go forward:

But lift thou up thy rod, and stretch out thine hand over the sea, and divide it: and the children of Israel shall go on dry ground through the midst of the sea. (Exodus 14:13–16)

Having the ability to go forward, with full faith in the Lord, takes daily practice. When the Lord commanded Nephi to build a ship, the young prophet simply asked where he could find ore for tools and got to work. When the Lord asked brother of Jared how he could have lights for his ships so the Jaredites could cross the oceans in darkness, he didn't sit on a log. Instead, the brother of Jared took action. He melted out sixteen transparent stones, took them up to the mountain, and only asked the Lord that which he could not do. In both Nephi's and the brother of Jared's examples, we know that throughout their long sagas, they both practiced over and over again asking the Lord for help, then acting upon the Lord's guidance. When all seems dark and you cannot see the way forward, you must practice moving forward one faithful step into the darkness after another. After years of relying on the Lord you will know, as did Moses, that the Lord will have your back even when things look hopeless and our enemies are at your doorstep.

Let us go up again unto Jerusalem, and let us be faithful in keeping the commandments of the Lord; for behold he is mightier than all the earth, then why not mightier than Laban and his fifty, yea, or even than his tens of thousands?

There let us go up; let us be strong like unto Moses; for he truly spake unto the waters of the Red Sea and they divided hither and thither, and our fathers came through, out of captivity, on dry ground, and the armies of Pharaoh did follow and were drowned in the waters of the Red Sea.

(1 Nephi 4:1–2)

Still I hope I shall always possess firmness and virtue enough to maintain (what I consider the most enviable of all titles) the character of an honest man.

—George Washington to Alexander Hamilton

Principle 5

Don't Be Afraid and Don't Back Down

HAVE YOU EVER CONSIDERED HOW OLD NEPHI WAS WHEN HE bravely acted alone in obtaining the brass plates of Laban? Though he was large for his age, he must have been a young teenager of only 13 or 14 years of age. Jewish tradition for a male's consent to marry is 13 years 1 Day, and if not married by the age of 20 a court would often require a man to marry. Nephi's older brother Laman was not married at the time, nor Lemuel, nor Sam. Even if Nephi had no sisters born between Laman and himself, Nephi must have been very young, yet incredibly valiant in keeping the commandments of the Lord. The young prophet must have been afraid of Laban's tens of thousands of warriors.

Nephi continually stood up to the wrath that came upon him each time he challenged his older brother's authority. Still, he never backed down. At times he was beaten and at other times he had his life threatened by his own siblings. Yet because he was "more faithful in keeping the commandments of the Lord—therefore he was favored of the Lord, for the Lord heard his prayers and answered them, and he took the lead of their journey in the wilderness" (Mosiah 10:13). His father, Lehi, recognized that it was Nephi's keeping of the commandments and his gifted leadership in the wilderness that kept the family from perishing (2 Nephi 1:24). If anything, Nephi never cowed down to the violent Laman, Lemuel, and the sons of Ismael. As Lehi described his manner:

> And ye [Laman & Lemuel] have murmured because he [Nephi] hath been plain unto you. Ye say that he hath used sharpness; ye say he hath been angry with you; but behold, his sharpness was the sharpness of the power of the word of God, which was in him; and that which ye call anger was the truth, according to that which is in God, which he could not restrain, manifesting boldly concerning your iniquities. (2 Nephi 1:26)

To our benefit, Nephi acted boldly, even though at times he was beaten and restrained by his older brothers. Yet, each time he did so, despite the bruises he suffered, the Lord came to his aid. The Lord will do the same to any righteous leader who stands up for the truth. As the phrase goes, "Act boldly and unseen forces will come to your aid."

If any example could compare to Nephi in courage and faith in God, it was the equally young David who stood tall against the giant warrior Goliath of Gath.

> And when the Philistine looked about, and saw David, he disdained him: for he was but a youth, and ruddy, and of a fair countenance.
>
> And the Philistine said unto David, Am I a dog, that thou comest to me with staves? And the Philistine cursed David by his gods.
>
> And the Philistine said to David, Come to me, and I will give thy flesh unto the fowls of the air, and to the beast of the field.
>
> Then said David to the Philistine, Thou comest to me with a sword, and with a spear, and with a shield: but I come to thee in the name of the Lord of hosts, the God of the armies of Israel, whom thou hast defied.
>
> This day will the Lord deliver thee into mine hand; and I will smite thee, and take thine head from thee; and I will give the carcases of the host of the Philistines this day unto the fowls of the air, and to the wild beasts of the earth; that all the earth may know that there is a God in Israel. (1 Samuel 17:42–46)

Taking a stand and not backing down takes heroic courage. Whether it is speaking up in a school board meeting or in challenging a violent enemy, it takes real courage. However, if you're on the Lord's team, you don't need to be afraid. In a BYU Idaho devotional talk titled "True Blue, Through and Through," Sheri L. Dew relates:

President Joseph F. Smith called integrity "the cornerstone of character" (4 April 1897 General Conference). And President Gordon B. Hinckley spoke of integrity this way: *"Men and women of integrity understand intrinsically that theirs is the precious right to hold their heads in the sunlight of truth, unashamed before anyone"* (*Standing for Something*, 29).

An incident in the life of President Joseph F. Smith bears out this point. In the fall of 1857, the nineteen-year-old Joseph F. was returning from his mission in Hawaii, and in California he joined a wagon train. It was a volatile time for the Saints. Johnston's Army was marching towards Utah, and many had bitter feelings towards the Church. One evening several hoodlums rode into camp, cursing and threatening to hurt every Mormon they could find. Most in the wagon train ran and hid in the brush. But Joseph F. thought to himself: "Shall I run from these fellows? Why should I fear them?" With that, he walked up to one of the intruders who, with pistol in hand, demanded, "Are you a Mormon?" Joseph F. Smith responded, "Yes siree; dyed in the wool; true blue, through and through." At that, the hoodlum grasped his hand and said, "Well you are the [blankety-blank] pleasantest man I ever met! Shake hands, young fellow. I am glad to see a man that stands up for his convictions" (See *Gospel Doctrine*, 518).[1]

While Latter-day Saints do not go looking for trouble, we are responsible for preaching the true gospel to every nation, kindred, and people. In the meridian of time, Peter didn't hide in some backwater village. Instead, he boldly headed for the Romans, the most powerful domain on earth at the time. Paul stood tall when he testified before thousands

1. Sheri L. Dew, "True Blue, Through and Through," Brigham Young University—Idaho devotional, 16 March 2004.

in Roman's eastern capital of Ephesus. In our times, Brigham Young declared: "Why should we worry about what others think of us, do we have more confidence in their opinions than we do our own?"

Captain Richard Whaley relates an incident that illustrates how important it is to stand up for what is right:

> Because DaNang was a rear area, there were college courses taught periodically and one of them was on Black-American History. An African American Major who had an "attitude" taught the course. Having received a BA in History, I decided to take the class and see what he had to teach. It turned out that I was the only non-Black in the class and the class had many of my "trouble-makers" attending.
>
> After two hours of 'hate-Whitey' and 'America is an evil nation' rhetoric from this Major and the others in the class, I had had it. I raised my hand and stood up to make my comment. I looked at all the class and said something to the effect: "For the past several hours, I have heard you condemning my forefathers for owning slaves. You need to know that my forefathers freed those slaves and paid their way to college in OH. You have, in essence, been teaching and preaching 'white slavery.' And that is just as wrong. Now, let me say this: if you or anyone ever walks up my driveway with the intent of enslaving or harming me or my family, I am going to put a bullet between your eyes, just as I would expect you to do if someone walked up your driveway with the same intent." Then I waited because I figured I was in real trouble now.
>
> The ringleader of the Blacks (a Staff Specialist from Chicago) stood up and said, "Captain, I can accept that." That was all. The tension was immediately reduced and we had a rather enjoyable class after that. I think I had established a sense of "fairness" with the minorities and they knew I wouldn't take anything from them and wasn't going to be intimidated, either. I also wouldn't allow anyone to abuse them because of race. (I had already given an Article 15 to a white Staff Sergeant for a racial comment against one of the black privates and that action reverberated throughout the company!)[2]

---

2. Richard, Whaley, "Vietnam Experiences 1971–1972, " email to author, May 29, 2020.

Few displays are as intimidating as the Moari Haka war dance. The demonstration of bravery originated when a foreign party of warriors would land their outriggers on a neighboring island. As tradition would have it, both the native warriors of the island and the new arrivals would face off on the beach. In turn each group of warriors would perform the Haka war dance to try to intimate the other party. As long as both groups of warriors did not show fear, in respect for each other, the parties would agree not to fight and conduct their trading business peacefully. As the old saying goes, "it's not the size of the dog in the fight; it's the size of the fight in the dog." These are the words of the celebrated New Zealand All Blacks Rugby team Haka:

Leader:
KA MATE! KA MATE!
We're going to die! We're going to die!
We were at war

Chorus:
KA ORA, KA ORA!
We're going to live! We're going to live!
But now there is peace.

Leader:
KA MATE! KA MATE!
We're going to die! We're going to die!
We thought we were all going to die

Chorus:
KA ORA, KA ORA!
We're going to live! We're going to live!
But now we are safe

All together:
TENEI TE TANGATA PU'RU-HURU
This is the man, so hairy
Because our leader, so strong and masculine,
NA'A NEI TIKI MAI WHAKA-WHITI TE . . .
Who fetched, and made shine he
Has unified us and brought back the sunny days of
. . . RA! UPANE! KA . . .

Indeed, we are going to live. For once we were dead, and now we are made alive because of our leader Jesus Christ. If a leader truly believes in his or her Savior, why should they fear? In the latter days has there been any greater example of not backing down than our beloved Prophet Joseph Smith? As written in *Saints*, Joseph was tarred and feathered one night and preached the gospel the next day.

"Call on your God for help," someone shouted. Joseph looked around and saw more men joining the mob. One man stepped out of a nearby orchard with a wooden plank, and the men stretched Joseph across it and carried him deeper into the meadow.

After they had gone some distance from the house, they tore away his clothes and held him down while a man approached with a sharp knife, ready to mutilate him. But the man took a look at Joseph and refused to cut him.

"Damn you," another man howled. He leapt on Joseph and raked his sharp fingernails across the prophet's skin, leaving it raw and lacerated. "That's the way the Holy Ghost falls on folks," he said.

Joseph could hear other men a short distance off, arguing over what to do with him and Sidney. He could not hear every word they said, but he thought he heard a familiar name or two.

Once the arguing stopped, someone said, "Let's tar up his mouth." Filthy hands forced his jaw open while a man tried to pour a bottle of acid down his throat. The bottle broke on Joseph's teeth, chipping one of them.

Another man tried to cram a paddle of sticky tar into his mouth, but Joseph shook his head back and forth. "Damn you!" the man cried. "Hold up your head." He jammed the paddle into Joseph's mouth until the tar oozed over his lips.

More men came with a vat of tar and poured it over him. The tar ran down his lacerated skin and through his hair. They covered him with feathers, dumped him on the cold ground, and fled the scene.

After they left, Joseph tore the tar from his lips and gasped for air. He struggled to his feet, but his strength failed him. He tried again and this time managed to stay upright. Stray feathers flitted in the air around him.

When she saw Joseph stumbling to the Johnsons' door, Emma fainted, sure the mob had mangled him beyond recognition. Hearing the commotion, several women in the neighborhood had rushed to the house. Joseph asked for a blanket to cover his battered body.

For the rest of the night, people tended to Joseph and to Sidney, who had lain in the meadow a long time, barely breathing. Emma scraped the tar from Joseph's limbs, chest, and back. Elsa Johnson, meanwhile, used lard from her pantry to ease the hardened tar from his skin and hair.

The next day, Joseph got dressed and preached a sermon from the Johnsons' doorstep. He recognized some of the men from the mob in the congregation, but he said nothing to them. In the afternoon, he baptized three people.[3]

We are also inspired by the great prophet's rebuking of the guards at the Liberty Jail. Again, in *Saints* we read:

Now each man tried to sleep with a shackle around his ankle and a heavy chain binding him to the other prisoners. The floor was hard and cold, and the men had no fire to keep them warm.

---

3. *Saints: The Story of the Church of Jesus Christ in the Latter Days, Volume 1, The Standard of Truth* (Salt Lake City: The Church of Jesus Christ of Latter-day Saints, 2018), 153.

Lying awake, Parley Pratt felt sick as their guards told obscene stories about raping and killing Saints. He wanted to stand up and rebuke the men—to say something that would make them stop talking—but he kept silent.

Suddenly, he heard chains clank beside him as Joseph rose to his feet. "Silence, ye fiends of the infernal pit!" the prophet thundered. "In the name of Jesus Christ, I rebuke you and command you to be still! I will not live another minute and hear such language!"

The startled guards gripped their weapons and looked up. Joseph stared back at them, radiating majesty. "Cease such talk," he commanded, "or you or I die *this instant!*"

The room went quiet, and the guards lowered their guns. Some of them retreated to the corners. Others crouched in fear at Joseph's feet. The prophet stood still, looking calm and dignified. The guards begged his pardon and fell silent until their replacements came.[4]

FINDING CALM IN THE STORM

Leaders don't panic. They stay calm in the heat of battle. When we are afraid our emotions blind our senses. Captain Whaley talks about being afraid before the battle, staying calm during the battle, and then feeling fear again once the bullets stop flying. Indeed fear is of the devil, a tool to keep one from thinking correctly. If you have faith in the Lord and serve Him, fear will not paralyze your thoughts and actions. You will be calm and decisive. In Psalms we are comforted: "The angel of the Lord encampeth round about them that fear him, and delivereth them" (Psalm 34:7). The following account is taken directly from my missionary journal:

---

4. Ibid, 368.

EXCERPT FROM MISSIONARY
JOURNAL OF GEORGE POTTER

Author on mission in Bolivia

La Paz, Bolivia 28 March 1970

After lunch we started a 30 hour fast to help us become more spiritual and to find a location for the new branch. We also hoped the fast will help us remember our Lord Jesus Christ and what He did for us this Easter and every other day of our earthly lives.

By the end of the day my life would be in the hands of the Lord.

That evening while trying to retrieve a soccer ball which passed our way from some boys playing, my companion didn't see a pile of sand in the darkness, tripped and smashed into a wall shoulder first. He was in pain and had some skin removed from his forehead. I take it that he was thereafter in much pain and in an irritating mood. Later that night we went out to Calicotto district to locate a referral. As we discovered, the address on the referral card did not exist. The trip to Calicotto took a half hour and was a waste of our valuable time. The day certainly was not going well for my companion; and at 12,000 feet above sea level, we were starting to feel the impact of our fast.

While we were waiting for a bus a dog kept barking at us from across the street. In frustration, my companion threw a rock at the dog which was barking from behind a tall iron rod gate. A few minutes later, a man came out from behind the gate and started yelling at my companion for chucking the rock at his dog. The language the man used was foul, basically calling my companion a stupid jerk for throwing a rock at his dog. My companion was in no mood to be chewed out by the man and said, "Shut up or I'll shut you up." A heated argument commenced with yelling from both parties. Neighbors and people on the street could hear the angry words being exchanged and started gathering around us.

One thing that always set my companion off was anyone referring to him as a "son of a b..." He had a serious case of over sensitive mother love. So when the man called my companion a "son of a b . . . ," my companion gave him a strong push. As a result the man came back at my companion with a fist ready for a fight. The man should have never tried that, for my companion was the middle weight golden gloves boxing champion of Utah. My companion punched the man in the nose and down he went. To my surprise the man didn't flee, but with a bleeding and probably broken nose tried to attack my companion.

By this time my companion realized what a mistake he had committed and tried to calm the man down while holding him off; yet the man kept swinging wildly at him. As a result, my companion finally lost him temper again and floored the man with a second punch; and again the man got up and continued attacking. By this time, spectators started entering the fight against my companion. I was just standing nearby observing the crazy happening my companion had gotten himself into. I was holding our scriptures and missionary flannel board which we used for giving discussions. Suddenly a truck stopped and a man got out gripping a metal pipe. I had no doubt that the pipe was intended for my companion's head; and it was time for me to drop what I was holding and take out the truck driver – which I did with one punch coming out of my hiding place in the shadows. The fight quickly became two missionaries against a small mob of at least two dozen Bolivians. I wasn't scared, and found the fight rather exciting. However, we were outnumbered and I was starting to lose my breath. The initial adrenaline rush was quickly fading and we were fighting at over two miles above sea level. I yelled to my companion, "let's get out of here, I am exhausted." "Me too," he yelled back and we started running down the street with the small mob in hot pursuit.

I didn't think I could hold out much longer when a *colectivo*, a taxi that drives down one designated street picking up and releasing passengers as it goes, came down the street heading in our direction. I figured I was going to be killed anyway, so I jumped out in front of the *colectivo*. Fortunately the man driving the old car hit the brakes and stopped just two feet in front of me. We jumped in the car and locked the doors and commanded the driver to "go"! The driver saw the mob coming and froze. The mob started beating the car and cracking the windows trying to get to us. Since I was in the front passenger's seat, I reached over, took the steering wheel, and put my foot on the gas slowy freeing the car from the grip of the angry mob.

The driver finally came to his senses and drove us into downtown La Paz. We stopped in the city and gave the man all the money we had to try to compensate him for the damage. I think he was just glad to see us go. Amazingly, we had no injuries from the fight, not even bleeding knuckles. I know we had been protected by divine intervention, even angels. It was a close call, *so we thought.*

29 March

Easter Sunday in La Paz. Pondering the Savior and his mission boosted my spirits. We also ended our 30+ hour fast. We went to a favorite Chinese restaurant and ordered several plates as an evening break-fast. After 30 hours our stomachs were so tight we couldn't begin to eat half of what we had ordered.

1 April – The April Fools were us

A very interesting day. We did some public relations work for the Church in the morning and later gave an investigator a discussion at the chapel of the La Paz Branch 1. The mission offices were on the second floor of the branch house. As we gave the discussion, we could see through the crack in the doorway that a half dozen Bolivian police headed up the stairs to the mission offices. Fortunately, they did not see us, for we found out later they carried with them arrest warrants for my companion and I and a court summons to a trail. After the police left, the assistants to the mission president came to see us, asking to talk with us after our discussion. They wanted to know what had happened on Saturday night. We explained that we had been involved in a street fight. Our mission President, Keith Roberts was visiting a branch in the jungle and was delayed returning because of heavy tropical rains. The assistants to the president telephoned President Roberts who directed us to do nothing until we had discussed the situation with the Church's attorney in La Paz. Apparently the police knew who we were from the Bible and other materials I had left on the steps of a neighbor's house when I had to intervene in the fight.

According to the court documents, my companion and I were supposed to appear the next day for a court hearing. When we talked to the attorney, Dr. Vacaflore, over the phone, he told us that we were not in the *good old US of A* and that things were very different in Bolivia – in other words – "wake up you naïve young men." He told us we were not to go to the hearing, that he would do that for us. He also told us quote, "You are no longer in Bolivia." What? "You have already been sent out of the country." He directed us not to return to our apartment in La Paz, but to immediately go into hiding.

2 April

Another day I will always remember. We went to see the attorney, Dr. Vacaflore, to learn what happened at the court hearing. He told us that when he got to the court room, there was no hearing or trial, just 15 police waiting to take us to a prison in the countryside. In fact, the judge had already issued a written order that the both of us should be taking to a prison in a remote area, beaten, starved and killed! Dr. Vacaflore told the judge that we had already fled the country. The judge didn't believe him. Our attorney asked why they wanted George Potter because he had not instigated the fight. The judge said that they were mostly after my companion, but if they got and killed George Potter that would also be good. We also found out from the attorney that the man my companion got in the fight with was a General in the Bolivian Army, and he probably paid the corrupt judge less than US$500 to have us "legally murdered."

We asked the attorney what we should do. He replied, "Get out of Bolivia any way you can and as soon as you can. However, he warned us that there is a police manhunt looking for you and the train station and airport are already on the lookout for you."

President Roberts, who was still rained in in the Amazon basin, decided to send us to Tupac, in the remote mountains near the Argentine border where the two missionaries assigned there ride horses and have dogs. Tupac is a group of isolated high-mountain villages where the missionaries are assigned to travel by horse to serve several tiny villages. We were to go there and if anyone asked about us, we were to ride the horses across the mountains into Argentina. When the attorney heard this plan he told us that it would be suicide because we would stick out like sore thumbs. The police would find us in no time.

In desperation, we decided to try to board the train south toward Argentina and then take buses across the border to freedom. We informed the mission office of our plans and they agreed to check out the train station for us. We took a taxi into central La Paz. Not trusting the driver and knowing there was a police manhunt for us, we did not tell the driver our destination. Along the way we asked if he could stop by the police station to give his brother his lunch. There was no lunch visible in the taxi. Sitting next to the driver, I told him that if he stopped at a police station I would kill him (of course I was only trying to scare him). I instructed him to drop us at a plaza where there were many other taxis. From there we hired another taxi and told the driver to take us to the train station. As we neared the train station, the office missionaries who had been posted at the station saw our taxi approaching and stopped us. They told us that the police were searching for us at the station. We were trapped with a death sentence hanging over us.

In the afternoon, the assistants to the mission president called the US Embassy and were told they could not help us. Later that night an official at the embassy called us from his private line and told us that the way they smuggled people out of Bolivia is to take the dirt road around Lake Titicaca to the Peruvian border. Normally, there was only one mail service to the remote border outpost each week and if we were lucky and reached the Bolivia/Peru border before the Bolivia Border Police got the notice to arrest us, we could escape into Peru. We had no other choice but to risk our lives and to get to the Lake Titicaca border as fast as possible.

3 April

Up at 5:30 a.m. and on our way toward Lake Titicaca and the dirt road that just might lead us to safety. We reached the lake and proceeding around the great body of water in the mission's VW van. The escape attempt was dusty and bumpy. If we got across the border we were instructed to go to the tiny LDS branch in Juliana, Peru and tell the missionaries there that they were being transferred back to La Paz, Bolivia. At that time, the small branches on the north side of Lake Titicaca, the Peruvian side of the lake, were still part of the Bolivia Mission. Of course, the elders in Juliaca had no idea we were coming, nor did we know if we would even make it through the border. As we neared the border, about 300 yards away, the van pulled to the side of the road and stopped. We were told that we needed to take our bags and walk the rest of the way to the border on foot. The Mission President didn't want other missionaries or the mission to be accused of helping us escape the law. That made sense, but wasn't very assuring.

We exited the van and carried our suitcases to the small hut that served as a border crossing on the Bolivian side of the border. When we reached the hut there were several armed border guards. We didn't need to talk to each other. We both were wondering if this would be our last minutes of freedom before imprisonment, a thorough beating and execution. We handed our passports to one of the border guards. It seemed to me that it took the policeman an hour to review my passport. Finally, after what probably took only a minute, the officer stamped my passport. I smiled and walked across the border into Peru.

6 May

I saw my companion off at the Juliaca airport. He boarded a vintage DC 3 airplane and flew off to Lima. We both thought that he was being transferred to another city in the Peru Mission. I learned later that this was certainly not the case. My companion's name had been sent by Interpol (International Police) in La Bolivia to their offices in Lima, Peru asking that if my companion was still in Peru and to have him arrested and extricated back to Bolivia. By the grace of God, Brother Jose Sousa, a member of the Peru Mission Presidency, worked for Interpol in Lima and the request came across his desk. Brother Sousa called the Peru Mission President Allen Litster and told him he had 24 hours to get my companion out of Peru or he would have to execute the request from La Paz. My companion finished his mission in California, and I was able to complete my mission in Peru knowing finally that the Bolivian authorities were no longer after me.

Even though my companion's anger caused an unfortunate set of events that could have ended our lives, there are two reasons why I included this true story in this book.

First, my companion was at fault; however, he was a dedicated and hardworking missionary. The Lord spared his life from corrupt officials (secret combinations) by having his Interpol arrest request sent to the desk of Jose Sousa and no one else.

Second, during those life-threatening days, I was totally without fear for my life. From the time of the fight until I reached the relative safety of Peru, I never once was afraid or panicked. My soul was calm and at peace. My mind was clear and I was able to make the right decisions when required, including two times when the police almost caught us in La Paz. I knew without doubt that during those perilous days, I was surrounded by angels and my soul was comforted by the Holy Ghost.

I admired our departed General Authority Seventy A. Theodore Tuttle. He was the General Authority in charge of the Bolivia and Peru Mission when I served in those countries. He called my mother twice to comfort her during my escape from Bolivia to Peru. He also interviewed me about the above incident and encouraged me about my mission and my future career plans. Yet my few dangerous days in Bolivia pale in comparison to those this valiant man experienced during World War II. Still, during dangerous times, we both experienced a calm reassurance that we would be safe. For thirty-six days as a young Marine Lieutenant, A. Theodore Tuttle fought inch-to inch to victory over the Japanese at Iwo Jima. Elder Tuttle recalls:

> It seems to me that from the very beginning I have had guidance in situations which made my safety more sure. . . .
>
> For almost five hours on D-Day we watched the naval bombardment of the island. You couldn't imagine that there would be anything left alive. All I could see was smoke and dust; it looked like all hell had broken loose. Prior to leaving the ship I gathered all the LDS men on the bow of the ship where we had a short prayer.
>
> When we headed for shore, it seemed like a practice problem. Sailing around in the rendezvous area we could see the whole drama before us.
>
> There were no bullets coming our way, and it appeared that everything was in our favor. We lifted our fire and it was then, when the enemy came out of their fox holes and entrenchments, that we found that they were alive. Then they rained down death and destruction on us.
>
> I stepped into three feet of water and started for shore just as a huge breaker pulled me and several others under with our carbines and mortars.
>
> We were on board ship a long time before going into combat, and in poor physical condition when we hit the

beach. I could only run about ten yards before I dropped from exhaustion. But I wasn't the only one. The whole southern end of the island is heavy sand. You would sink a couple of inches into it wherever you stepped; it was like running through a wheat bin, carrying a fifty-pound pack. When I landed there were already a lot of shell holes in which to fall, and most of them were full of marines when I got there. I struggled ahead under the weight of my pack and other gear. Every now and then the fire would let up and we could get up and run a little ways. By jumping in one shell hole after another, I finally gained a more suitable position. It took me a couple of hours to get three hundred yards to where I was supposed to go.

From then on, it was just a matter of not being where they happened to be shooting. Mortar shells dropped without warning. It was an inexpressible sensation to be in your hole and feel shells land all around you. Often they were so close that sand and rocks were hurled on me. It still seems a miracle to me how any of us got across that beach alive.

Although my life was almost constantly in danger, I was never injured. I had many close calls, but it seems I was watched over and protected by a power higher than my own.[5]

MORE THAN EVENING THE ODDS AGAINST SATAN

God will honor those who honor Him and serve Him. Those leading others during the years prior to the Lord's Second Coming will undoubtedly find themselves involved in situations where neighbors are killing each other, if not involved in outright physical or spiritual battles. It is also likely that the forces of the righteous will be greatly outnumbered by wicked masses seeking the blood and souls of the righteous. How can Latter-day Saint leaders prevail against Satan's armies and angry mobs? I believe the solution is found in honoring

---

5. Paul H. Kelly and Lin H. Johnson, *Courage in a Season of War: Latter-day Saints Experience World War II* (Self-published, 2002), 428–431.

God and sacrificing for His Son's Kingdom. Consider the example of the faithful men and women of the Mormon Battalion.

At great sacrifice to them and their families, the members of the Mormon Battalion provided the Church with the financial means necessary for the first Latter-day Saint exodus to the Salt Lake Valley. Brigham Young called their sacrifice the "present and temporal salvation" of the Saints. President Young blessed the members of the battalion. He promised them that their "lives should be spared and [their] expedition result in great good, and [their] names be handed down in honorable remembrance to all generations." He further promised them "that they would have no fighting to do."[6] Despite the fact that the battalion served during the Mexican American War, and came very close to ongoing battles, as they approached each encounter, the battles stopped and the enemy surrendered. Indeed, being on God's side brings forth unseen forces. As Elisha told his fearful young servant who had seen the enemy's great host of horses and chariots, "Fear not: for they that be with us are more than they that be with them. And Elisha prayed, and said, Lord, I pray thee, open his eyes, that he may see. And the Lord opened the eyes of the young man; and he saw: and, behold, the mountain was full of horses and chariots of fire round about Elisha" (2 Kings 6:16–17).

In the dangerous times ahead, it would be a very incompetent leader if he or she loses faith in the Lord's power to preserve. As President Russell M. Nelson has taught: "As you choose to let God prevail in your lives, you will experience for yourselves that our God is 'a God of miracles' [Mormon 9:11]."[7] Our Lord has proved over and over again that He will fight beside us. The Book of Mormon provides a wonderful example of the Lord's power to preserve. When the Nephites were outnumbered by the Lamanite armies and were struggling to survive, 2,000 young stripling warriors came forth to support their host nation. We know well the story of how these young men were taught by their mothers to not doubt their faith in the Lord. The

---

6. Brandon J. Metcalf, "Four Things to Know about the Journey of the Mormon Battalion," *Church History,* 21 March 2019, https://history.churchofjesuschrist.org/content/historic-sites/journey-of-the-mormon-battalion?lang=eng, accessed 15 December 2020.

7. Russell M. Nelson, "Let God Prevail," October 2020 general conference.

Lamanite youth asked Helaman to be their leader. Battle after battle the stripling warriors fought with unmovable faith and great courage, even to the point where in one battle all 2,000 were wounded, but none perished (Alma 57:24). The miracle was a direct result of their faith in Christ (Alma 57:26). Helaman was so impressed by the 2,000 young Lamanite warriors that he called them his sons (Alma 56:10).

Of course, being preserved by faith in the Lord still exists in our day, and will be the power that will preserve many righteous leaders during the tribulation. In an article entitled "Latter-day stripling warriors," Brad Taylor writes of the Korea Seoul Mission's touching visit to sacred ground. He called those the missionaries remembered as modern-day stripling warriors, and the leader as a Helaman-like role model:

> The battle is called the "Miracle at Gapyeong." The heroic incident took place on May 25, 1951, in South Korea when a small battalion of 240 brave young soldiers from small-town southern Utah Latter-day Saint homes found themselves suddenly under attack by 4,000 Chinese and North Korean soldiers. It was a terrifying and completely unexpected attack. They were given the understanding that they were to provide artillery support to allied soldiers positioned ahead at the North Korean enemy line. But there were critical miscommunications and in fact, there was no buffer between the Utah soldiers and the enemy.
>
> They were shocked and terrified to discover that they were being directly attacked, and drastically outnumbered. The battle is accurately described as "a ferocious hand-to-hand battle fought in the early morning darkness." At dawn, Lt. Frank Dalley and Captain Ray Cox led their Latter-day Saint battalion into battle. They courageously fought their way through the Gapyeong Valley, destroying Chinese machine gun forts and inflicting hundreds of enemy casualties. "I just kept firing my .50 caliber (machine gun) until the barrel melted," said artillery soldier Elmo Robinson.
>
> Despite having a better than 16x advantage (4,000 vs. 240), the Chinese/North Korean opposition finally gave up and

attempted to retreat by climbing up the surrounding mountains to the north. In the end, more than 350 Chinese and North Korean enemies were killed, and another 830 were taken prisoner but *not one of the Latter-day Saint soldiers was killed.*

Many of the Chinese and North Korean soldiers that had been taken prisoner were asked how they could be so completely defeated by a such small battalion of only 240 young men? Their reply was "we shoot them, but they don't fall down."

One of the many spiritual aspects of this valiant group's battle was that this 213th Battalion had been promised by the president of the St. George Utah Temple that they would return home safely if they lived true and faithful to their God. These young men rose to that occasion and were recognized as a standout group who lived their lives with exactness and courage. Many of the family and friends in St. George, Cedar City, Richfield, Fillmore, and Beaver accurately compared this group to Helaman's stripling warriors (Alma 56).

Their leader, Lieutenant Colonel Frank Dalley, held many similarities to Helaman. He was a man of devout Latter-day Saint faith, who was old enough to be a father to these young boys age 17 to 23. He knew their families and felt a paternal responsibility to take care of them. He felt that if even one of those boys died, he wouldn't be able to face their parents back home in Southern Utah. He spent hours in prayer pleading with the Lord to help him to know how to lead and protect them from harm's way. It was well known by all in Dalley's battalion that when the flag was raised at his tent, he was in prayer and communication with God and that he was not to be disturbed.

Regarding that terrifying attack in 1951, Dalley later said on CBS Evening News with Edward R. Murrow: "For moments I supposed I was almost dazed, then instinctively my thoughts turned to God, and I knew that our safety was in the hands of our Maker. I humbly asked for help . . . and I feel sure that I was guided by a Supreme Being."[8]

Looking forward, we should not fear. For faithful leaders, there is no need to be panic-stricken of the violence encounters that are foretold. If it is the Lord's will and we place our trust in Him, our people will be preserved. In the days of Armageddon, the Lord has promised to slay the army of two hundred million (Joel 3:14, Revelation 9:16; 16:14,16).

DON'T GIVE UP ON GOD'S MIRACLES

"God has provided a means that man, through faith, might work mighty miracles; therefore he becometh a great benefit to his fellow beings" (Mosiah 8:18). Not backing down also means never giving up on the Lord. When all seems hopeless, the leader needs to keep driving forward. By example he or she needs to put their shoulder to the wheel and keep pushing, even when there appears to be no trail forward. Remember the accounts of the Utah pioneers who thought they could pull their handcarts no further, just to realize that angels began helping them pull the load. If the leader doesn't believe that the Lord is a "God of miracles . . . yesterday, today, and forever" (2 Nephi 27:23), how can he or she expect their followers to maintain faith when all seems lost? Miracles will happen, but only "according to their faith" (2 Nephi 27:23).

In apocalyptic times, the plans you had for your family and business might dissolve amongst the chaos, violence, and disease. Gary Roberts learned from experience the need to pray for God's help and to keep moving forward. He relates:

Wow, when the enormity of the gift of 800,000 acres of land (containing cobalt, copper, manganese, oil, gold, diamonds, and timber resources worth more than all the other natural resources in Zaire) hit me, I was overwhelmingly grateful to Our Heavenly Father for His love. So, after receiving the land

---

8. Brad Taylor, "Latter-day stripling warriors: The Korea Seoul Mission's touching visit to sacred ground," *LDS Living*, 11 December 2020.

offer from Willy Mishiki, I had my lawyers draw up transfer of ownership documents. Once the documents were signed, I began the process of creating investment vehicles to place the land and secure the investments to develop the property.

I contacted my bankers and potential investment partners to discuss this opportunity. In the beginning of this process, Willy Mishiki joined me in these meetings. It helped the discussions when he described the politics of Zaire and the opportunities that existed for development.

While we were making the investment rounds, Zaire's President Laurent Kabila was killed by one of his security guards. His son, Joseph Kabila, was installed to replace him, and his late father's rebel partners went back into the countryside to fight the son Joseph's new government. This news was bad enough, but when I found out that the rebels went back to the region that was given to me to launch their war effort, I had to immediately put a new plan into operation. The first step being to get on my knees and asked Heavenly Father to open the right doors for me and to guide me in what to do and say.

First, I contacted all of my potential investors and gave them the latest news. I asked for their patience while I attempted to see if anything could be done. Second, Willy and I strategized on the best options that were available to us. We knew that the rebels would need capital to fight. One option for the rebels would be to steal the gold and diamonds from the region and sell it. The closest point for the sale of these precious metals was probably Uganda. Third, we needed to make contact with Ugandan officials to get their assistance. Finally, we needed to convince the rebels to negotiate and not drag the country into a civil war.

I made an appointment to meet with the Ugandan Ambassador to the United States in Washington, DC. She was a very warm and gracious lady. I briefly explained the situation and what I was attempting to do. She had to cut our meeting short and asked if we could meet later that evening at her home for dinner.

At the ambassador's home, I was greeted by a young teenage girl who showed me into the living room. The ambassador appeared shortly thereafter, and we continued our conversation. She said that she was going to speak to her husband who was in Uganda for advice on who could help me. We went to dinner. At dinner we were surrounded by five young ladies. One of the ladies asked if I believed in God and to which church I belonged. I replied, "Yes, I believe in God and I am a member of the Church of Jesus Christ of Latter-day Saints." The ambassador then began by saying that she had been baptized in Sweden during her last ambassadorial tour and that the young lady that asked me the question was getting baptized in a few days. The young lady asked if I would confirm her a member of the church. I said that I would love to, but I needed to interview her before performing the ordinance. We agreed to meet that Saturday for the interview. The ambassador said that she would have more information about who my contact would be on Saturday.

Saturday I went back to the ambassador's home and interviewed the young lady. After the interview, I met with the ambassador and she said that after consulting with her husband, they agreed that Caleb Akandwanaho, aka General Salim Saleh, was the man that I needed to see. The ambassador had already spoken to the general's wife, Jovial, and she was prepared to help me.

The next day was the day for the young lady to get baptized. It was at the chapel that President Ezra Taft Benson attended years earlier while working in Washington DC as the Secretary of Agriculture. Willy Mishiki attended the ceremony and sat next to the ambassador. It was a very special event.

I called Jovial Akandwanaho. She was prepared for my call. As it turned out, the general was responsible for securing the borders with Zaire and was very familiar with the situation. He was also the President of Uganda's brother and a war veteran. I arranged to meet the general in Kampala, Uganda, as soon as possible.

I flew to Kampala to meet the general. Jovial met me at the airport and personally drove me to my hotel. After depositing me at the hotel, Jovial said that her manager, Andrew Segoya, would pick me up the next day at 10 a.m. to meet the general.

Promptly at 10 a.m., Andrew, a tall man with the build of a bodyguard, greeted me in the lobby of my hotel and drove me to the general's home. Once we passed the front gate and guards, I was taken to the main house to meet Jovial. She then had me escorted to the grand patio to meet the general.

The general was exactly what I expected: impressionable, direct, and no nonsense. He wanted to know what I wanted from him. I told him I needed to contact the rebel leaders to get them to the negotiating table with Joseph Kabila. The general knew all the players quite well. As I later discovered, he was intimately involved with the rebels. He offered me the use of his offices and aides. If I needed anything else, his wife would reach him to get it. That was the only time I met with the general.

True to his word, the general provided me with his aides and facilities. I was able to reach the rebel leaders' lieutenants and open negotiations.

I left Uganda with a greater understanding of how to solve the crisis and was extremely grateful to the general, Jovial, and their aides in assisting me in getting me to the players.

When I returned to the States, I contacted the rebel leaders and my bankers to meet in a neutral location. After much discussion, we selected Abu Dhabi in the United Arab Emirates. I opened an account with the National Bank of Abu Dhabi. I invited the rebel leaders to meet in Abu Dhabi in October 2003.

Five leaders arrived in Abu Dhabi and we got down to business. After two days of intense discussions. we reached agreement. It was decided that I would report back to President Kabila on our meetings and that he would make the next move.

I flew to Kinshasa and met with President Kabila, his principal political advisor, and the Central Bank Governor.

The president agreed to the conclusions of the agreement with the rebel leaders. The political advisor was tasked to get back to the rebel leaders. Once this was done and the rebel leaders were satisfied with outcome, I was able to get back to seeking financing for my land project.

1. Lean on the Holy Ghost to guide you when you don't immediately see a path forward. When you get the witness to act, do it right away.

2. Never forget that Heavenly Father always has a plan to get the job done, so why can't it be with you? So why can't you be the instrument in His hands?[9]

As Abraham Lincoln put it: "I am a slow walker, but I never walk back."

Acting boldly, staying calm and not giving up in the presence of danger and hopeless odds might not save you from getting bruised and bloodied or even thrown in a crude prison, but it just might convince an obnoxious school board to believe you and stop them authorizing an unsound or unholy curriculum.

> *And the day shall come that the earth shall rest, but before that day the heavens shall be darkened, and a veil of darkness shall cover the earth; and the heavens shall shake, and also the earth; and great tribulations shall be among the children of men, but my people will I preserve.*
> *(Moses 7:61)*

---

9. Gary Clay Roberts, "Two stories for your consideration in the book," email to author, July 18, 2020.

From the end of the earth will I cry unto thee, when my heart is overwhelmed: lead me to the rock that is higher than I.

—Psalm 61:2

Principle 6

Be Guided by a Higher Purpose

WE LIVE IN A REMARKABLE TIME WITH THE OPPORTUNITY TO HELP gather Israel and build the highway through the desert for the Lord's Second Coming. During the trials and tribulations that will come, we must never lose sight of the great purpose for which we were born into this dispensation. Isaiah declared:

Arise, shine; for thy light is come, and the glory of the Lord is risen upon thee.

For, behold, the darkness shall cover the earth, and gross darkness the people: but the Lord shall arise upon thee, and his glory shall be seen upon thee.

And the Gentiles shall come to thy light, and kings to the brightness of thy rising. (Isaiah 60:1–3)

President Russell M. Nelson reminded the Relief Society of their grand mission in the latter days:

Admittedly, the Lord has spoken of our day in sobering terms. He warned that in our day "men's hearts [would fail] them" and that even the very elect would be at risk of being deceived. He told Prophet Joseph Smith that "peace [would] be taken from the earth" and calamities would befall mankind.

Yet the Lord has also provided a vision of how remarkable this dispensation is. He inspired the Prophet Joseph Smith to declare that "the work of . . . these last days, is one of vast magnitude. . . . Its glories are past description, and its grandeur unsurpassable."[1]

To maintain enduring energy and a resilient and positive attitude through dark days, leaders will need to fortify themselves in a righteous cause. He or she must forget their own sufferings and sacrifices and think of others. Hugh Nibley summed it up in these words: "True leaders are inspiring because they are inspired, caught up in a higher purpose, devoid of personal ambition, idealistic, and incorruptible.[2]" Writing of his own achievements, Nibley stated:

> While I have been commended for some things, they were never the things which I considered most important—that was entirely a little understanding between me and my Heavenly Father, which I have thoroughly enjoyed, though no one else knows anything about it. . . . I would rather be a doorkeeper in the House of the Lord than mingle with the top brass in the tents of the wicked.[3]

The sustaining power of being engaged in the Lord's cause was taught to the sisters of the Church by Dallin H. Oaks in the October 2020 General Conference:

> "For after much tribulation come the blessings" (D&C 58:4).
>
> Sisters, I testify that these promises, given in the midst of persecutions and personal tragedies, apply to each of you in your troubling circumstances today. They are precious and remind each of us to be of good cheer and to have joy

1. Russell M. Nelson, "Embrace the Future with Faith," October 2020 general conference. (Quoting or referencing: Luke 21:26, D&C 45:26, Matthew 24:24, Joseph Smith-Matthew 1:22, D&C 1:35, D&C 1:17, 2Timothy 3:1–5).

2. Hugh Nibley, "Leaders and Managers," Brigham Young University commencement address, 19 August 1983, speeches.byu.edu.

3. "The Best Possible Test," *Brother Brigham Challenges the Saints*, edited Don E. Norton and Shirley S. Ricks, Vol. 13 in *The Collected Works of Hugh Nibley* (Salt Lake City: Deseret Books/FARMS, 1994), 535–37. (Hugh is paraphrasing Psalms 84:10).

in the fulness of the gospel as we press forward through the challenges of mortality.

Tribulations and challenges are common experiences of mortality. . . . With His help and our faithfulness and endurance, we will prevail. Like the mortal life of which they are a part, all tribulations are temporary. . . .

Think of those early members! Again and again, they were driven from place to place. Finally they faced the challenges of establishing their homes and the Church in a wilderness. Two years after the initial band of pioneers arrived in the valley of the Great Salt Lake, the pioneers' grip on survival in that hostile area was still precarious. Most members were still on the trail across the plains or struggling to get resources to do so. Yet leaders and members were still of hope and good cheer.

Even though the Saints were not settled in their new homes, at October 1849 general conference a new wave of missionaries was sent out to Scandinavia, France, Germany, Italy, and the South Pacific. At what could have been thought their lowest level, the pioneers rose to new heights. And just three years later, another 98 were also called to begin to gather scattered Israel. One of the Church leaders explained that these missions "are generally, not to be very long ones; probably from 3 to 7 years will be as long as any man will be absent from his family."[4]

It was a vision of a promised land that sustained Lehi's family in the extreme desert of Arabia, as well as the pioneers who followed Brigham Young into a barren landscape. As we face the difficult challenges in the dark years ahead, we must keep an eternal perspective and a vision of what we are asked to accomplish. Whatever the trials we may face, we can overcome them all by realizing that we are part of the building of a New Jerusalem, preparing the way for the glorious Second Coming of the Lord, and earning our station in the presence of our Father in Heaven. The Lord has promised: "And they shall overcome all things. Wherefore, let no man glory in man, but

---

4. Dallin H. Oaks, "Be of Good Cheer," October 2020 general conference.

rather let him glory in God, who shall subdue all enemies under his feet. These shall dwell in the presence of God and his Christ forever" (D&C 76:60–62).

FREE AGENCY AND HOPE IN CHRIST

No one will follow a leader who lives under a dark and gloomy cloud. Followers are inspired by optimistic thinkers who can even exhibit a sense of humor when all is going wrong. But how did the early Latter-day Saint pioneers maintain a cheerful attitude and positive outlook under such miserable circumstances? The answer to this question is key for leaders in the violent years to come, for they will face conditions far worse than those experienced by the pioneers. To make matters worse, too many people believe they are limited in their ability to overcome difficult circumstances in order to achieve great goals. They have been taught that they are only the product of their environment. The eternal truth is that we have been placed in a rough second estate to learn to exercise our agency and to have faith in Christ.

The legendary scholar Stephen R. Covey was a genuine champion in teaching how to overcome environmental determinism by exercising one's God given free agency. One of his favorite examples was Victor Frankl. Dr. Covey relates Frankl's use of agency in his book *The 7 Habits of Highly Effective People*:

> Frankl was a determinist raised in the tradition of Freudian psychology, which postulates that whatever happens to you as a child shapes your character and personality and basically governs your whole life. The limits and parameters of your life are set, and, basically, you can't do much about it.
>
> Frankl was also a psychiatrist and a Jew. He was imprisoned in the death camps of Nazi Germany, where he experienced things that were so repugnant to our sense of decency that we shudder to even repeat them.
>
> His parents, his brother, and his wife died in the camps or were sent to the gas ovens. Except for his sister, his entire family perished. Frankl himself suffered torture and innumerable indignities, never knowing from one moment to the next if his

path would lead to the ovens or if he would be among the "saved" who would remove the bodies or shovel out the ashes of those so fated.

One day, naked and alone in a small room, he began to become aware of what he later called "the last human of the freedoms"—the freedom his Nazi captors could not take away. They could control his entire environment, they could do what they wanted to his body, but Victor Frankl himself was a self-aware being who could look as an observer at his very involvement. His basic identity was intact. *He could decide within himself how all of this was going to affect him.* Between what happened to him, or his stimulus, and his response to it, was his freedom or power to choose that response.

In the midst of his experiences, Frankl would project himself into different circumstance, such as lecturing to his students after his release from the death camps. He would describe himself in the classroom, in his mind's eye, and give his students the lessons he was learning during his very torture.

Through a series of such disciplines—mental, emotional, and moral, principally using memory and imagination—he exercised his small, embryonic freedom until it grew larger and larger, until he had more freedom than his Nazi captors. They had more *liberty*, more options to choose from in their environment; but he had more *freedom*, more internal power to exercise his options. He became an inspiration to those around him, even to some of the guards. He helped others find meaning in their suffering and dignity in their prison existence.

In the midst of the most degrading circumstances imaginable, Frankl used the human endowment of self-awareness to discover a fundamental principle about the nature of man: *Between stimulus and response, man has the freedom to choose.*[5]

---

5. Stephen R. Covey, *The 7 Habits of Highly Effective People*, (New York: Simon & Schuster, 1989), 76–77.

Burdened down with strenuous trials, the early Latter-day Saint pioneers achieved a marvelous work. Their exodus from Nauvoo to the Salt Lake Valley has been referred to as the Trail of Hope, for without "faith, hope, and charity, you can do nothing" (D&C 18:19). Their leader, Brigham Young, continually instilled in the saints the hope that they were building an ensign to the nations high in the mountains. The prophet gave the pioneers hope when all seemed hopeless. Regardless of their troubles, the Saints prevailed because they believed they were preparing a land for their inheritance in a place prepared for them in the west, and a "man must hope, or he cannot receive an inheritance in the place which thou hast prepared" (Ether 12:32). During the incredibly difficult times ahead, leaders, as did Brigham Young, will need to be a fountain of hope for their followers. Such hope will always be accessible to a righteous leader through the gift of the Holy Ghost (Moroni 8:26).

AN INSPIRING LEADER SEEKS HIGHER GROUND

Nephi was no stranger to adversity and tribulations. He led his family through an eight-year journey in a hellish wilderness. He endured the pains and sorrows of a dysfunctional family—his brothers attempting to take his life on more than one occasion. He built a new civilization from scratch and led his people into blood battles against his own kin (see Mosiah 10:13–16, 1 Nephi 7:16; 16:37; 2 Nephi 5). Yet through all these challenges, Nephi never seems to have admitted defeat— rather he pressed forward and became an inspiring and beloved king. He understood well the principle of eternal progress. He taught:

> And now, my beloved brethren, after ye have gotten into this strait and narrow path, I would ask if all is done? Behold, I say unto you, Nay; for ye have not come thus far save it were by the word of Christ with unshaken faith in him, relying wholly upon the merits of him who is mighty to save.
>
> Wherefore, ye must press forward with a steadfastness in Christ, having a perfect brightness of hope, and a love of God and of all men. Wherefore, if ye shall press forward, feasting

upon the word of Christ, and endure to the end, behold, thus saith the Father: Ye shall have eternal life. (2 Nephi 31:19–20)

A proactive leader like Nephi will never accept the status quo mantra. They will press forward and proactively elevate their people to an even higher cause. Martin Luther King Jr. stated, "A genuine leader is not a searcher for consensus, but a molder of consensus." What inspiring cause will help your people endure the tough times ahead? What banner will they fight for?

The inspiration that drove Japanese American Saiji Zakimi during World War II was a love for his country and need for self-respect and dignity for his people. He stated, "I didn't worry about dying. I was willing to give my life for my country."[6] Saiji was wounded twice during the war. He relates his experience:

When I saw the Japanese planes attacking Pearl Harbor, I thought, *Those men look just like me.* My ROTC unit was immediately conscripted into the Home Guard and set to work guarding key installations in the area twenty-four hours a day. One month later all those of Japanese ancestry were discharged from their assignment. This decision deeply offended me, for this is my country, too; I was born on American soil, and according to the law of the land, I was a United States citizen. Following the attack on Pearl Harbor there was intense reaction against Americans of Japanese descent. As a group of former ROTC students, we petitioned the powers that be to allow us to serve. We felt that we had to act, to do something to demonstrate our loyalty to the United States of American. We became the Varsity Victory Volunteers and were stationed at Schofield Barracks, where we did Army duty without pay. About a year later we were told, "Okay, we can trust you," and our 4-C classifications, (meaning "enemy alien, not fit for service") was changed. We were formed into the 442nd Regimental Combat Team. The shoulder patch for

6. Paul H. Kelly and Lin H. Johnson, *Courage in a Season of War: Latter-day Saints Experience World War II*, (Self-published, 2002), 56.

our unit was a coffin with a torch of liberty inside, and our motto was "Go for Broke."

By war's end the 442nd, and its subordinate elements, became the most highly decorated single combat unit of its size in the history of the United States: eight Presidential Distinguished Unit Citations and 18,143 individual decorations, including one Medal of Honor; 52 Distinguished Service Crosses; 560 Silver Stars, and 28 Oak Leaf Clusters in lieu of a second Silver Star; 4000 Bronze Stars; and at least 9,486 Purple Hearts.

The 442nd became renowned for bravery. In the Vosges Mountains of northeastern France, a unit of Texans was trapped by Germans. Another Texas unit had been unable to rescue them, so we were moved to France to attempt the rescue.

I had not yet found The Church of Jesus Christ of Latter-day Saints and knew nothing of the Book of Mormon. I now think of the experience as being like the Stripling Warriors under Helaman in the Book of Mormon. It seems a miracle that none of us was killed, as this fighting was especially bitter and bloody.

The 442nd took more than 800 casualties in reaching the Texans, a unit of about 250 men. [7]

The Lamanite stripling warriors, whom Helaman called his sons, were able to inspire others to this day through their faith that they transformed into action. Holding onto the faith that their mothers taught them, the two thousand and sixty young men fought like lions. They honored their parents by protecting the Nephites. Helaman wrote of their cause:

Yea, and they did obey and observe to perform every word of command with exactness; yea, and even according to their faith it was done unto them; and I did remember the words which they said unto me that their mothers had taught them.

---

7. Ibid, 56–57.

. . . And now, their preservation was astonishing to our whole army, yea, that they should be spared while there was a thousand of our brethren who were slain. And we do justly ascribe it to the miraculous power of God, because of their exceeding faith in that which they had been taught to believe—that there was a just God, and whosoever did not doubt, that they should be preserved by his marvelous power.

Now this was the faith of these of whom I have spoken; they are young, and their minds are firm, and they do put their trust in God continually. (Alma 57: 21, 26–27)

As Latter-day Saints, it should be easy for us to lead with a higher cause and a divine purpose that will allow our family and community to prevail over Satan's fear tactics. As the Prophet Joseph Smith stated:

The standard of truth has been erected. No unhallowed hand can stop the work from progressing; persecutions may rage, mobs may combine, armies may assemble, calumny may defame, but the truth of God will go forth boldly, nobly, and independent till it has penetrated every continent, visited every clime, swept every country, and sounded in every ear, till the purposes of God shall be accomplished and the great Jehovah shall say the work is done.[8]

General Moroni understood this principle and expressed it when attempting to convince the defeated Lamanite Zerahemnah to stop the war, covenant to keep the peace, and return to his own land:

. . . Behold, Zerahemnah, that we do not desire to be men of blood. Ye know that ye are in our hands, yet we do not desire to slay you.

Behold, we have not come out to battle against you that we might shed your blood for power; neither do we desire to bring any one to the yoke of bondage. But this is the very

---

8. *Saints: The Story of the Church of Jesus Christ in the Latter Days, Volume 1, The Standard of Truth* (Salt Lake City: The Church of Jesus Christ of Latter-day Saints, 2018), Epigraph.

cause for which ye have come against us; yea, and ye are angry with us because of our religion.

But now, ye behold that the Lord is with us; and ye behold that he has delivered you into our hands. And now I would that ye should understand that this is done unto us because of our religion and our faith in Christ. And now ye see that ye cannot destroy this our faith.

Now ye see that this is the true faith of God; yea, ye see that God will support, and keep, and preserve us, so long as we are faithful unto him, and unto our faith, and our religion; and never will the Lord suffer that we shall be destroyed except we should fall into transgression and deny our faith.

And now, Zerahemnah, I command you, in the name of that all-powerful God, who has strengthened our arms that we have gained power over you, by our faith, by our religion, and by our rites of worship, and by our church, and by the sacred support which we owe to our wives and our children, by that liberty which binds us to our lands and our country; yea, and also by the maintenance of the sacred word of God, to which we owe all our happiness; and by all that is most dear unto us— (Alma 44:1–6)

A RIGHTEOUS CAUSE SEPARATES THE GOOD FROM THE EVIL

Having a righteous cause brings forth vision and insight. The wars in the last days will be fought in clear daylight, as well as in dark places and in the shadows. Without the help of the Holy Ghost, how will a leader know who is their real enemy? How will a leader know the root cause being used by Satan to instigate hate? If your cause is righteous, you will receive righteous discernment.

For example, think of the chaotic uncertainty in a mob of rioting demonstrators. How will you be able to distinguish who are the real instigators among the innocent? How will you know what it will take to neutralize their anger? Will you simply arrest everyone who is demonstrating, which will undoubtedly turn many peaceful demonstrators into resentful victims? It has always been a ploy of Satan to place wolves in sheep's skins among the flocks. Take the example of the Zoramites who were made captains over the unwilling Lamanite warriors. The Zoramites were perverted dissenters who separated themselves from the Nephites (Alma 30:25, 31:1) and were the ones who persecuted the converts of Alma (Alma 31:26–34, 41; 35:3–6). They were appointed captains over the disinclined Lamanites (Alma 48:5) to inspire them to fight courageously (Alma 43:43 44). The Zoramites were the real instigators, not the reluctant Lamanite soldiers.

A leader must have the inspired vision to see who are their real enemies, the wolves among the flocks. Among the innocent prowl angry antagonists, infiltrators, and saboteurs. A leader in the chaotic last days will need to have the wisdom to know who is their enemy and the best approach to deal with them.

> The light of the body is the eye: if therefore thine eye be single, thy whole body shall be full of light. (Matthew 6:22)

Unfortunately, in fearful and violent situations, it is not always easy to feel the inspiration of the spirit. However, knowing that your cause is righteous, you can be confident you are doing the right thing. Brigham Young noted:

> If I do not know the will of my Father, and what He requires of me in a certain transaction, if I ask Him to give me wisdom concerning any requirement in my life, or in regard to my own course, or that of my friends, my family, my children, or those that I preside over, and get no answer from Him, and then do the very best that my judgment will teach me, He is bound to own and honor that transaction, and He will do so to all intents and purposes.[9]

---

9. Brigham Young, *Journal of Discourses*, Vol. 3:205.

PRESS FORWARD HAVING HOPE IN CHRIST

Can you imagine how different the history of the world would be if Moses said to himself halfway through the Red Sea, "Maybe this isn't a good idea?" What if Joseph Smith had decided the restoration of the true religion wasn't worth the persecution he received for testifying of it? What if Brigham Young had taken one look at the barren Salt Lake Valley and said, "This can't be the place." When you are confident you are doing the right thing . . . just do it.

The last days will be more terrifying than any time since the creation. Having a righteous purpose breeds hope when all seems lost. In turn, hope can grow into faith, and faith brings forward miracles. Conversely, without hope, people lose faith and are lost in the chaos. A leader will need to keep his or her followers positive and moving forward through it all. As Napoleon stated, "A leader is a dealer in hope." If parents, teachers, Church and community leaders become discouraged, resentful, and feel hopeless, Satan has won the battle.

In his book, *For Times of Trouble,* apostle Jeffry R. Holland relates this story about the necessity of having hope:

> In a good-natured conversation around the dinner table, the host said that receiving the delightful dessert that had been prepared depended upon his guests' answering a gospel question correctly, namely, "What virtue, what strength is it that no man or woman can live without?"
>
> Guest number one said, faith—no one could really live without faith in God.
>
> The host replied that faith in God was certainly the most fundamental of religious virtues and that living a truly good life or a saved life or a happy life would certainly require faith. But, no, faith was not the answer. Unfortunately, he knew many people who lived without faith in anything and, though that fact was unfortunate, it nevertheless indicated that life could go on without faith because it did for them.
>
> The second guest answered love—that no one could really live without love in his or her life.
>
> Again the host qualified the answer, saying that undoubtedly that was true if we were speaking about the love

of God, but his question was about virtue we have, not that God has. Unfortunately, he said, there were lots of people who lived without love toward anyone or from anyone—and yet they continue to live.

"No," he said in answer to his own question, "I truly believe the most essential ingredient in life and the virtue that lets other blessings like faith and love flourish is *hope*. This doesn't mean that hope is the greater of the virtues (the Apostle Paul went on record as saying that love was the greatest of these three) but it may mean that in a sense hope is the most essential of the three at least initially because it can give rise to the other two.

All of us need to believe that things will get better. No matter how dark the night or how long the struggle, we all need to believe that the dawn will come and that the tears of the night will be dried in the rays of the morning sun.[10]

Through the difficulties ahead, leaders will need to keep their people focused on a positive outcome, a righteous goal or purpose. Leaders need to ensure that their people have a cause to fight for, hope for, and a reason for staying alive. For forty years, Moses kept the children of Israel determined to reach a land of milk and honey. Lehi's family murmured in the hellish wilderness, yet they eventually endured the journey knowing there was a promised land waiting for them. The early Latter-day Saints crossed the mountains and plains of North America one footstep at a time, praying they would make it to mount Zion. At the end of times, what *higher cause* can there be than to live to witness the Second Coming and to help build a New Jerusalem?

Leaders during the Apocalypse must be more than dealers in hope. Starting with hope, they must turn it into faith in Christ. It will take miracle after miracle to get your people to New Jerusalem and the Millennium. To those who lead during the end of times, Moroni gave a personalized warning and a blessed promise:

---

10. Jeffrey R. Holland, *For Times of Trouble* (Salt Lake City: Deseret Book, 2012), 66–67.

And the reason why he [God] ceaseth to do miracles among the children of men is because that they dwindle in unbelief, and depart from the right way, and know not the God in whom they should trust.

Behold, I say unto you that whoso believeth in Christ, doubting nothing, whatsoever he shall ask the Father in the name of Christ it shall be granted him, and this promise is unto all, even unto the ends of the earth. (Mormon 9:20–21)

When the battles rage, having a righteous cause is paramount. In the long run, good causes will prevail over evil intentions. For example, more than superior numbers and weapons, the Union soldiers of the North defeated the Confederate Armies of the South in the American Civil War because they had a higher and more righteous cause—the elimination of the evil of slavery in the United States. While many historians rationalize that the southern states fought for reasons other than slavery, let's be clear, all their justifications are rooted in the evils of slavery and the economic gains therefrom. In 1861, while visiting the Union troops in the thick of the Civil War, Julia Ward Howe wrote a poem that encompassed the cause the Union soldiers fought for. It was an anti-slavery anthem. When President Abraham Lincoln heard it sung for the first time, he wept. It became known as the "Battle Hymn of the Republic":

Mine eyes have seen the glory of the coming of the Lord:
He is trampling out the vintage where the grapes of wrath are stored;
He hath loosed the fateful lightning of His terrible swift sword:
His truth is marching on.

I have seen Him in the watch-fires of a hundred circling camps,
They have builded Him an altar in the evening dews and damps;
I can read His righteous sentence by the dim and flaring lamps;
His day is marching on

I have read a fiery gospel writ in burnished rows of steel;
"As ye deal with my contemners, so with you my grace shall deal;
Let the Hero, born of woman, crush the serpent with his heel,
Since God is marching on."

He has sounded forth the trumpet that shall never call retreat;
He is sifting out the hearts of men before His judgment-seat:
Oh, be swift, my soul, to answer Him! Be jubilant, my feet!
Our God is marching on.

In the beauty of the lilies Christ was born across the sea,
With a glory in his bosom that transfigures you and me:
As he died to make men holy, let us die to make men free,
While God is marching on.[11]

The Lord is my shepherd; I shall not want.

He maketh me to lie down in green pastures:
he leadeth me beside the still waters.

He restoreth my soul: he leadeth me in the paths
of righteousness for his name's sake.

Yea, though I walk through the valley of the shadow
of death, I will fear no evil: for thou art with me; thy
rod and thy staff they comfort me. (Psalm 23:1–4)

---

11. Julia Ward Howe, "The Battle Hymn of the Republic," *The Atlantic Monthly*, Vol IX, February 1862. https://cdn.theatlantic.com/assets/media/img/posts/2017/05/battlehymn_original/f18a47fea.jpg.

Then shall two be in the field; the one shall be taken, and the other left. Two women shall be grinding at the mill; the one shall be taken, and the other left.

—Matthew 24:40–41

Principle 7

Next Man Up—
Next Women Up

ONE SHALL BE TAKEN AND ONE SHALL BE LEFT. HAVE YOU WONDERED which one will be taken and which one will be left? Will it be the righteous one that is taken up to meet Christ and the evil one left to suffer? Or will it be the other way around? Whichever way it is, the Lord gave a clear warning to both men and women of the gravity of the events that will face those left behind. However, no one knows when the calamites will happen (Matthew 24:42), and no one knows if they will be taken or left behind. Furthermore, there is no guarantee that even if you are exceptionally righteous that you will not be a victim of the violence in last days (Revelation 6:9). The Lord has declared in the latter days: "Therefore, be not afraid of your enemies, for I have decreed in my heart, saith the Lord, that I will prove you in all things, whether you will abide in my covenant, even unto death, that you may be found worthy" (D&C 98:14).

Another possibility is that you will be one of those who are selected to prepare Zion for the Lord. If you are so blessed, you might be called suddenly to leave your community and join the 144,000 assigned to build the New Jerusalem. What is important for the leader of a family, a priesthood quorum, a Relief Society, a community, a tribe, or a nation is that you need to develop and prepare leaders to fill leadership roles in case you or others are suddenly here today and gone tomorrow.

DEVELOPING LEADERS TO REPLACE YOU AND OTHERS

Throughout history outstanding leaders have identified and then developed leaders to take their place. The Lord mentored Peter, James, and John; teaching them vital lessons as He ministered on earth. Paul was tutored by the Lord in the wilderness of Sinai (Galatians 1:11, 12, 15–17). Moses selected Joshua and developed his student's leadership skills over a 40-year period in a desert classroom. Nephi taught his younger brother Jacob to lead the Church.

An example in our era is how Joseph Smith helped transform the house painter Brigham Young into a powerful leader, even a modern Moses. Through difficult assignments like Zion's Camp and his early mission to England, Brigham Young was prepared to be an ideal successor who could boldly lead the Saints through the trials they would encounter as they fled Nauvoo, cross the American wilderness, and raise a progressive community in a barren wasteland. Joseph even continued mentoring Brigham Young from the other side of the veil.[1] Shortly after Joseph's death, Brigham recounted a dream he had where Joseph Smith gave him personal instruction. President Young said,

> Joseph stepped toward me, and looking very earnestly, yet pleasantly said: "Tell the people to be humble and faithful, and be sure to keep the spirit of the Lord and it will lead them right. Be careful and not turn away the small still voice; it will teach them what to do and where to go; it will yield the fruits of the Kingdom. . . . Tell the brethren if they will follow the spirit of the Lord they will go right."[2]

Leadership guru Professor Dave Ulrich has published over 30 books on leadership, organization, and human resources. A member

---

1. *Teaching of the Presidents of the Church: Brigham Young*, (Salt Lake City: The Church of Jesus Christ of Latter-day Saints, 1997), 345.
2. Ibid, 41.

of the Church, Dave is generally accepted as the leading consultant and educator in the field of corporate human resource development. He has advised and performed research with over half of the Fortune 200 companies and has consulted in over 80 countries. Together with his colleagues Norm Smallwood and Kate Sweetman, Dave Ulrich conducted extensive interviews with a wide range of successful CEOs, academics, senior executives, and experienced consultants. Over and over again, the professionals they interviewed suggested five leadership competency domains that were essential for organizations to grow. These five domains became their "Leadership Code," and the basis for their book, *The Leadership Code: Five Rules to Lead.* Of the hundreds of books I have read on leadership, *The Leadership Code* is one of the most effective for coaching leaders on how to improve their performance and how to balance their leadership behavior. The five leadership competency domains of the Leadership Core are: Strategist, Executor, Talent Manager, Human Capital Developer, and Personal Proficiency.[3] For the purposes of this chapter, I will briefly discuss some elements of Leadership Code Rule #4: "Build the next generation."

RULE 4: BUILD THE NEXT GENERATION

A leader begins to develop the next generation of leaders by "mapping the workforce." Simply put, the leader needs to identify what leadership positions are critical for the organization to thrive and who are the best candidates to fill each of those positions when the positions need to be filled. In the context of the violent last days, a leader should map out which positions will need backup leaders when the current leader is suddenly gone. This needs to be mapped for all important positions— since one will be taken and one will be left. What positions do you need to prepare candidates for? A list could look like this:

- Father of the family
- Mother of the family
- Bishop and organizational presidents and teachers
- Relief Society President

---

3. Dave Ulrich, Norm Smallwood, & Kate Sweetman, *The Leadership Code: Five Rules to Lead By* (Boston: Harvard Business Press, 2008).

- Mayor
- Fire Chief
- Police Chief
- Community patrol director
- Emergency response director
- Extended (family tribe) Chief
- Leadership positions at my workplace

Once you have identified the critical positions, you need to have "Individual Development Plans" for each candidate who could possibly be called upon to fulfill the leadership role. Of course, the leader would do this only for those roles for which he or she has a stewardship, i.e. a stake president developing a set of possible replacement bishops. In the family context, a mother needs to train one or more of her daughters to take her place if she is taken. The father needs to prepare one or more sons to fill his shoes during very difficult times.

It then requires leadership to make the tough decision as to which candidate is best suited to fill each critical position. For example, when the Lord chose Brigham Young, He must have understood the outcomes expected of him—to successfully lead an impoverished people into a desert wilderness and to build there an ensign to the nations.

To identify the right person for the right leadership position, one must map all the critical positions that might need filling and then to determine what are the outcomes expected of that position and the required skills needed to obtain those outcomes. The mapping process continues by identifying each best candidate's skills to determine how they match up against the skills required for the desired outcomes. Where is each candidate strong and where are they weak in the necessary skills, including leadership competencies? Ulrich warns: "There are some people who are better at critical jobs than others, but it takes leadership to make these tough decisions."[4]

Have you identified who are the best candidates for each of the critical positions you are responsible for? Each position has its own challenges and skill set requirements. As Lehi became fragile while leading his family in the wilderness, taking exception to tradition of

---

4. Ibid.

placing the oldest son as the leader, he allowed Nephi to take his place as the head of the family (Mosiah 10:13). Although at the time Nephi led with "sharpness" (2 Nephi 1:26), his bold plainness was probably one of the leadership competencies the Lord recognized in Nephi that made him the right leader for the terrible conditions the family endured in the wilderness. Of course, Nephi was also chosen for the position by the Lord because of his faithfulness in keeping the commandments (1 Nephi 2:19–20). Fortunately for the family, if it weren't for Nephi's leadership, the family would have perished in the desert (2 Nephi 1:24). Despite being the fourth son, Nephi was the right person with the right skills for the right job at the right time.

Once you have identified the best person available for filling each critical position, you must perform three important leadership development steps. First, prepare what leadership development experts call a critical position heat-map. A heat-map is a color-coded table that uses color to indicate highest readiness and lowest readiness scores of each "best person available." That is, for each position use a numerical scale to score how the best candidate rates against each of the competencies he or she will need to perform in the position they are candidates to fill. The scoring can be on an absolute or a percentage scale so long as it indicates how ready the person is to perform as a leader—that is, the ability to obtain the desired outcomes. It helps to make the colors intuitive, i.e. green colors are "ready now to perform", yellow colors as "still needing some training," and red colors as "not ready." Heat-maps can easily be built using a computer spreadsheet. Once the map is developed, at a glance the leader can see which positions have "ready now to perform," positions where some training is needed, and positions that are "in jeopardy" because there is no one ready to take the place of the leader who could be taken at any moment.

Second, in those positions where the best person available is not "ready now," the leader needs to personally coach each candidate to expedite their development. Leadership coaching is a collaborative, individualized relationship between a leader and the coach. Developmental coaching is about improving skills and knowledge as well as developing sound emotional intelligences. An effective coach helps the coachee see their own strengths, weaknesses, and potentials, and supports the individual in developing an action plan for growth. The best example of a coach is the Lord. Michelle D. Craig, First Counselor in the Young Women General Presidency, explains: "Jesus Christ sees people deeply. He sees individuals, their needs, and who they can become. Where others saw fishermen, sinners, or publicans, Jesus saw disciples."[5] An example of a last day's coach could be a mother helping her daughter learn the leadership roles and skills needed to help her family survive in case she, the mother, is taken. Regardless of the position in question, coaching is a partnership—one in which both sides work to prepare the candidate for the necessary behaviors and leadership competencies they will need to effectively lead when called upon.

Third, the leader must be a mentor or they must select a mentor to train each best candidate the skills needed to perform in the position in question. A mentor is a skilled person who guides a less experienced person by building a trusting relationship and modeling the desired skills. An effective mentor understands that his or her role is to be dependable, engaged, authentic, and tuned into the skills the mentee needs to learn from them. The word mentor comes from the character "Mentor" in Homer's epic tale, *The Odyssey*. Mentor was a trusted friend of Odysseus, the king of Ithaca. There will be many critical skills needed to survive the years of the tribulation. An example of mentoring could be a father teaching his sons how to hunt for food or purify water. Other examples could be training community leaders how to pacify an angry mob or how to put out a raging fire when there is no fire department.

A TWO-WAY STREET—KNOW THYSELF AND DEVELOP THYSELF

Not only will leaders in the last days need to groom replacements— the next man or women up—they must prepare themselves to fill the leadership positions of others who might be "taken." Besides creating your own individual development plan to prepare yourself for each of the possible positions you might find yourself in, one of the most

5. Michelle D. Craig, "Eyes to See," October 2020 general conference.

effective ways to develop the leadership skills you will need is to model your behavior after a leader who is highly effective in that position. Such a person is known as a leader role model. Whether the position in question is a head nurse or a family patriarch, modeling the behavior of someone you know who is highly successful in that position is an effective and fast way to become prepared.

You might ask: "What is modeling?" It is simply observing the behavior and decision making of a leader in variant situations, and then practicing emulating the behaviors that have been shown to be effective. Likewise, a wise man or woman studies carefully the leadership strengths and weakness of those above, around, and below them and then model the effective behavior and avoid the ineffective behavior.

Using historical examples can also be useful. General George Patton was a passionate student of military history. He studied the actions and decisions of military leaders throughout history and used the information he gained to know what worked and what didn't work to obtain victory. Indeed, the scriptures, both ancient and modern, provide righteous leader role models we can emulate.

Whichever leader you believe is a good leader role model for the position you are preparing for, observe them carefully and take note of what your leader role model does with others in each of the five leadership domains (rules) identified by Ulrich, Smallwood, and Sweetman. That is, what do your leader role models do to:

Rule 1: Shape the future

This rule is embodied in the strategist dimension of the leader. Strategists answer the question "Where are we going?" and make sure that those around them understand the direction as well. They not only envision, but can also create a future. They figure out where the organization needs to go to succeed, they test these ideas pragmatically against current resources (money, people, organizational capabilities), and they work with others to uncover how to get from the present to the desired future.

Rule 2: Make things happen

The executor dimension of the leader focuses on the question, "How will we make sure we get to where we need to go?" Executors translate strategy into action and know how to make change positive. Executors assign accountability, know which key decisions to take and which to delegate, and ensure that teams work well together.

Rule 3: Engage today's talent

Leaders who optimize talent today answer the question "Who goes with us on our business journey?" Talent managers know how to identify, build and engage talent to get results now. Talent managers identify what skills are required, draw talent to their organizations, engage them, communicate extensively, and ensure that employees turn in their best efforts. Talent managers generate intense personal, professional and organizational loyalty.

Rule 4: Build the next generation

Leaders who are human capital developers answer the question, "Who stays and sustains the organization for the next generation?" . . . Just as good parents invest in helping their children succeed, human capital developers help future leaders succeed. Human capital developers throughout the organization build a workforce plan focused on future talent, understanding how to develop potential talent, and help employees see their future careers within the company.

Rule 5: Invest in yourself

At the heart of the leadership code—literally and figuratively—is personal proficiency. Effective leaders cannot be reduced to what they know and do. Who they are as human beings has everything to do with how much they can accomplish with and through other people.

Leaders are learners—from success, failure, assignments, books, classes, people and life itself. Passionate about their beliefs and interests, they expend an enormous personal energy and attention on whatever matters to them. Effective leaders inspire loyalty and good will in others because they themselves act with integrity and trust. Decisive and impassioned, they are capable of bold and courageous moves. Confident in their ability to deal with situations as they arise, they can tolerate ambiguity.[6]

THE AMAZING POWER OF MODELING

No one is born with all the leadership competencies they need to be a highly successful leader. Everyone has their natural strengths and weakness. However, a leader can become competent in the leadership strengths of other leaders they model. Alexander the Great studied to be a military leader under his father Philip II of Macedonia. While Philip was a skilled military commander (Executor), he had no vision or strategy beyond his homeland of Macedonia and possessed only the limited talent management skills of a feudal king. Alexander modeled the military skills of his father, but also mastered how to leverage these by being an inspiring visionary and having remarkable talent management skills. The combination of Alexander's leadership competencies allowed him to conquer the known world.

Publius Cornelius Scipio Africanus was a Roman general and consul who is considered one of the best military commanders and strategists of all time. He led Rome to victory during the Second Punic War. His greatest military achievement was the defeat of Hannibal at the Battle of Zama in 202 BC. Scipio Africanus mentored under his father the Roman general Scipio I. He learned from his father how to command a Roman legion. However, he also observed firsthand how his father was defeated by Hannibal. To avenge Roman and his father's defeat, Scipio Africanus studied carefully the military strategies and tactics of his enemy Hannibal. Throughout his victories of Spain and his North African campaign, Scipio Africanus emulated

---

6. Dave Ulrich and Nate Smallwood, "Cracking the Leadership Code: A Journey Through Leadership," *The RBL Group,* 9 November 2018. https://www.rbl.net/insights/articles/cracking-the-leadership-code-a-journey-through-leadership, accessed 8 December 2020.

the battle tactics of Hannibal and by so doing eventually defeated the great Carthaginian commander.

Undoubtedly, the paramount opportunity of all would be to be mentored and coached by our Father in Heaven. God is the perfect leader role model, and ultimately, we should try to acquire His godly leadership competencies. Adam received personal coaching and mentoring from Heavenly Father. The Prophet Joseph Smith taught that Adam lived 1,000 years, less six months. Since his life after leaving the garden amounted to 930 years, he must have been with the Father in the garden for roughly seventy years (see Genesis 5:5). Of Adam's time in the Garden of Eden, Joseph Fielding Smith wrote: "He [Adam] was in the presence of God. He saw him just as you see your father."[7] It would seem that observing God the Father would have provided our first earthly father an ideal leader role model.

Enoch received a similar majestic blessing. His leader role model and coach was Jesus Christ. Even though Enoch lived during a time of great wickedness, he inspired his people to become a Zion community, so righteous that they were taken into heaven. What is certain, Enoch didn't accomplish this alone. Enoch saw the Lord and walked with Him continually for 365 years (D&C 107:49).

For our own survival and that of our family, it is vital that in the last days we have our Father in Heaven and His son Jesus Christ as our primary leadership coaches—letting them teach us through daily inspiration what we need to be to lead as they would. We must hear them. We must let them prevail in our lives. President Russell M. Nelson has taught:

> Now, my dear brothers and sisters, it takes both faith and courage to let God prevail. It takes persistent, rigorous spiritual work to repent and put off the natural man through the Atonement of Jesus Christ (Mosiah 3:19). It takes consistent, daily effort to develop personal habits to study the gospel, to learn more about Heavenly Father and Jesus Christ, and to seek and respond to personal revelation.

---

7. Joseph Fielding Smith, *Conference Report*, October 1926, 177.

During these perilous times of which the Apostle Paul prophesied (see 2 Timothy 3:1–13), Satan is no longer even *trying* to hide his attacks on God's plan. Emboldened evil abounds. Therefore, the only way to survive spiritually is to be determined to let God prevail in our lives, to learn to hear His voice, and to use our energy to help gather Israel. [8]

We might not be able to see God and His Son face-to-face, like Adam and Enoch; however, if a leader lives righteously and are in tune to divine revelations and the constant companionship of the Holy Ghost, he or she can receive the same perfect leadership coaching as the ancients. President Nelson warns: "In coming days, it will not be possible to survive spiritually without the guiding, directing, comforting, and constant influence of the Holy Ghost."[9]

EMULATING A LEADER-ROLE MODEL TAKES PRACTICE AND PERSISTENCE

Behaviors and decision making are visible. That is, they are observable in others. For example, courage is only exhibited. It has to be displayed to exist in the minds of others. Courage is not a hidden character, it is something people have to see you do. But what if you do not believe you have courage? By emulating of a leader role model, you can with time develop courageous behavior. You won't suddenly become a tower of bravery, but with time, modeling the same behavior over and over, you will become courageous. In time, you will feel courageous and others will see your courage because you act in a courageous manner.

For example, assume you believe you cannot stand up to a lawless mob. However, you witnessed how your neighbor successfully did just that. The next time you face the angry mob, just do exactly what he did—model his behavior. At first you might not have the same level of desired outcome; however, it probably ended in results better than

---

8. Russell M. Nelson, "Let God Prevail," October 2020 general conference.
9. Russell M. Nelson, "Revelation for the Church, Revelation for Our Lives," April 2018 general conference.

if you had not emulated the courageous neighbor. Over time and by practicing the same behaviors, you will gain the leadership competency and will achieve the same desired outcomes.

Through persistent practice, leadership competencies can be developed. The key is don't be afraid to try a new behavior. Do not be afraid to lead. President Spencer J. Kimball was fond of saying, "Do it." When practicing a new behavior, the most important step, and the most difficult step, is the first step. Think of the leadership ascension of Nephi. He led his family in the wilderness, captained a ship across two oceans, became a beloved king, successfully led his people in war, and the founded a marvelous library—the Book of Mormon. Yet, his first act of leadership was confronting his reluctant older brothers and convincing them to return to the house of Laban. We can only wonder what would have become of Nephi if he had not taken that first step.

The life of President Heber J. Grant is a wonderful role model for persistence and self-improvement. We read from the *Teaching of the Presidents of the Church*:

> President Heber J. Grant often quoted the following statement, which is sometimes attributed to Ralph Waldo Emerson: "That which we persist in doing becomes easier for us to do—not that the nature of the thing is changed, but that our power to do is increased." President Grant exemplified this truth, particularly in serving the Lord. Despite hardships such as poverty and the early death of his father, he persisted in keeping the commandments, fulfilling his Church callings, and doing all he could to build the kingdom of God on the earth.
>
> We can accomplish any worthwhile goal if we are persistent.
>
> . . . God has given to some people ten talents; to others, he has given one; but they who improve the one talent will live to see the day when they will far outshine those who have ten talents but fail to improve them.

Trustworthiness, stick-to-it-iveness, and determination are the qualities that will help you to win the battle of life.[10]

If you continue to model the leadership competencies that are required for the positions you might suddenly need to fill if others are taken, you will be the right leader with the right skills at the right time in the end of times.

> . . . Jesus saith to Simon Peter, Simon, son of Jonas, lovest thou me more than these? He saith unto him, Yea, Lord; thou knowest that I love thee. He saith unto him, Feed my lambs.
>
> He saith to him again the second time, Simon, son of Jonas, lovest thou me? He saith unto him, Yea, Lord; thou knowest that I love thee. He saith unto him, Feed my sheep.
>
> He saith unto him the third time, Simon, son of Jonas, lovest thou me? Peter was grieved because he said unto him the third time, Lovest thou me? And he said unto him, Lord, thou knowest all things; thou knowest that I love thee. Jesus saith unto him, Feed my sheep. (John 21:15–17)

---

10. *Teachings Of Presidents Of The Church: Heber J. Grant,* (Salt Lake City: The Church of Jesus Christ of Latter-day Saints, 2020), 35–36.

*My concern is not whether God is on
our side; my greatest concern is to be
on God's side, for God is always right.*

—Abraham Lincoln

Principle 8

Be Humble but Be Excellent

The Prophet Mormon declared, "Behold, the pride of this nation, or the people of the Nephites, hath proven their destruction except they should repent" (Moroni 8:27). It's an ominous warning to those in leadership positions in the last day. If you are arrogant and prideful, like the Nephites, you and your people are doomed. Fortunately, the prophet provided the cure, "And the remission of sins bringeth meekness, and lowliness of heart; and because of meekness and lowliness of heart cometh visitations of the Holy Ghost" (Moroni 8:26).

The Lord has stated in our era, "We have learned by sad experience that it is the nature and disposition of almost all men, as soon as they get a little authority, as they suppose, they will immediately begin to exercise unrighteous dominion. Hence many are called, but few are chosen" (D&C 121:39–40). A loose rephrasing might be, "Hence many are proud managers, but few are humble leaders."

President Benson opened his famous general conference talk on pride with these words:

> In the premortal council, it was pride that felled Lucifer, "a son of the morning." (2 Ne. 24:12–15; see also D&C 76:25–27; Moses 4:3.) At the end of this world, when God cleanses the earth by fire, the proud will be burned as stubble and

the meek shall inherit the earth. (See 3 Ne. 12:5, 3 Ne. 25:1; D&C 29:9; JS—H 1:37; Mal. 4:1.)[1]

As the American prophet Samuel warned a doomed Nephite society:

> Yea, heavy destruction awaiteth this people, and it surely cometh unto this people, and nothing can save this people save it be repentance and faith on the Lord Jesus Christ, who surely shall come unto the world, and shall suffer many things and shall be slain for his people.
>
> Therefore, thus saith the Lord: Because of the hardness of the hearts of the people of the Nephites, except they repent I will take away my word from them, and I will withdraw my Spirit from them, and I will suffer them no longer, and *I will turn the hearts of their brethren against them.* (Helaman 13:6, 8, emphasis added)

The bad news is that the hearts of the enemies of the Saints in the latter days will be bent on destroying them: "Ye hear of wars in far countries, and you say that there will soon be great wars in far countries, but ye know not the hearts of men in your own land" (D&C 38:29). The good news is that the Lord will soften the hearts of oppressors and unbelievers before the day of His coming (D&C 124:8–9). Indeed, if the Saints are humble and repent, the Lord will soften the hearts of our enemies.

> Yea, and we may see at the very time when he doth prosper his people, yea, in the increase of their fields, their flocks and their herds, and in gold, and in silver, and in all manner of precious things of every kind and art; sparing their lives, and delivering them out of the hands of their enemies; *softening the hearts of their enemies that they should not declare wars against them.* (Helaman 12:2, emphasis added)

---

1. Ezra Taft Benson, "Beware of Pride," April 1989 general conference.

BATTLE PROVEN HUMILITY

It can be argued that the most hellish years of the history of the United States were those during the bloody Civil War. Through the bloody years of death and destruction, the war's most successful general was the humble General Ulysses S. Grant. The Union General is considered the father of modern warfare. To this day Grant is the most studied military leader at West Point. Author Mike Lively writes of this remarkable leader:

> Humility is a trait we should all strive to cultivate. The best leaders throughout history, especially in the U.S. military, were humble. Humility helps us to not get lost in our own egos, to value others more dearly, and to better lead and serve. In the annals of American military history, it would be difficult to find a more humble leader than Ulysses S. Grant. Grant possessed an unusual amount of humility, knowledge of self, and a resultant ability to constantly acknowledge and learn from his own mistakes. His generalship during the Civil War exemplified servant leadership, and from it we can take examples of humility which we can use to be better leaders and people. . . .
>
> While Grant's humility was on display in his interactions with superiors, it was extremely pronounced in how he treated his subordinates, especially once he was promoted to lieutenant general of all Union forces in 1864. Grant could have, as most other generals would, remained in Washington D.C. while prosecuting the war. It was the hub of government and the Secretary of War as well as the president would've been close, not to mention the comforts of life available to a man of such high station. Grant decided to stay with his men, on the move, always close to the action. He slept on the ground with them, forgoing the extravagance of the usual general's quarters despite having attained the highest formal generalship in American history. He wore a private's jacket with lieutenant general's ranks instead of a formal general's uniform.

He encouraged alternative viewpoints from subordinate generals. He welcomed criticism from General Sherman about his own strategies, understanding that conveyance of humility and delegation of responsibility were essential to efficient operations. He took blame from subordinates when things went wrong and gave praise to them when things went right. . . .

Grant made humility his moniker, his style, remaining true to himself as he led. His subordinates responded well, and this attitude resonated throughout Union forces. We can all take a page out of Grant's book whenever we have a leadership role. Forgoing benefits of one's station, not taking slights to heart, and encouraging healthy disagreement all foster a better organizational climate, and help us not get too caught up in our own heads. By putting his ego aside, Grant was able to lead and live better. He would show his humility and humanity in an even more revealing fashion towards his enemies. . . .

Grant was always humble. He treated his superiors with deference and respect, he always placed himself on the same level as his subordinates, and he showed honor and compassion to his enemies. In so doing, he effectively led Union forces to triumph over the Confederacy, and won the Civil War.[2]

HUMILITY THROUGH LISTENING

As the example of General Grant shows, humility is exhibited by listening to and learning from others. Indeed, there is no higher act of respect than listening. Captain Whaley relates:

The racial problems within the Command continued to increase and finally resulted in a large demonstration led by

---

2. Matt Lively, "To Lead, Be Humble—Ulysses S. Grant," *Medium: Start it up*, 19 August 2019, https://medium.com/swlh/to-lead-be-humble-ulysses-s-grant-b3374233a99f#:~:text=Grant%20was%20always%20humble.,and%20won%20the%20Civil%20War, accessed 19 June 2020.

some of the guys in my unit. The Colonel was furious and wanted to know what we Company Commanders were going to do. I suggested he allow me to deal with those whom I was identifying that were in my command and the others do the same. But, I told him that there was a perception amongst many of the minorities that they weren't being treated fairly in promotions, etc. I suggested as a way to diffuse the tension, that he go out and disburse the demonstrators and appoint someone to listen to their complaints. That would give us time to work within our companies. He refused to take personal action but did set up the ombudsman approach and I went out and conveyed that to the demonstrators. He also (thinking about what had happened a few months before I suspect), ordered that the officers set up a walking patrol amongst themselves in their company areas for the next couple nights. So, I got my Platoon Leaders together and discussed how to comply.

It was decided that we would NOT carry a weapon, as that would indicate we were afraid of our soldiers and I did not believe that US officers should ever be afraid of those whom they lead. I also took the first shift, as I knew if there was going to be trouble that was when it was most likely to happen.

That night as I was walking through the area, I heard footsteps behind me. I turned but couldn't see anyone as it was very dark, so I continued on towards a lighted corner and stepped around the corner waiting to see who was following me and why. At this point, I was beginning to wonder if not having our weapons was such a smart thing. Suddenly, coming around the corner was a Black soldier who had been a rehabilitation transfer into my company. He had been in trouble and this was his last chance. We had talked when he came in and I told him that this was a new unit and his past was over; what he did in the future was what was important. I gave him a moderately responsible position and he appreciated that. Now, he was in front of me carrying a club I used to beat off wild dogs that he had taken out of my office.

I asked him what he was doing and why did he have my club? He told me that I was walking through the "brothers" area and he was going to make sure nothing happened to me. I thanked him but assured him that I could handle myself. I told him the "brothers" might not like him guarding me. He just smiled and said he was going to make sure I was not hurt and that he had not forgotten that I had treated him fairly and it was the least he could do for me. He followed me for the next two nights and nothing happened. He also came under considerable verbal "abuse" by his "brothers" but that didn't deter him.[3]

Don't speak down at people! The Lord chose fishermen to lead His church, and a young uneducated lad to restore it in the latter days. The Islamic prophet Muhammad taught his followers how to be effective influencers. He instructed his disciples to first determine who was the person in the room that had the least knowledge and intelligence and then to speak to the entire group at that person's level of understanding. You might disagree with Muhammad's message, but the effectiveness of this leadership principle is undeniable. Within a hundred years of his death his followers ruled an empire larger than ancient Rome.

THE GOOD SHEPHERD WILL PROTECT HIS SHEEP

Humility combined with courage through faith in Christ can protect you from your attackers. Samuel the Lamanite was shielded from the adversary's arrows. Moroni taught: "And neither at any time hath any wrought miracles until after their faith; wherefore they first believed in the Son of God" (Ether 12:18). The great George Washington was a humble and faithful Christian. He was always quick to give credit to the divine being that protected him in battle after battle. For example, we have the account of his involvement in the battle at Fort Duquesne

---

3. Richard, Whaley, "Vietnam Experiences 1971–1972, " email to author, May 29, 2020.

during the French Indian War. Washington had repeatedly warned his British superior offices to not fight in the traditional European style. They ignored his advice. The Joseph Smith Foundation provides this summary of the battle from David Barton's book, *The Bulletproof George Washington*:

> But these were British veterans; they knew exactly what to do. The problem was, they were veterans of European wars. European warfare was all in the open. One army lined up at one end of an open field, the other army lined up at the other end, they looked at each other, took aim, and fired. No running, no hiding, But here they were in the Pennsylvania woods with the French and Indians firing at them from the tops of trees, from behind rocks, and from under logs.
>
> When they came under fire, the British troops did exactly what they had been taught; they lined up shoulder-to-shoulder in the bottom of that ravine—and were slaughtered. At the end of two hours, 714 of the 1300 British and American troops had been shot down; only 30 of the French and Indians had been shot.
>
> There were 86 British and American officers involved in that battle; at the end of the battle, George Washington was the only officer who had not been shot down off his horse—he was the only officer left on horseback.
>
> Following this resounding defeat, Washington gathered the remaining troops and retreated back to Fort Cumberland in western Maryland, arriving there on July 17, 1755.
>
> The next day, Washington wrote a letter to his family explaining that after the battle was over, he had taken off his jacket and had found four bullet holes through it, yet not a single bullet had touched him; several horses had been shot from under him, but he had not been harmed. He told them:
>
> "By the all-powerful dispensations of Providence, I have been protected beyond all human probability or expectation."
>
> Washington openly acknowledged that God's hand was upon him, that God had protected him and kept him through that battle. However, the story does not stop here. Fifteen years

later, in 1770—now a time of peace—George Washington and a close personal friend, Dr. James Craik, returned to those same Pennsylvania woods. An old Indian chief from far away, having heard that Washington had come back to those woods, traveled a long way just to meet with him.

He sat down with Washington, and face-to-face over a council fire, the chief told Washington that he had been a leader in that battle fifteen years earlier, and that he had instructed his braves to single out all the officers and shoot them down. Washington had been singled out, and the chief explained that he personally had shot at Washington seventeen different times, but without effect. Believing Washington to be under the care of the Great Spirit, the chief instructed his braves to cease firing at him. He then told Washington:

"I have traveled a long and weary path that I might see the young warrior of the great battle. . . . I am come to pay homage to the man who is the particular favorite of Heaven, and who can never die in battle."[4]

The message is clear. Have faith in Christ and believe in His miracles. You will need them as doomsday approaches. Just remember, when gangs of thugs are approaching your house, it won't be the time to proudly show that you earned an "A" in English literature. Be humble, listen to them, and reply to them in a language they will understand. As a result, you will soften their hearts.

A SOFT WORD TURNS AWAY WRATH

America's first highly influential diplomat was Benjamin Franklin. He counseled his son:

> . . . [W]hen I advanced anything that may possibly be disputed, the words, *certainly, undoubtedly,* or any others that give the air of positiveness to an opinion: but rather say, I conceive

---

4. David Barton, "Inspiring Narrative," *Wiki: The Bulletproof George Washington—The Joseph Smith Foundation*, https://josephsmithfoundation.org/the-bulletproof-george-washington/, accessed 10 August 2020.

or apprehend a thing to be so and so; it appears to me, *or I should think it so or so,* for such and such reasons; or *I imagine it to be so*; or it is so, *if I am not mistaken.* This habit, I believe, has been of great advantage to me when I have had occasion to inculcate my opinions, and persuade men into measures that I have been from time to time engaged in promoting; and as the chief ends of conversation are to *inform* or to be *informed,* to *please* or to *persuade,* I wish well-meaning, sensible men would not lessen their power of doing good by a positive, assuming manner, that seldom fails to disgust, tends to create opposition, and to defeat every one of those purposes for which speech was given to us, to wit, giving or receiving information or pleasure. For, if you would inform, a positive and dogmatic manner in advancing your sentiments may provoke contradiction and prevent a candid attention. If you wish information and improvement from the knowledge of others, and yet, at the same time, express yourself as firmly fixed in your present opinions, modest, sensible men, who do not love disputation, will probably leave you undisturbed in the possession of your error. And by such a manner, you can seldom hope to recommend yourself in *pleasing* your hearers, or to persuade those whose concurrences your desire.[5]

For violent situations, Franklin's eloquent advice can be restated, "If you talk arrogantly to people who are against your position, you'll only inflame the situation and probably get yourself killed." If you want the common good to prevail and to deescalate a potentially violent encounter, speak modestly (humbly) and with diffidence to the angry mob leaders. Franklin went on to quote the Pope: "For want of modesty is want of sense."[6]

A soft answer turns away wrath: but grievous words stir up anger.

5. Benjamin Franklin, *Autobiography of Benjamin Franklin: 1706–1757,* (United States: Applewood Books, 2008), 22–23.
6. Ibid, 24.

The tongue of the wise useth knowledge aright: but the mouth of fools poureth out foolishness.

The eyes of the Lord are in every place, beholding the evil and the good.

A wholesome tongue is a tree of life: but perverseness therein is a breach in the spirit. (Proverbs 15:1–4)

Who can forget President Ezra Taft Benson's warning to the Latter-day Saints:

The Doctrine and Covenants tells us that the Book of Mormon is the "record of a fallen people." (D&C 20:9.) Why did they fall? This is one of the major messages of the Book of Mormon. Mormon gives the answer in the closing chapters of the book in these words: "Behold, the pride of this nation, or the people of the Nephites, hath proven their destruction." (Moro. 8:27.) And then, lest we miss that momentous Book of Mormon message from that fallen people, the Lord warns us in the Doctrine and Covenants, "Beware of pride, lest ye become as the Nephites of old." (D&C 38:39.)

. . . Let us choose to be humble. We can do it. I know we can.

My dear brethren and sisters, we must prepare to redeem Zion. It was essentially the sin of pride that kept us from establishing Zion in the days of the Prophet Joseph Smith. It was the same sin of pride that brought consecration to an end among the Nephites. (See 4 Ne. 1:24–25.)

Pride is the great stumbling block to Zion. I repeat: Pride *is* the great stumbling block to Zion. [7]

When the Nephites were humble, the Lord protected them from the Lamanites and the corrupt judges placed in power by the conspiring Gadianton robbers. The same protection will be provided to those who faithfully serve the Lord. Finally, our Savior will stop Satan from using corrupt government officials to destroy those who humbly serve Him.

---

7. Ezra Taft Benson, "Beware of Pride," April 1989 general conference.

Certainly, humility was a characteristic that made Grant, Washington, and Moroni great leaders. However, they were also extremely competent generals who were feared by their enemies.

BE EXCELLENT—COMPETENT IN YOUR LEADERSHIP AND KNOWLEDGEABLE IN THE SKILLS YOU NEED

"Learn to be good for something," said Brigham Young. Abraham Lincoln applied the principle to one's career, "Whatever you are, be a good one." No one respects a leader who is not technically competent in the craft or sphere of influence which he or she is trying to lead others. The film *Gladiator* depicts the bloodthirsty arena of the Roman circus. The character General Maximus was not respected by the other gladiators because of his eloquent speeches. He gained their allegiance and the applause of the audience because he knew how to kill.

If you want to be a leader of welders, be the best welder you can. If you want to be a leader of farmers, produce the best crops. When the Lord wanted to call fishermen to follow him, He showed He was a better fisherman by filling their nets with fish. People admire and will follow competency.

Captain Whaley could shoot, a skill which probably saved him from having to kill or be killed. It was also one of his competencies that gained the respect of the rioting whites and blacks in his company.

A day or two after assuming command, my exuberant Executive Officer decided we needed to all be familiarized with our assigned weapons, so with my approval, he set up a range and the company all went out to fire. I was first, of course, and an interesting thing happened. I took three shots at the target and put three rounds through the bullseye with my .45 pistol. I had never before, nor since, done that. I recall the troops being highly impressed that the "old man" can really shoot! This turned out, I believe, to be significant later.

As we began to clean up the drug and discipline problems, the First Sergeant and I got our first anonymous threats.

Sadly, this wasn't unknown and, in fact, every Company Commander had been "jumped" at one time by a "soldier." I had no intention of allowing that to happen. As I was driving to a location one day, I commented to my driver that I sure wished the guys would clean house on the druggies. Well, he took that as license to do so.

Richard Whaley in Vietnam

That night I got a frantic call from the CQ over the field phone to my hooch saying there was a riot in the barracks. Now, there had been serious riots prior to my assuming command where blacks had broken into an arms room and stolen some weapons and began shooting at whites. I immediately grabbed my weapon and called for some help from the new S4 whom I felt I could trust to cover me.

I had put out a motto to the unit that: "You never put on your weapon unless you intend to use it and you never draw it unless you are prepared to die." So, when I came running into the Company area where the crowd was, someone noted that I had my weapon on. He yelled: "It's the old man and he can shoot!" The crowd began to fade back.

The troops had surrounded a couple of the whites and were going to beat them up. My arriving on the scene stopped the fracas but now, the blacks wanted their weapons so they could take action. I told them they could not be armed and that I would protect them the remainder of the night. I ordered the crowd to disperse, which they did, and then ordered the CQ to get two guards posted to cover these guys.

One of the blacks started to mouth off so I ordered him to get into his room and poked him in the stomach. He snarled at me, "We're going to get you." I told him, "Be my guest, but don't miss, because if you do, I'll kill you." He pops up, "You'll get court-martialed." To which I responded, "You'll never know as you'll be dead." He went into his room and I resolved the problems the next morning. However, I did sleep with a loaded, cocked .45 for the next two weeks. I figure that these punks knew I was deadly serious and they knew I could shoot so they didn't follow through with their threats and I was the only company commander who was never jumped.[8]

"Ye shall know them by their fruits. Do men gather grapes of thorns, or figs of thistles?" (Matthew 7:16). Competency is a foundational attribute for anyone trying to lead people. Generally speaking, you cannot lead people who question your level of competency. They simply won't trust you. Who is going to trust someone to lead them if they do not believe they are capable? Would you trust your life to a heart surgeon whose patients tend to die during their operations?

COMPETENT LEADERSHIP IN A CHAOTIC WORLD

Just having a degree in management does not make you a leader, especially one with the skills needed to survive the events of the Great Tribulation. Recent studies indicate that most MBA graduates might be able to manage routine assignments, but they are not prepared to lead organizations. The executives who hire them find MBA graduates lacking interpersonal and leadership skills. For example, A Hay Group study found that the leadership skills of communications and team building were valued by 93% of executives, only 51% of MBA graduates agreed.[9]

Development Dimensions International conducted a comprehensive analysis of leadership assessment data from more than 15,000 leaders. The study collected data from five levels of leaders, ending at the C-Suite. The assessments were collected from over 300 companies in over 20 industries and 18 countries. The results showed that for

8. Richard, Whaley, "Vietnam Experiences 1971–1972, " email to author, May 29, 2020.
9. Amelia Hopkins, "Are Employers Satisfied with MBA's Skillsets?", *TOPMBA*, 3 November 2017, https://www.topmba.com/jobs/are-employers-satisfied-mbas-skillsets, accessed 6 January 2021.

organizational performance, as measured by net profit and return on investment, the five most important skills are entrepreneurship, business savvy, driving execution, decision-making, and leading change. These five leadership skills are only slightly covered in schools of business. Further, the assessment data showed disturbingly low levels of leader readiness in shaping strategy, building a high-performance culture, and enhancing organizational talent. The five lowest-rated business drivers point to a lack of capability to improve talent and performance, make big organizational enhancements and taking a business in a new direction. In other words, today's managers can manage in calm waters, but lack the ability to navigate organizations through difficult times and changing environments. They can manage the "here and now," but cannot lead in ambiguous times and stormy business environments.[10] It would appear then that today's business managers are ill prepared to lead others in the rough years that are on the horizon.

LEADERSHIP COMPETENCIES BASED ON PRINCIPLES

What are the competencies you believe you will need to have to be respected as a leader when the years of tribulation arrive at your doorstep? Conditions will vary depending on your circumstances and location, so you will need to develop your own set of leadership competencies that are based on righteous principle. Make a list of the competencies, pray about them, and practice leading by applying these principle driven competencies. Tad R. Callister, former Sunday School general president, wrote:

> Why is it more effective to teach principles than rules? There are at least two key reasons: First, rules are often limited to one or perhaps a few specific situations, while principles generally have much broader application. Second, principles create an environment that maximizes agency while rules tend

---

10. Evan Sinar, "The Truth About Leadership Skill Gaps," *Chief Learning Officer*, 22 June 2017, https://www.chieflearningofficer.com/2017/06/22/the-truth-about-leadership-skill-gaps/, accessed 6 June 2021.

to minimize agency by restricting, sometimes even dictating our choices.[11]

Stephen M.R. Covey provides an example of the principle-based leadership competency of building trust in an organization. He writes:

Ultimately you'll want to make sure that leadership paradigms are aligned with the principles that create trust. When leaders fundamentally don't believe people can be trusted, they create systems and structures that reflect that belief, such as hierarchy, multiple layers of management, and cumbersome processes. In turn, these systems and structures ultimately help produce the distrusting behaviors that validate the leaders' perceptions that people can't be trusted in the first place. It becomes a vicious, downward cycle.

{T}he surest way to make [a man] untrustworthy is to distrust him and show your distrust. —Henry Stimson, Former U.S. Secretary of State

. . . By contrast, when leaders such as David Packard, Blake Nordstrom, and David Neeleman fundamentally believe that people can be trusted, they create systems and structures that reflect that belief, such as open storage bins, one-page employee manuals, and home reservationists. These systems and structures reinforce and ultimately help produce the trusting behaviors that validate the leaders' perceptions that people can be trusted to begin with. Thus, the paradigms and the behaviors work together to create a virtuous, upward cycle.[12]

Certainly, building trust with others will be a critical leadership skill for the years ahead. It is based on the righteous principle of faith in others. Here are just a few suggestions for competencies that could be mastered through applying righteous principles. They are leadership skills that could ultimately save your life:

11. Tad R. Callister, "Principles versus rules," *Church News: Living Faith,* 3 August 2020, https://www.thechurchnews.com/living-faith/2020-08-03/tad-r-callister-principles-rules-agency-189931, accessed 26 July 2021.
12. Stephen M.R. Covey, *The Speed of Trust: The One Things that Changes Everything,* (New York: Simon & Schuster, 2006).

- relationship building with people who are different than you
- negotiation skills
- communication skills
- survival and preparedness proficiency
- self-defense and weapons training
- effective and quick decision-making
- organizing and directing
- first-aid application
- missionary work

Again, your list of competencies should be aligned to your principles and customized for what you believe will be the environment your family and community will face in the dark years ahead.

LEADERS MAGNIFY THEIR CALLINGS

Being a church leader can help you practice the leadership competencies you will need in the future. However, just holding a position in the Church does not make you a leader. For the most part, officers in the Church do just that—*they hold offices*, and they are charged with keeping their offices running smoothly under the directives of people in higher offices. For example, a bishop holds the "office" of bishop in the Aaronic Priesthood. He is the president of the Aaronic Priesthood, not the "leader" of the Aaronic priesthood. The bishop's duties are spelled out in the Doctrine and Covenants. The bishop is to hold the keys of the ministering of angels and the preparatory gospel, to preside, to minister, to care for the poor, to manage the storehouse, to aid in the disposition of tithings, and to be a judge in Israel, all under the stewardship of people in higher offices. The bishop's responsibilities are extremely important and for which we are grateful for their faithfulness in their callings. However, his duties are for the most part administrative and *managerial*. Indeed, the Doctrine and Covenants uses the concept of stewardship, and does not even mention the words *leadership* or *leader*.

On the one hand, if a bishop is not a competent manager of the ward, the ward suffers, and it is unlikely he will also be an effective spiritual leader of the people in his ward. On the other hand, if he is a wonderful manager of the duties of his office, the ward will run smoothly, but it's no guarantee he is a remarkable spiritual leader who inspires his members to higher spiritual plains and to resist the evils and idols of the world.

Some might question why so many bishops tend to have university diplomas and professional careers. The answer is quite obvious once you understand that most church callings are managerial in nature and people who have managed work and people in their daily work can generally perform at a high level the managerial responsibilities for the Church. However, good managers are not necessarily outstanding leaders. In his BYU commencement address called "Leaders and Managers," Hugh Nibley warns the Brigham Young University graduates about thinking their degrees are diplomas in leadership. Indeed, they are often the exact opposite:

> At the present time, Captain Grace Hopper, that grand old lady of the Navy, is calling our attention to the contrasting and conflicting natures of management and leadership. No one, she says, ever managed men into battle. She wants more emphasis in teaching leadership. But leadership can no more be taught than creativity or how to be a genius. The *Generalstab* tried desperately for a hundred years to train up a generation of leaders for the German army, but it never worked, because the men who delighted their superiors, i.e., the managers, got the high commands, while the men who delighted the lower ranks, i.e., the leaders, got reprimands. Leaders are movers and shakers, original, inventive, unpredictable, imaginative, full of surprises that discomfit the enemy in war and the main office in peace. For managers are safe, conservative, predictable, conforming organization men and team players, dedicated to the establishment.
>
> . . . There is necessarily some of the manager in every leader (what better example than Brigham Young?), as there should be some of the leader in every manager. Speaking in the temple to the temple management, the scribes and Pharisees all in their official robes, the Lord chided them for one-sidedness: They kept careful accounts of the most trivial sums brought

into the temple, but in their dealings they neglected fair play, compassion, and good faith, which happen to be the prime qualities of leadership. The Lord insisted that *both* states of mind are necessary, and that is important: "This ye must do [speaking of the bookkeeping] but not neglect the other." But it is "the blind leading the blind," he continues, who reverse priorities, who "choke on a gnat and gulp down a camel" (see Matthew 23:23). So vast is the discrepancy between management and leadership that only a blind man would get them backwards. Yet that is what we do. In that same chapter of Matthew, the Lord tells the same men that they do not really take the temple seriously while the business contracts registered in the temple they take very seriously indeed (see Matthew 23:16–18). I am told of a meeting of very big businessmen in a distant place, who happened also to be the heads of stakes, where they addressed the problem of "how to stay awake in the temple." For them what is done in the house of the Lord is mere quota-filling until they can get back to the real work of the world.

. . . That Joseph Smith is beyond compare the greatest leader of modern times is a proposition that needs no comment. Brigham Young recalled that many of the brethren considered themselves better managers than Joseph and were often upset by his economic naiveté. Brigham was certainly a better manager than the Prophet (or anybody else, for that matter), and he knew it, yet he always deferred to and unfailingly followed Brother Joseph all the way while urging others to do the same, because he knew only too well how small is the wisdom of men compared with the wisdom of God.[13]

Regardless of how large or small a calling, a Church *leader* will not just manage their callings, but truly "magnify" them. An example of remarkable leadership in the Church is President Russell M. Nelson who made 32 major changes in the practices and policies of the Church during his first year as president. President Nelson doesn't

---

13. Hugh Nibley, "Leaders and Managers," Brigham Young University commencement address, 19 August 1983, speeches.byu.edu.

manage the Church under the Lord's guidance; he proactively changes the Church as he *"Hears Him."*

Of course, we need competent managers throughout the Church. People who faithfully minister in their callings day-in-day-out. However, as Satan continues to tighten his grip on the world, and targets the Church's members, in particular its youth, the more spiritual leaders need to overcome the forces of evil through inspiring and power leadership.

Let your light so shine before men, that they may see your good works, and glorify your Father which is in heaven.
(Matthew 5:16)

PART TWO

Preparing to Lead in the End of Days

The Lord told us how with simple, but stunning, reassurance:

"If ye are prepared ye shall not fear."

—President Russell M. Nelson,
quoting Doctrine and Covenants 38:30[1]

---

1. Russell M. Nelson, "Embrace the Future with Faith," October 2020 general conference.

To be prepared for war is one of the
most effectual means of preserving peace.

—George Washington, First Annual Address
to both Houses of Congress, 1790

Chapter 9

Physical Preparedness and Building a Zion Community

Time is running out! Six decades ago, Ezra Taft Benson warned:

> In the light of these prophecies there should be no doubt in the mind of any priesthood holder that the human family is headed for trouble. There are rugged days ahead. It is time for every man who wishes to do his duty to get himself prepared— *physically*, *spiritually*, and *psychologically*—for the task which may come at any time, as suddenly as the whirlwind.[1]

Recently, President Russell M. Nelson warned the Saints: "The adversary *never* stops attacking. So, we can never stop preparing. The more self-reliant we are—*temporally*, *emotionally*, and *spiritually*—the more prepared we are to thwart Satan's relentless assaults."[2]

The pied piper of advanced technology has deadened our senses to the perils of our current lifestyle. We marvel at the speed and ease of living in a high-tech world. We ask "Hey Siri" in our cell phones to order a pizza and it arrives a few minutes later. We transfer funds

---

1. Ezra Taft Benson, in Conference Report, October 1961, 70, emphasis added.
2. Russell M. Nelson, "Embrace the Future with Faith," October 2020 general conference, emphasis added.

throughout the world from our smart refrigerator. Our watch tells us our blood pressure. Grandparents living in one part of the world can see and talk to their grandchildren in another part of the globe without leaving their couch. In the dead of winter in the Northern Hemisphere we can eat fresh grapes from the Southern Hemisphere and think nothing of it. Yes, it is wonderful, but exceedingly fragile.

In reality, we live in constant jeopardy! The thin veneer of these wonders can come crashing down in an instant. Our very existence is vulnerable to a number of real threats, including cyber wars, solar blasts, massive storms and droughts due to climate change, nuclear war, earthquakes, plagues, etc. How closely have you studied the security of your electricity source? Think for a minute. Where does your food supply originate—local farms or industrial agricultural projects in far off nations? If an earthquake disrupted your water supply, where could you find clean drinking water? Retired General Jeffrey Burton served on a seven-state emergency response committee. To say the least, the results of the committee's study were sobering. The committee concluded that if the Walmart trucks were not moving within 72 hours, people would be killing each other for food.[3]

Perhaps the most important question for a leader to ask is, "Who will be there to help us when we need help to fend off murderous mobs?" No one will be able to stand alone during the years of the tribulation. As a result, a leader must build strong interpersonal relationships that can be called upon to provide help for his or her community. Leadership guru Stephen R. Covey writes of personal relationships, "You can't get the fruits without the roots."[4] In other words, interdependent and mutually beneficial relations are established over time. Relationships that can provide real help in times of distress are based on long-established trust and the leader having a thorough understanding of the other party's needs, abilities, and resources. Ideally, they are based on integrity and a Christian love for all mankind. Given these elements, mutually beneficial aid can be obtained in what Stephen Covey calls Win/Win relationships:

---

3. Jeffrey Burton, conversation with the author, Salem, Utah, 3 November 2020.
4. Stephen R. Covey, *The 7 Habits of Highly Effective People*, (New York: Simon & Schuster, 2004), 376.

Win/Win is a frame of mind and heart that constantly seeks mutual benefit in all human interactions. Win/Win means that agreements or solutions are mutually beneficial, mutually satisfying. With a Win/Win solution, all parties feed good about the decision and feel committed to the action plan. Win/Win sees life as a cooperative, not a competitive arena. Most people tend to think in terms of dichotomies: strong or weak, hardball or softball, win or lose. But that kind of thinking is fundamentally flawed. It's based on power and position rather than on principle. Win/Win is based on the paradigm that there is plenty for everybody, that one person's success is not achieved at the expense or exclusion of the success of others.[5]

Win/Win agreements are hard enough to negotiate in today's greedy and competitive society. Mutually beneficial arrangements will be far more difficult to navigate during the dark days of the Great Tribulation where evil is reigning, people are suffering, essential resources for survival are extremely scarce, and one person's very survival might depend on robbing the food and water from another family. In such distressing and violent conditions, human nature is likely to resort to Loss/Win or even Lose/Lose behavior as witness in the last days of the Jaredites and Nephites. Yet, it is my belief that a leader's ability to negotiate Win/Win agreements with family, friends, wards, stakes, communities, and even opposing forces will be essential for survival. One must be for all, and all must be for one. President Henry B. Eyring has counseled: "[W]e must notice the tribulation of others and try to help. That will be especially hard when we are being sorely tested ourselves. But we will discover as we lift another's burden, even a little, that our backs are strengthened and we sense a light in the darkness."[6] Being sure that others Win, at the same time we do, is the spirit of "ministering," which President Nelson calls "a newer, holier approach to caring for and ministering to others;" as he explains: "Effective ministering efforts are enabled by the innate gifts

---

5. Ibid, 217–218.
6. Henry B. Eyring, "Tested, Proved, and Polished," October 2020 general conference.

of the sisters and by the incomparable power of the priesthood. We all need such protection from the cunning wiles of the adversary."[7]

THE IMPORTANCE OF BEING OF ONE HEART AND ONE MIND

Jeffrey R. Holland reminds us:

> God expects us to be unified as His children and as His Church. He expects us to "dwell together in unity."
>
> Indeed, one of the greatest characteristics of the latter-day Zion is that the people will be "of one heart and one minds, and [dwell together] in righteousness." In His magnificent Intercessory Prayer, Christ pled for that unity in the lives of His disciples. Later the New Testament Saints did believe and "were of one heart, and of one soul."
>
> We are, as members of the Church, the body of Christ. He expects unity of purpose and sublimation of selfishness when the health of the whole body is at stake. This helps the entire enterprise—as well as the individuals in it—to fend off difficult times or triumph over them when they come.[8]

Being one as a community is at the core of our faith. Elder Quentin L. Cook explains: "*Unity* is also a broad, comprehensive term but most certainly exemplifies the first and second great commandments to love God and love our fellowmen. It denotes a Zion people whose hearts and minds are 'knit together in unity' (Mosiah 18:21, Moses 7:18)."[9] It would follow then that if the Zion of the Lord's Second Coming will be the New Jerusalem in Jackson County, Missouri (D&C 45:66–67), its leaders will need to have a high level of emotional intelligence and exceptional trustworthiness to unify their followers as one.

---

7. Russell M. Nelson, "Ministering", April 2018 general conference.

8. Jeffrey R. Holland, *For Times of Trouble* (Salt Lake City: Deseret Book, 2012), 144.

9. Quentin L. Cook, "Hearts Knit in Righteousness and Unity," October 2020 general conference.

TEMPORAL PREPAREDNESS

Ezra Taft Benson warned, "The revelation to produce and store food may be as essential to our temporal welfare today as boarding the ark was to the people in the days of Noah."[10] President Nelson advises:

> If preparation is our key to embracing this dispensation and our future with faith, how can we best prepare?
>
> For decades, the Lord's prophets have urged us to store food, water, and financial reserves for a time of need. The current pandemic has reinforced the wisdom of that counsel. I urge you to take steps to be temporally prepared. But I am even more concerned about your spiritual and emotional preparation.
>
> In that regard, we can learn a lot from Captain Moroni. As commander of the Nephite armies, he faced opposing forces that were stronger, greater in number, and meaner. So, Moroni prepared his people in three ways.
>
> First, he helped them create areas where they would be safe— "places of security" he called them. Second, he prepared "the minds of the people to be faithful unto the Lord." And third, he never stopped preparing his people—physically or spiritually.[11]

PLACES OF SECURITY

According to President Nelson, a place of security is *"anywhere* you can feel the presence of the Holy Ghost and be guided by Him."[12] A spiritual refuge could be found in a righteous home, trusting in the inspired priesthood leadership of a ward or stake, or being found worshipping in a temple of the Lord.

A physical place of security is another matter. In General Moroni's case, it meant embankments, forts, and high walls (Alma 48:8). Consider once again the calamities of the end of times. It would

---

10. Ezra Taft Benson, "Prepare for the Days of Tribulation," October 1980 general conference.
11. Russell M. Nelson, "Embrace the Future with Faith," October 2020 general conference.
12. Ibid.

appear that all people who can, will be living in caves and neighbors will be killing one another. As a leader, what preparations have you made to physically secure your family and community in such conditions? Captain Moroni armed his people. Does your community have the collective means to protect its citizens from hooligans and armed mobs? Do you have neighborhood watches organized? Have you led citizen groups to discuss with the civil authorities what would happen if police and national guard forces are overwhelmed? Where will your family go if your house is destroyed by one of a multitude of the tribulation's natural disasters? Do you have a solid home or place where extended family members can come to find safety, warmth, food, and other necessary resources required of a place of security? The list is daunting—but one a leader needs to carefully plan.

PUTTING YOUR HOUSE IN ORDER

It's hard to help others if you need help yourself. A leader should start his/her preparations by evaluating if their own house is in order. For decades, the Church leaders have asked *all* members to "fend off difficult times or triumph over them" by being prepared. To confront the evils of secret combinations in the last days, Ezra Taft Benson taught:

> [M]ost important of all, each member of the priesthood should set his own house in order. This should include:
>
> 1. Regular family prayer, remembering especially our government leaders.
>
> 2. Getting out of debt.
>
> 3. Seeing that each member of the family understands the importance of keeping the commandments.
>
> 4. Seeing that the truth is shared with members of the family, with neighbors, and with associates.
>
> 5. Seeing that each member is performing his duties in the priesthood, in the auxiliary organizations, in the temple, and in the civic life of the community.

6. Seeing that every wage earner in the home is a full tithepayer and fulfilling other obligations in financial support of the kingdom.

7. Providing a one-year supply of essentials.

In doing these things a member of the Church is not only making himself an opponent of the adversary, but a proponent of the Lord.[13]

Being prepared requires self-reliance, so we can provide the spiritual and temporal needs of our family, as well as for others, in time of crisis. Self-reliance is far more than a welfare program. It is an essential way of life that is required if one desires salvation in this life and the next. Marion G. Romney stated: "Let us work for what we need. Let us be self-reliant and independent. Salvation can be obtained on no other principle."[14]

The doctrines and principles of the Church's self-reliance program are delineated in the Leader's Guide, found on the Church's website:

> Self-reliance is defined as "the ability, commitment, and effort to provide the spiritual and temporal necessities of life for self and family. As members become self-reliant, they are also better able to serve and care for others" (Handbook 2, 6.1.1). Three key teachings can help us understand how to lead self-reliant lives:
>
> First, self-reliance is an essential commandment in the plan of salvation. President Spencer W. Kimball taught: "The Church and its members are commanded by the Lord to be self-reliant and independent. (See D&C 78:13–14.) The responsibility for each person's social, emotional, spiritual, physical, or economic wellbeing rests first upon himself, second upon his family, and third upon the Church if he is a faithful member thereof" (*Teachings of Presidents of the Church: Spencer W. Kimball* [2006], 116).

---

13. Ezra Taft Benson, in Conference Report, October 1961, 75.
14. Marion G. Romney, "In Mine Own Way," October 1976 general conference.

Second, God can and will provide a way for His righteous children to become self-reliant. "And it is my purpose to provide for my saints, for all things are mine" (D&C 104:15).

Third, all things, including temporal concerns, are spiritual matters to God (see D&C 29:34). As we commit to living the gospel more fully, we can become more self-reliant both temporally and spiritually. President Dieter F. Uchtdorf taught: "The two great commandments—to love God and our neighbor—are a joining of the temporal and the spiritual. . . . Like two sides of a coin, the temporal and spiritual are inseparable" (Dieter F. Uchtdorf, "Providing in the Lord's Way," *Ensign* or *Liahona*, Nov. 2011, 53).

Some of the gospel principles that can help us be more self-reliant include increasing faith in Heavenly Father and Jesus Christ, becoming more obedient, repenting of our mistakes, using our agency righteously, and serving others. . . .

The stakes of Zion are places of security that protect all who enter. The purpose of the stake is to be "a defense, and . . . a refuge from the storm, and from wrath when it shall be poured out . . . upon the whole earth" (D&C 115:6). Stakes are gathering places where Church members can serve and strengthen each other, become unified, and receive priesthood ordinances and gospel instructions (Handbook 1, introduction).

The Lord said to priesthood leaders, "I have given unto you . . . the keys . . . for the work of the ministry and the perfecting of my saints" (D&C 124:143). President Dieter F. Uchtdorf taught: "The Lord's way of self-reliance involves in a balanced way many facets of life, including education, health, employment, family finances, and spiritual strength. . . . What this means is that, in large measure, you're going to have to figure it out for yourself. Every family, every congregation, every area of the world is different" ("Providing in the Lord's Way," *Ensign* or *Liahona*, Nov. 2011, 55).[15]

---

15. "Self-Reliance Initiative," *Leader's Guide for the Self-Reliance Initiative,* (Salt Lake City: The Church of Jesus Christ of Latter-day Saints, 2017), 2–3.

Being prepared in all ways is a gospel principle and the key to a bright outlook. President Russell M. Nelson has declared: "I am not saying that the days ahead will be easy, but I promise you that the future will be glorious for those who are prepared and who continue to be instruments in the Lord's hands."[16]

Self-reliance is Zion based and where all things are placed before the bishop (D&C 72:15). Zion, if its members obey the commandments, will be a place of defense and refuge (D&C 97:25, 115:6). Indeed, if a leader can help form a true Zion in his community, where everyone obeys the commandments and are "pure in heart," the Lord has promised "all that fight against Zion shall be destroyed" (1 Nephi 22:14).

CREATING AND MAINTAINING "ONENESS"

The catch is that to be a Zion, all involved must be of one in faith, obedience, purpose, and purity. The power of "oneness" in the Lord is more powerful than any weapon made by man. Being "One" is far different and far more difficult to achieve than just functioning as an effective "team." It requires every person in the group or community being totally committed to the achievement of the final objective with all their hearts, minds, strengths, and resources. In a Zion, all have a common unifying enemy, Satan and his dark angels. At the helm of Zion is one ultimate leader, our Savior.

One sign of a unified "oneness" is that the leader is at the front with his troops. General Washington, General Patton, or King Leonidas led at the frontlines, not from the "team leader's" secure office. "All Israel and Judah loved David, because he went out [to battle] and came in before them" (1 Samuel 18:16). While our forces might be unseen, if we are righteous, it will be the Lord who will lead the fight against Satan in the last days (D&C 98:37; 105:14; 109:28, Daniel 10). As generals, lieutenants, foot soldiers, or fathers and mothers, we must lead from the front. It is only by example that you can unify your followers, as did King David in unifying both Israel and Judah. A leader

---

16. Russell M. Nelson, "Embrace the Future with Faith," October 2020 general conference.

can build oneness by following our ultimate leader Jesus Christ and showing by example that he or she has eyes single to the glory of God.

In military history, a valuable lesson of the importance of "being one" and "staying one" comes from the account of the Persian invasion of Greece. The historian Herodotus recorded the battle of freedom-loving Greeks against the far superior forces of their enemy. Led by 300 Spartans with 6,000 other Greeks from other areas of Greece, the Greek army blocked the invading army of 100,000 Persians in a narrow gap in the mountains called Thermopylae. All the citizens of the Greek domains feared for their lives. The Thessalians had already sought safety by aligning with the Persian king Xerxes. Against such odds some Greek cities decided to put aside their rivalries and band together.

Under king Leonidas, the 300 Spartans and the soldiers from the other Greek cities dug in at Thermopylae. Behind a defensive wall the Greeks were able to fight off wave after wave of Persian warriors. Fighting as one, the Greeks prevented the Persians from taking the pass. During the first two days of bloody battle the Persians had suffered thousands of casualties.

However, the Greek's fortunes changed. Among their number was a traitor who informed the Persian king of a secret passage around the pass which allowed the Persian soldiers to go around the Spartans so they could attack from both sides.

On the morning of the third day of battle, Leonidas, the Spartan leader, realized they had been betrayed and chose to fight to the end, knowing that his men could never win the battle. He told the remaining Greek soldiers to flee whilst they could, however many stayed behind to fight to the death with their Spartan brothers.[17]

The message for us in the last days from the battle to Thermopylae is obvious. Even though we will be overwhelmed by far superior numbers, if we stay as a united family, a faithful ward, or a community that is one, we can be victorious regardless of the size of the forces of evil. However, if the oneness is betrayed, the enemy can prevail. This principle was recorded over and over again in the pages of the Book of Mormon. When the Nephites were one in the faith, they always

---

17. Kate Lohnes, "Battle of Thermopylae," Britannica, *https://www.britannica.com/ event/Battle-of-Thermopylae-Greek-history-480-BC*, assessed August 15, 2021.

prevailed against greater forces. However, when the Nephites had dissenters or fought among themselves, they were overrun.

In a real crisis it is vital that we think of everyone in our community. Just one discontent traitor can destroy our community. In the turbulent times ahead, we must all be Good Samaritans. We must be willing to share what we have. When our community is in need, the last thing to do is to circle the wagons and shoot inward. We must help one another if we are to survive, be it from an earthquake, battle, plague, or an evil designing foe that is out to destroy us. Being one means taking care of everyone. Again, it requires having the leadership ability to build Win/Win relationships, understand the needs of the members of the community, to organize care, and to inspire followers to have sustained faith and hope in the Lord. It requires being an outstanding priesthood, relief society, family, or community leader. A modern term for this kind of leadership is "Servant Leadership."

SERVANT LEADERSHIP

Bekele Geleta, former Secretary General of the International Federation of Red Cross and Red Crescent (IFRC), stated: "Leaders are stewards at the team level whenever they work to ensure individuals within the organization interact well with each other."[18] He writes of a group he advised:

> It's 7 am on a Saturday. Jet-lagged and tired, eight of us are gathered in a private room at West Point's picturesque Jefferson Hall. We've been told to discuss our individual views on the role of stewardship for leaders. The diversity between the eight of us is astounding. Amongst us, the former head of the world's largest humanitarian organization, a Swiss soldier who served on peacekeeping tours in Kosovo, a few student-activists from

---

18. Aaron Churchill, Brian Barney, Alexa Hazel, Debra Kelsall, Sandy Mouch, Dominique Verdun, "What is Stewardship, and should all great leaders practice it?" *New York Times inEducation*, https://nytimesineducation.com/spotlight/what-is-stewardship-and-should-all-great-leaders-practice-it/#:~:text=Leaders%20are%20stewards%20at%20the,done%20peacekeeping%20tours%20in%20Kosovo, accessed 21 June 2020.

some of North America's foremost university campuses, an engineer designing the next-step in modern prosthetics, an athletic trainer, and two West Point cadets. We certainly brought to bear a diverse set of perspectives on leadership. Yet from each of our personal experiences we derived a common sentiment regarding the act of stewardship. We all agreed that good stewardship allows any organization to continually develop and adjust to an ever-changing world. . . .

Leaders are stewards at the team level whenever they work to ensure individuals within the organization interact well with each other. A great example of team stewardship comes from the experience of the Swiss group member who had done peacekeeping tours in Kosovo. Early on during one tour he noticed his team was losing motivation. Personality conflicts also arose amongst the team. In order for the team to succeed, it was important that this lack of motivation and the team conflicts did not translate to their interaction with the local population. So managing the interaction between individuals was key. For our Swiss group member, this involved setting agreed-upon codes of conduct, periodically explaining the "why" of their missions, and ensuring equal working hours. These actions improved team effectiveness and avoided future misunderstandings. Stewardship begins with ensuring individual well-being, transitions into a focus on team effectiveness, and ultimately leads to a need for institutional-level considerations.

. . . The act of stewardship by leaders in an organization can be invaluable. Truly, achieving relevance and in a globalizing world, ensuring that individuals work well in effective teams, and establishing environments where individuals can improve their sense of well-being are all good acts of stewardship. To the eight of us in that room at West Point, it seemed that effective leadership always involved some level of stewardship. In our reflections we agreed that acts of stewardship are often a requirement for great leadership.[19]

---

19. Ibid.

Cristina Potter relates the story of her grandfather who was a successful merchant in the Philippines until the Japanese invaded the Islands during WWII.

> The Japanese occupied my grandparent's small town. In a very real way, that meant starvation, for the Japanese robbed our people of any food they could find. The people were starving, including my relatives. My grandfather took it upon himself to provide food for the people in the town. Every night he would disobey the Japanese curfew, slip passed the guards and hike deep into the jungle. If caught he would be put to death. In the moonlight he cleared a space in the forest, planted, nurtured, and eventually harvested vegetables—not just for his own family, but for the entire town.[20]

It was the inspired Nephite leader Gidgiddoni who not only prepared the Nephites with a seven-year food supply, but also taught his people that if they stayed as one, they could defeat the powerful Gadianton robbers. His inspired leadership made it impossible for the army of Gadianton robbers to destroy the righteous:

> And the robbers could not exist save it were in the wilderness, for the want of food; for the Nephites had left their lands desolate, and had gathered their flocks and their herds and all their substance, and *they were in one body*.
>
> Therefore, there was no chance for the robbers to plunder and to obtain food, save it were to come up to open battle against the Nephites; and the Nephites *being in one body*, and having so great a number, and having reserved for themselves provisions, and horses and cattle, and flocks every kind, that *they might subsist for the space of seven years*, in the which they did hope to destroy the robbers from off the face of the land. (3 Nephi 4:3–4, emphasis added)

If ye are not one ye are not mine. (D&C 38:27)

---

20. Cristina Potter, as told to the author in personal conversation, October 1, 2018.

We are never defeated unless we give up on God.

—Ronald Reagan

Chapter 10

Emotional Preparedness to Overcome Satan's Demons

Just prior to the Lord visiting the Nephites, Samuel the Lamanite warned them that demons and angels of Satan were surrounding them (Helaman 13:37). These same evil forces are alive today and their intentions are to destroy you and your family through *anger, sorrow, guilt, fear,* and a multitude of other cunning emotional tools. To lead others against the forces of darkness in the last days, you must develop a self-mastery against Satan's emotional demons. Developing a spiritual defense against these debilitating emotions can only be accomplished having a high emotional intelligence through the personal ministering of our Lord Jesus Christ.

I attended a conference in the Middle East where Elder Jeffrey Holland began his talk by discussing how difficult it must be living in a faraway country without family and one's normal support systems. He asked if there was anyone in the audience who had no one in their family who was experiencing major problems. Elder Holland then asked if so, he would like to have a picture of them so he could put it on the cover of the Church News. Elder Holland then noted that everyone in the Church or a family member of theirs was experiencing a major problem, including every General Authority.

In most of these cases, it is Satan who is to some degree behind these problems. Lucifer is still receiving recruits, either willingly or unconsciously, to act as his demons. They are real, and they won't go away. In trying to disrupt the Lord's coming to the Nephites and Lamanites, we read:

> And it came to pass that thus passed away the ninety and fifth year also, and the people began to forget those signs and wonders which they had heard, and began to be less and less astonished at a sign or a wonder from heaven, insomuch that they began to be hard in their hearts, and blind in their minds, and began to disbelieve all which they had heard and seen—
>
> Imagining up some vain thing in their hearts, that it was wrought by men and by the power of the devil, to lead away and deceive the hearts of the people; and thus did Satan get possession of the hearts of the people again, insomuch that he did blind their eyes and lead them away to believe that the doctrine of Christ was a foolish and a vain thing. (3 Nephi 2:1–2)

The leader of the Gadianton robbers, Giddianhi revealed the purposes of Satan and his secret combinations when he wrote to Lachoneus, "I swear unto you with an oath, that on the morrow month I will command that my armies shall come down against you, and they shall not stay their hand and shall spare not, but shall slay you, and shall let fall the sword upon you even until ye shall become extinct" (3 Nephi 3:8). In the days prior to the Second Coming don't expect to find relief from these destructive forces by relying on the courts and lawyers. If Satan employs the same strategies that he used before the Lord's first coming in the New World, many latter-day judges and lawyers will be greedy demons themselves. We can see this shadowing in the years prior to the Lord's first appearance in the Americas.

> Now there were many of the people who were exceedingly angry [at the prophets] because of those who testified of these things; and those who were angry were chiefly the chief judges, and they who had been high priests and lawyers; yea, all those who were lawyers were angry with those who testified of these things.

Now it came to pass that those judges had many friends and kindreds; and the remainder, yea, even almost all the lawyers and the high priests, did gather themselves together, and united with the kindreds of those judges who were to be tried according to the law.

And they did enter into a covenant one with another, yea, even into that covenant which was given by them of old, which covenant was given and administered by the devil, to combine against all righteousness. (3 Nephi 6:21, 27–28)

From the history of the Nephites, it appears that Satan's strategy is to first corrupt the judicial systems of government and then destroy the entire Nephite administration. Later in the same year, and only three years prior to the Lord's coming to the Nephites, the rest of their government dissimulated. The people became polarized, and law and order became dysfunctional:

. . . [T]he thirtieth year, they did destroy upon the judgment-seat, yea, did murder the chief judge of the land.

And the people were divided one against another; and they did separate one from another into tribes, every man according to his family and his kindred and friends; and thus they did destroy the government of the land.

And every tribe did appoint a chief or a leader over them; and thus they became tribes and leaders of tribes. (3 Nephi 7:1–3)

How far removed is "destroying upon the judgment-seat and killing the chief judge" from the mob's attack on the United States Congress and the calls of killing the Vice President of the United States on January 6, 2021? How different is it from the mobs who killed the Nephite prophets, covenanted to kill the Lord's people and "did set at defiance the law and the rights of their country; another to destroy the governor," than of the anarchist mobs who took control of parts of Portland and Seattle in 2020 (3 Nephi 6:27–30)?

Again, we can expect Satan to use the same strategy to destroy national governments before the Lord's Second Coming as he has used successfully in the past. Remember again, Prophet Joseph Smith declared:

"Even this nation will be on the verge of crumbling to pieces and tumbling to the ground and when the Constitution is on the brink of ruin this people will be the staff upon which the nation shall lean and they shall bear the Constitution away from the very verge of destruction."[1]

How does Satan blind a leader's eyes and direct an entire society down the road to destruction? It is often through human emotions. It is impossible for a leader to have a clear vision if they are constantly depressed, angry, or afraid. It is equally impossible to choose the right while these emotions plague one's reasoning. Even more dangerous, how can a leader be sensitive to the guidance of the still small voice of the Holy Ghost when they are angry or afraid? Without the Holy Spirit, our decisions are compromised and our actions tend to make things worse. Without divine guidance, people simply surrender their judgment to what they hear on the media or from angry friends. In the worst case, leaders simply react to the mob mentality that rules the streets.

ANGER

While in an emotionally charged state caused by anger or fear, it is impossible to be an effective leader against the forces that are trying to destroy you, your family, your community, and your nation. President Thomas S. Monson taught that anger is Satan's tool for "[t]o be angry is to yield to the influence of Satan. No one can *make* us angry. It is our choice."[2] If anger is a matter of personal choice, how can we control our emotions when so many destroyers, demons, and monsters are impacting our lives on a daily basis? How is your emotional state when you enter your workplace, talk with your spouse or children when things are heated, or watch the discouraging events on the evening news? President Monson continued:

> Recently as I watched the news on television, I realized that many of the lead stories were similar in nature in that the

---

1. D. Michael Stewart, "What do we know about the purported statement of Joseph Smith that the Constitution would hang by a thread and that the elders would save it?" *Ensign*, June 1976.
2. Thomas S. Monson, "School Thy Feelings, O My Brother," October 2009 general conference.

tragedies reported all basically traced back to one emotion: *anger*. The father of an infant had been arrested for physical abuse of the baby. It was alleged that the baby's crying had so infuriated him that he had broken one of the child's limbs and several ribs. Alarming was the report of growing gang violence, with the number of gang-related killings having risen sharply. Another story that night involved the shooting of a woman by her estranged husband, who was reportedly in a jealous rage after finding her with another man. Then, of course, there was the usual coverage of wars and conflicts throughout the world.[3]

Does it seem like your nation is experiencing the kind of days experienced by the Nephites before the Lord appeared to them?

And it came to pass that the people began to wax strong in wickedness and abominations; and they did not believe that there should be any more signs or wonders given; and Satan did go about, leading away the hearts of the people, tempting them and causing them that they should do great wickedness in the land. (3 Nephi 2:3)

Here is just a short list of some of the multitude of demons trying to keep us from being inspired leaders:

- Co-workers whose alcohol or drug abuse endangers us and make our working conditions at best difficult and at worse hazardous.
- Bipolar spouses or other family members who are contrite one day and the next day go on a binge of immorality and extravagant spending.
- Greedy lawyers who try to financially destroy us with unfounded law suites.
- A boss who discriminates against us because of our faith, race, or sex or who makes our lives miserable in other ways.
- Dissenters from the Church who try to lead away other members, even your family and dearest friends.

---

3. Ibid.

- Drug pushers who entice children into a hellish addiction that will destroy their lives and bring sorrow and deep pain to those who love them.
- Sexual predators preying on the very young, innocent, and weak.
- Parents who kill their own spouses and children; and likewise, children murdering their parents and siblings.
- Corrupt government leaders who stuff their pockets while ignoring the needs of the people they were elected to represent.
- Fake friends and colleagues who swindle people out of their lifetime savings.
- Internet thieves who steal your ID and run up tens of thousands of dollars in debts, all in your name.
- Good people drowning in co-dependent relationships where their free agency is severely compromised.
- Strongman government leaders who put their nation's treasury funds into their own offshore numbered bank accounts or who sell out their countries to communist governments.
- Etc., etc.—for the list of today's demons can go on and on.

Just reading the above list probably made you angry, mad, and even afraid. These are not the best emotions to have while trying to lead with clear vision and inspired decision-making. President Monson cites:

> The Apostle Paul asks in Ephesians, chapter 4, verse 26 of the Joseph Smith Translation: "Can ye be angry, and not sin? let not the sun go down upon your wrath." I ask, is it possible to feel the Spirit of our Heavenly Father when we are angry? I know of no instance where such would be the case.
>
> From 3 Nephi in the Book of Mormon, we read: "There shall be no disputations among you. . . ."
>
> If we desire to have a proper spirit with us at all times, we must choose to refrain from becoming angry. I testify that such is possible.[4]

---

4. Ibid.

The question begs to be asked: How does a leader control his own anger and help his family, friends, and associates to do the same? The Mayo Clinic's prescription for controlling anger consists of ten anger management recommendations:

1. Think before you speak

In the heat of the moment, it's easy to say something you'll later regret.

2. Once you're calm, express your anger

State your concerns and needs clearly and directly, without hurting others or trying to control them.

3. Get some exercise

Physical activity can help reduce stress that can cause you to become angry.

4. Take a timeout

Give yourself short breaks during times of the day that tend to be stressful.

5. Identify possible solutions

Instead of focusing on what made you mad, work on resolving the issue at hand. Is your partner late for dinner every night? Schedule meals later in the evening. Remind yourself that anger won't fix anything.

6. Stick with 'I' statements

To avoid criticizing or placing blame—which might only increase tension—use "I" statements to describe the problem.

7. Don't hold a grudge

Forgiveness is a powerful tool. If you can forgive someone who angered you, you might both learn from the situation and strengthen your relationship.

8. Use humor to release tension

Lightening up can help diffuse tension. Use humor to help you face what's making you angry and, possibly, any unrealistic expectations you have for how things should go.

9. Practice relaxation skills

When your temper flares, put relaxation skills to work. Practice deep-breathing exercises, imagine a relaxing scene, or repeat a calming word or phrase, such as "Take it easy."

10. Know when to seek help

Learning to control anger is a challenge for everyone at times. Seek help for anger issues if your anger seems out of control.[5]

Certainly twenty-first-century anger management tools are helpful for managing one's emotions when someone cuts you off in traffic or when your teenage child refuses to stop gaming on his computer or when you hear of a judge allowing a rapist to go free or when your bank refuses to provide you a loan or when the candidate from the "wrong" party wins the election or, for that matter, any other anger triggers of our day. However, anger management for leaders during the hard times ahead will required more effective remedies.

ADVANCED ANGER MANAGEMENT FOR THE END OF TIMES

In the years preceding the Lord's Second Coming, things will be very tough. There will be a multitude of things going wrong at the same time and lives being shattered around us. Satan will tempt you to resort to anger or to bow to fear. During these calamities and heart-breaking events, it will be critical that leaders make inspired decisions with the "proper spirit." That would seem to be common sense but

---

5. Mayo Clinic Staff, "Anger management: 10 tips to tame your temper," *Mayo Clinic: Healthy Lifestyle, Adult Health*, 29 February 2020, https://www.mayoclinic.org/healthy-lifestyle/adult-health/in-depth/anger-management/art-20045434, accessed 18 December 2020.

consider for a moment what you might experience during the years of the Great Tribulation. Here are a few speculations of some of the circumstances a leader might have to endure without getting angry:

- Your family is starving, and you can't find fresh water for your crying children (Revelation 6:5–6; 8:10–11; 16:4–7).
- Your neighbors are killing each other and threatening your family (Revelation 6:5–8).
- Close friends in your ward have been murdered standing up for their faith in Christ (Revelation 6:9–11).
- Your house was destroyed by a massive forest fire, and you need to move your family to a cold and dirty cave (Revelation 8:7, 15).
- The sky is darkened as a result of a comet hitting the earth—now you family is freezing in the new norm of a dusty ice age (Revelation 6:12–13; 8:10–11).
- An enormous earthquake disrupted all your utilities, including natural gas, electricity, and the internet (Revelation 16:18).
- Your sons and daughters have been enlisted to fight wars and rumors of war (Revelation 12:7; 13:7; 17:14).
- Huge hailstorms have destroyed your orchard, garden, and nearby farms (Revelation 16:20).
- A solar flare destroys all electronics in motor vehicles and computers resulting in no powered transportation for vital resources and causing skin boils (Revelation 16:8–9).
- Your spouse is suddenly taken away—leaving you a single parent (Matthew 24:20).
- The few remaining medical services are overwhelmed with plague victims (Revelation 16:1–2).
- People you work with and associate with have been tortured for five months by hideous locust and now wish they were dead. (Revelation 9:1–10).
- All remaining banking and retail services are controlled by Satan (Revelation 13:16–18).
- You are slowing getting weaker and weaker from nuclear radiation poisoning (Matthew 24:15).

Here are two advanced anger management tools missed by the Mayo Clinic. First, despite whatever happens, a leader must "praise

God" and teach his or her followers not to turn their anger towards Heavenly Father. The prophet Job lost everything. His three friends tried to convince him that his misfortunes were caused by God's anger and a punishment for sins. Job would not accept their counsel, but praised God and declared that, "Though he slay me, yet will I trust in him" (Job 13:15). Near the end of King David's violent and sorrowful life he wrote:

> For his [God's] anger endureth but a moment; in his favour is life: weeping may endure for a night, but joy cometh in the morning.
>
> And in my prosperity I said, I shall never be moved.
>
> Lord, by they favour thou hast made my mountain to stand strong: thou didst hide thy face, and I was troubled.
>
> I cried to thee, O Lord; and unto the Lord I made supplications.
>
> What profit is there in my blood, when I go down to the pit? Shall the dust praise thee? shall it declare thy truth?
>
> Hear, O Lord, and have mercy upon me: Lord, be thou my helper.
>
> Thou hast turned for me my mourning into dance: thou hast put off my sackcloth, and girded me with gladness;
>
> To the end that my glory may sing praise to thee, and not be silent. (Psalm 30:5–12)

King David's reflections on his life brought him to the knowledge of the second key to a higher form on anger management—gratitude. In the same Psalm he taught: "Sing unto the Lord, O ye saints of his, and give thanks at the remembrance of his holiness;" and "O Lord my God, I will give thanks unto thee for ever" (Psalms 30:4, 12). President Russell M. Nelson understands how having gratitude can help us during trying times to avoid anger and maintain the righteous emotion of joy. During difficult days of the Covid-19 pandemic, the president offered his message on the healing power of gratitude. He counseled the world:

> As a man of science and as a man of faith, the current worldwide pandemic has been of great concern to me. As a

man of science, I appreciate the critical need to prevent the spread of infection. I also honor the devoted service of health care professionals and grieve for the many whose lives have been upended by COVID-19.

As a man of faith, however, I view the current pandemic as only one of many ills that plague our world, including hate, civil unrest, racism, violence, dishonesty, and lack of civility.

Skilled scientists and researchers are laboring diligently to develop and distribute a vaccine against the coronavirus. But there is no medication or operation that can fix the many spiritual woes and maladies that we face.

There is, however, a remedy—one that may seem surprising—because it flies in the face of our natural intuitions. Nevertheless, its effects have been validated by scientists as well as men and women of faith.

I am referring to the healing power of *gratitude.*

. . . Over my nine and a half decades of life, I have concluded that *counting* our blessings is far better than *recounting* our problems. No matter our situation, showing gratitude for our privileges is a fast-acting and long-lasting spiritual prescription.

Does gratitude spare us from sorrow, sadness, grief, and pain? No, but it does soothe our feelings. It provides us with a greater perspective on the very purpose and joy of life.[6]

GODLY SORROWS AND THE EXCRUCIATING PAIN OF DISENGAGEMENT

More heartrending than physical death is the anguish felt by separation from loved ones in this life. Our fondest dreams and "eternal joy" are returning home with our earthly family to the waiting arms

---

6. Russell M. Nelson, "The Healing Power of Gratitude," posted by The Church of Jesus Christ of Latter-day Saints on YouTube, 20 November 2020, https://www.youtube.com/watch?v=i51gcWCs-Ho. Transcript accessed 18 December 2020 at https://assets.ldscdn.org/ac/ce/acce1d6a5b114c8c6eb33605830000a4176eb859/prayer_of_gratitude_video_and_awareness_materials.pdf.

of heavenly parents. In contrast is the remorse from being separate from loved ones now and for eternity. According to the Dartmouth University Stress Test, the distress suffered from divorce or martial separation is only exceeded by the death of a spouse.[7] Living in Saudi Arabia, I witnessed how agonizing it was for Latter-day Saints to live far away from parents, siblings, and children. As a missionary in Latin America, I mourned with converts who were disowned by their families because they joined the true faith.

As appalling as some might believe, leaders in the dark years ahead will see in an increasing rate of separation from toxic family and friends. The breach of love will be either involuntary or, in many cases, voluntary. Like the pied piper of evil, Satan will draw away loved ones to the point they will reject their family, friends, and fellow church members. We all know the pain of having loved ones go astray.

Perhaps even more sorrowful is when we will need to voluntarily disengage from our own loved ones who have joined Satan's ranks. Otherwise, they will spiritually, emotionally, and physically drag us down until we are dysfunctional as leaders and will draw away other loved ones. We can only imagine how painful it was for Nephi to finally separate from his elder brothers. For years he tolerated their hatred of him, ever hoping they would eventually turn toward the light. It was only at the warning of the Lord that his brothers would kill him that Nephi finally separated from Laman and Lemuel (2 Nephi 5:5).

President Thomas S. Monson taught, "We cannot be neutral; there is no middle ground. The Lord knows this; Lucifer knows this. As long as we live upon this earth, Lucifer and his hosts will never abandon the hope of claiming our souls."[8] Unfortunately, Satan will claim many souls of those we love. As the righteous diligently endeavor to live the gospel of Jesus Christ, some family members and dear friends will elect to direct their lives into Satan's camp and will turn against the righteous. The line that separates the good from the wicked sorrowfully runs straight through family and friendship ties. Today, no Latter-day

---

7. T.H. Holmes and T.H. Rahe, "The Social Readjustment Rating Scale," *Journal of Psychosomatic Research*, 11:213, 1967. Accessed 23 December 2020 at https://www.dartmouth.edu/eap/library/lifechangestresstest.pdf.

8. Thomas S. Monson, "The Three Rs of Choice," October 2010 general conference.

Saint family is immune, and things are only going to get worse. Already we read of apostates killing their own spouses and children. The news is full of accounts where children kill their parents just to get money for their next hit of illegal drugs. Whether such behavior is classified as satanic or psychotic, and as sorrowful as it might be, some relationships will become so spiritually and physically dangerous that leaders will need to separate themselves from those they love. It seems that we are all destined to experience to a very small degree the sorrow our heavenly parents experienced in the pre-existence when they needed to cast out one-third of their children because they followed Lucifer (D&C 29:36).

Righteous leaders in the years to come can only pray that the number of their own lost ones will be less than one in three. Elder Jeffrey R. Holland's words help us understand our need to withdraw from venomous relationships and the full meaning of the divine requirement to forgive all men:

> He [the Lord] did *not* say, "You are not allowed to feel true pain or real sorrow from the shattering experiences you have had at the hand of another." *Nor* did He say, "In order to forgive fully, you have to reenter a toxic relationship or return to an abusive, destructive circumstance."[9]

In other words, leaders and others will need to have the faith, hope in Christ and internal fortitude to end relationships with family and loved associates who are dragging them and others down to their level. Leaders will need to have the emotional health to endure the pains of disengagement and at the same time to uplift others by having a positive attitude and hope in Christ. It won't be easy.

GUILT

Dealing with the disabling emotion of guilt is especially difficult for Latter-day Saints who struggle to live up to the expectations of heavenly parents and a perfect elder brother. Guilt can be a real burden that is hard to lift from our shoulders and request through repentance

---

9. Jeffrey R. Holland, "The Ministry of Reconciliation," October 2018 general conference.

the grace of our Savior. Part of His boundless Atonement is that the Lord was "a man of sorrows, and acquainted with grief" because "we hid as it were our faces from him" (Isaiah 53:3). With eternal thanksgiving we need to always remember Him, for "he was wounded for our transgressions, he was bruised for our iniquities: the chastisement of our peace was upon him; and with his strips we are healed" (Isaiah 53:5). As Alma taught: "If thou believest in the redemption of Christ thou canst be healed" (Alma 15:8). Don't we all long to hear the words the Lord spoke to Enos, "thy sins are forgiven thee, and thou shalt be blessed" (Enos 1:5). "And I, Enos, knew that God could not lie; wherefore, my guilt was swept away" (Enos 1:6).

Add to the guilt we feel because of our imperfections, will be the remorse leaders will experience due to events they will not be responsible for during the Great Tribulations. Leaders will require a high degree of emotional intelligence and spiritual understanding to function as an effective leader. M. Russell Ballard has counseled:

> [E]liminate guilt. I hope it goes without saying that guilt is not a proper motivational technique for leaders and teachers of the gospel of Jesus Christ. We must always motivate through love and sincere appreciation, not by creating guilt. I like the thought "Catch others doing something right."[10]

Eliminating guilt from our own motives and the actions of others will not be easy when the chaotic events of the end of times rain down upon us. Here are just a few scenarios to tempt a leader to harbor guilt:

You are the head nurse in a hospital. The greatest earthquake ever has flooded your emergency room. The physicians and facilities are overwhelmed. It is your job to decide who should be admitted for treatment, who will be dismissed with minor injuries, and whose injuries are so severe that they should be turned away and left to die.

You are a military commissioned or non-commissioned officer. Half of the young soldiers you lead against Satan's forces are killed (one is taken and one is left). The men and women who fall in battle under your command leave behind spouses and children.

---

10. M. Russell Ballard, "Oh Be Wise," October 2006 general conference.

Your neighbor begs you for food, water, and shelter. Your heart wants you to give them relief, yet the Spirit warns you that your stewardship is to your own family, and you must say no.

A child has fallen into Satan's camp and is drawing away his/her siblings and endangering your entire family. After much prayer and fasting, you must turn away the child and disengage.

A list of scenarios can go on and on. These types of tragedies might be based on a lack of judgment or simple human error, but none of them are a result of intentional sin. Still, one would be heartless if they did not feel a sense of guilt for what occurred. Yet guilt can itself overwhelm a leader who cannot learn to put it aside. Friends of mine suffered terrible abuse from a child. The pain and guilt was so consuming that they are barely able to run the company they owned. I advised them to meet with Dr. Taylor Hartman, the author of *The Color Code* and *The People Code* and a gifted counselor. Paraphrasing Hartman, he gave the following advice to them. "Completely stop all communications with your toxic daughter. You are allowed to grieve 15 minutes each morning for your loss, and then stop thinking of her the rest of the day. It is not your *fault*. Stop letting your daughter manipulate you because she's pulling at your guilty feelings." It was hard advice to follow, but it was effective and allowed my friends to stop dwelling in constant pain and guilt, to clear their minds and to get back to running a large family business.

Our beloved prophet Russell M. Nelson is a renowned heart surgeon. He also understands how to help us overcome the emotion of guilt when we feel we have made errors. He has taught:

> James gave a practical standard by which mortal perfection could be measured. He said, "If any man offend not in word, the same is a *perfect* man."
>
> Scriptures have described Noah, Seth, and Job as *perfect* men. No doubt the same term might apply to a large number of faithful disciples in various dispensations. Alma said that "there were many, exceedingly great many," who were pure before the Lord.
>
> This does not mean that these people never made mistakes or never had need of correction. . . .

Mortal perfection can be achieved as we try to perform every duty, keep every law, and strive to be as perfect in our sphere as our Heavenly Father is in his. If we do the best we can, the Lord will bless us according to our deeds and the desires of our hearts.

. . . Recently I studied the English and Greek editions of the New Testament, concentrating on each use of the term *perfect* and its derivatives. Studying both languages together provided some interesting insights, since Greek was the original language of the New Testament.

In Matt. 5:48, the term *perfect* was translated from the Greek *teleios*, which means "complete." *Teleios* is an adjective derived from the noun *telos*, which means "end." The infinitive form of the verb is *teleiono*, which means "to reach a distant end, to be fully developed, to consummate, or to finish." Please note that the word does not imply "freedom from error"; it implies "achieving a distant objective." In fact, when writers of the Greek New Testament wished to describe perfection of behavior—precision or excellence of human effort—they did *not* employ a form of *teleios*; instead, they chose different words.[11]

Living among the Muslims for almost three decades, I accepted many invitations to visit families mourning the death of a loved one. To my surprise these occasions were not filled with tears and words of grief. When I tried to express my condolences, I received replies like this: "It is fine my friend, *Inshallah*"—meaning "it is God's will." If we consider the big picture and realize that even if we feel some degree of responsibility for someone's death or the need to disengage from a loved one, we can minimize the guilt we feel, and continue to function effectively as a leader. President Nelson recently related this personal story:

Not long ago, the wife of one of our grandsons was struggling spiritually. I will call her "Jill." Despite fasting, prayer, and

---

11. Russell M. Nelson, "Perfection Pending," October 1995 general conference.

priesthood blessings, Jill's father was dying. She was gripped with fear that she would lose both her dad and her testimony.

Late one evening, my wife, Sister Wendy Nelson, told me of Jill's situation. The next morning Wendy felt impressed to share with Jill that my response to her spiritual wrestle was one word! The word was *myopic*.

Jill later admitted to Wendy that initially she was devastated by my response. She said, "I was hoping for Grandfather to promise me a miracle for my dad. I kept wondering why the word myopic was the one he felt compelled to say."

After Jill's father passed on, the word myopic kept coming to her mind. She opened her heart to understand even more deeply that myopic meant "nearsighted." And her thinking began to shift. Jill then said, "Myopic caused me to stop, think, and heal. That word now fills me with peace. It reminds me to expand my perspective and seek the eternal. It reminds me that there is a divine plan and that my dad still lives and loves and looks out for me. Myopic has led me to God."

. . . By choosing to let God prevail, she is finding peace.[12]

By letting God prevail, leaders can withstand Satan's attempts to discourage them by making them feel guilty for past imperfections and errors. He, our Lord, has the whole world in His hands, even during the tragedies and sorrows of the Great Tribulation. If leaders remember that reality, they can continue to motivate their followers with love and a vision of a bright outlook. Further, the leader can teach their followers to overcoming their own disenabling feelings of guilt and despair through hope in Christ.

FEAR

With stars falling to earth, earthquakes stronger than ever before, neighbors killing neighbors, famine, and people wishing to die, no wonder men's hearts will fail them in the very last days. As the Lord's coming draws near, fear will abound. Even if a leader can find

---

12. Russell M. Nelson, "Let God Prevail," October 2020 general conference.

solace knowing that the long-awaited Millennium will so arrive, he or she will be surrounded by people so afraid they will be acting liked caged animals. To have any hope of leading people in such dire circumstances, leaders must first manage their own fear. Ralph Waldo Emerson wrote, "Fear defeats more people than any other one thing in the world." Any military commander who has led soldiers into battle can tell you that fear is one of Satan's foremost weapons against righteous leadership. Kevin J. Worthen, president of Brigham Young University, has counseled:

> We need to recognize that the feeling of despair and hopelessness that characterizes irrational fear is a tool of the adversary. Indeed, it is one of his primary tools. I am convinced that just as we have articles of faith, Satan and his minions must have articles of fear to aid them in their work. They might read something like this: "We believe that the first principles of despair and damnation are doubt God, doubt yourself, doubt others, and, most of all, be afraid—be very afraid of the future."[13]

With the world seemingly falling apart around us, how does a leader resist Satan's attempts to trap them in a state of debilitating fear? How does a leader devotedly obey God's repeated commandment to "not fear?" Of course, the answer is, first, to have faith in the Lord, and second, to inspire faith in those who you are responsible for. President Gordon B. Hinckley taught, "Fear is the antithesis of faith."[14] President Russell M. Nelson confirms: "[F]aith is the antidote for fear."[15] We know who the leader must have faith in—Jesus Christ. If he does, then he will also have faith in himself.

But what are the core elements of that faith that will sustain a leader in the violent days of the Tribulation?

First and foremost, leaders will need to have faith in the Atonement of our Savior. They need not fear death, for the Lord has risen; and

---

13. Kevin J. Worthen, "Fear Not," Brigham Young University devotional, 12 September 2017, speeches.byu.edu, accessed 3 January 2021.
14. Gordon B. Hinckley, "God Hath Not Given Us the Spirit of Fear," *Ensign*, October 1984.
15. Russell M. Nelson, "Let Your Faith Show," April 2014 general conference.

they realize that death is just a portal back to loved ones; and if worthy, eternal life with our eternal family.

Second, leaders will need to have faith that if they trust and follow the guidance of our Church Leaders, they will be victorious for "though the heavens and the earth pass away, my word shall not pass away, but shall all be fulfilled, whether by mine own voice or by the voice of my servants, it is the same" (D&C 1:38).

Third, leaders will need to have faith that the Lord will be with them in all their physical and spiritual battles. They must trust the word the Lord gave His leaders in ancient Israel:

> Thou whom I have taken the ends of the earth, and called thee from the chief men thereof, and said unto thee, Thou art my servants; I have chosen thee, and not cast thee away,
>
> Fear thou not; for I am with thee: be not dismayed; for I am thy God: I will strengthen thee; yea, I will help thee; yea, I will uphold thee with the right hand of my righteousness.
>
> Behold, all they that were incensed against thee shall be ashamed and confounded: they shall be as nothing; and they that strive with thee shall perish. (Isaiah 41:9–11)

Kevin J. Worthen provides four suggestions on how to manage irrational fear:

> First, recognize and remember that this kind of "fear comes not of God, but . . . from [Satan,] the adversary of truth and righteousness." . . .
>
> Second, we can increase the amount of faith and decrease the amount of fear in our lives by serving others more. As the *Lectures on Faith* indicate, faith is a "principle of action." . . .
>
> Third, we can increase the amount of faith in our lives if we understand that, as Elder Neil L. Andersen once observed, "Faith is not only a feeling; it is a decision." . . .
>
> Fourth, even if we recognize that faith is a choice and that we are facing that choice, we may doubt our ability to make that choice—especially in pressure situations. Too many of us too often worry whether we are capable of choosing faith when it really counts. If that is a concern, I urge you to recognize

that you already exercised incredible faith in Christ at a most critical juncture in your eternal journey.

You are all familiar with the scene. We were gathered together in a Grand Council in which our Father in Heaven described His plan for us to become like Him. . . .

It was the strength of our testimonies in Christ that allowed us to overcome Satan. It was our faith in Jesus Christ. Think about it. At that time the blood of the Lamb had not yet been shed and the Atonement had not yet been performed. All we had was the promise of our Heavenly Father and Christ that Jesus would perform His role perfectly. It all rose or fell on that. And we had the choice of whether we would believe in that promise in those circumstances. All we had was our faith in Him. But in that critical time, we all chose to be governed by faith and not by fear.[16]

If there is ever a time that a leader will feel that he or she are walking in the shallows of death, it will be during the Great Tribulation. Yet, they can stand stout and fearless holding tight to the promises of their Lord: "What time I am afraid, I will trust in thee. In God I will praise his word, in God I have put my trust; I will not fear what flesh can do unto me" (Psalm 56:3–4).

LEADERS WILL NEED TO HAVE THE RIGHT SPIRIT

During the tumultuous years preceding the coming of Christ, leaders will need to make the right decisions at the right time, each and every time. Making correct decisions under such circumstances will be trying. To do so, leaders will need to have the right spirit and a clear and logical mind, follow carefully and completely the steps in effective problem solving, and call upon God for enlightenment in each step in the problem-solving process. The Lord advised Oliver Cowdery:

---

16. Kevin J. Worthen, "Fear Not," Brigham Young University devotional, 12 September 2017, speeches.byu.edu, accessed 3 January 2021.

Behold, you have not understood; you have supposed that I would give it unto you, when you took no thought save it was to ask me.

But, behold, I say unto you, that you must study it out in your mind; then you must ask me if it be right, and if it is right I will cause that your bosom shall burn within you; therefore, you shall feel that it is right.

But if it is not right you shall have no such feeling, but you shall have a stupor of thought that shall cause you to forget the thing which is wrong; . . . (D&C 9:7–9)

Singer and song writer, Chuck Girard, penned these thoughtful lyrics to his song *Slow Down*:

In the midst of my confusion
In the time of desperate need
When I am thinking not too clearly
A gentle voice does intercede

Slow down, slow down, be still
Be still and wait, on the Spirit of the Lord
Slow down and hear His voice
And know that He is God

In the time of tribulation
When I'm feeling so unsure
When things are pressing in about me
Comes a gentle voice so still, so pure

Slow down, slow down, be still, my child
Be still and wait, on the Spirit of the Lord
Slow down and hear His voice
And know that He is God
And know that He is God[17]

During the Black Lives Matters protest in Salt Lake City on July 9, 2020, the city saw the calm and reasoned response to mob violence

---

17. Chuck Girard, "Slow Down," *Chuck Girard*, Good News Records, CD, 1975.

by Salt Lake District Attorney Sim Gill as reported in the Deseret News the next morning:

> [District Attorney Sim Gill] surveyed the damage to his office Friday morning.
>
> "It was an unlawful and irresponsible disregard for civic dialogue and community collaboration. The building will be repaired, our work will continue. The vandalism of a few won't discourage or distract us from continuing our work in the community as we seek improvement, reform, understanding and respect throughout our community," Gill's office said in a prepared statement Friday.[18]

The following day the Deseret News reported that the estimated damage to the District Attorney's building was two hundred thousand dollars and that four protesters had been arrested.

With the right spirit, calm emotions and a clear mind, a leader can solve tough problems using the steps of effective problem-solving. Any solution should start with consolation and information gathering and should be constructed carefully and each step prayerfully considered. The classical steps in effective problem solving become even more powerful when supported by divine guidance. Each step requires one or more prayers:

1. Discern that there is an urgent threat and if immediate action is required.
2. If an emergency, what action is needed *now* to keep things from getting worse?
3. If not an emergency, gather data and other pertinent information.
4. Analyze the date to define correctly the nature of the problem and its root cause.
5. Set a goal that, if achieved, will solve the problem.

---

18. Pat Reavy, "Mayor, D.A., police taking precautions after receiving 'credible threats,'" *Deseret News*, 10 July 2020.

6. Study and evaluate possible courses of action (solutions) that will achieve the goal—throw out any possible solutions that will likely not achieve the goal.
7. Select the most effective and efficient solution(s) to achieve the goal.
8. Develop an action plan and resource budget to implement the best solution(s).
9. Implement the plan.
10. Evaluate the success of your implementation and make any required adjustments.

Finally, at times our pain, anger, and despair can feel like a runaway train leaving us mentally and spiritually paralyzed. There is only one person who fully understands what is happening to us and can instantly provide the peace we need to have to function as an effective leader. We read in Psalm:

They mount up to the heaven, they go down again to the depths: their soul is melted because of trouble.

They reel to and fro, and stagger like a drunken man, are at their wits' end.

Then they cry unto the Lord in their trouble, and he bringeth them out of their distresses.

He maketh the storm a calm, so that the waves thereof are still.

Then are they glad because they be quiet; so he bringeth them unto their desired haven. (Psalm 107:26–30)

And behold, the Lord passed by, and a great and strong wind rent the mountains, and brake in pieces the rocks before the Lord, but the Lord was not in the wind: and after the wind an earthquake; but the Lord was not in the earthquake:

And after the earthquake a fire; but the Lord was not in the fire: and after the fire a still small voice.
(1 Kings 19:11–12)

If we ever forget that we are One Nation Under God, then we will be a nation gone under.

—Ronald Reagan

Chapter 11

Spiritual Preparedness— Leading in Righteousness

THE LORD'S DIVINE LEADERSHIP SCHOOL IS THE LATTER-DAY SAINT missionary program. Bar none, it is the toughest and most effective leadership program on earth. Its students are the Lord's leadership apprentices who learn how to inspire people twice their age and with twice their experience. Applying the Holy Spirit, these young leaders perform the most difficult leadership function—helping people change their lives. The Lord laid down the standard qualifications for those seeking to lead people through the conversion process of rebirth. Unfortunately, not all who enter the missionary field reap success, and not all graduate as righteous leaders. However, if these young elders and sisters earnestly apply the standards set by the Lord, they will have begun their journey to becoming a righteous leader in Zion.

"And faith, hope, charity and love, with an eye single to the glory of God, qualify him [her] for the work" (D&C 4:5).

Faith

Hope

Charity

Love

Eye single to the glory of God

Once qualified as a righteous leader, what does it take to be truly effective? The Lord continued: "Remember faith, virtue, knowledge, temperance, patience, brotherly kindness, godliness, charity, humility, diligence. Ask, and ye shall receive; knock, and it shall be opened unto you" (D&C 4:6–7).

The Lord has warned his leaders:

No power or influence can or ought to be maintained by virtue of the priesthood, only by persuasion, by long-suffering, by gentleness and meekness, and by love unfeigned;

By kindness, and pure knowledge, which shall greatly enlarge the soul without hypocrisy, and without guile—

Reproving betimes with sharpness, when moved upon by the Holy Ghost; and then showing forth afterwards an increase of love toward him whom thou hast reproved, lest he esteem thee to be his enemy;

That he may know that thy faithfulness is stronger than the cords of death. (D&C 121:41-44)

Brigham Young said:

To be gentle and kind, modest and truthful, to be full of faith and integrity, doing no wrong is of God; goodness sheds a halo of loveliness around every person who possesses it, making their countenances beam with light, and their society desirable because of its excellency. They are loved of God, of holy angels, and of all the good earth, while they are hated, envied, admired, and feared by the wicked.[1]

BROTHERLY KINDNESS

Do we try to apply brotherly kindness in our lives today? If we do not practice it today, how much more difficult will it be in the future when our enemies attack our homes and kill our loved ones? Retaining that

---

1. "Developing Christlike Attitudes toward Others," *Teachings of Presidents of the Church: Brigham Young*, (Salt Lake City: The Church of Jesus Christ of Latter-day Saints, 1997), 219.

virtue will be extremely difficult in the darkest of the last days. The Lord said:

> Blessed are ye, when men shall revile you, and persecute you, and shall say all manner of evil against you falsely, for my sake.
>
> Rejoice, and be exceeding glad: for great is your reward in heaven: for so persecuted they the prophets which were before you. (Matthew 5:11–12)

> Ye have heard that it hath been said, Thou shalt love they neighbor, and hate thine enemy.
>
> But I say unto you, Love your enemies, bless them that curse you, do good to them that hate you, and pray for them which despitefully use you, and persecute you; (Matthew 5:43–44)

Brotherly kindness is developed over a lifetime of genuinely seeking of the welfare of others. It is more than just striving for Win/Win solutions. Brotherly kindness means truly loving all our brothers and sisters despite their behavior. As noted before, at times leaders might need to disengage from those they love—but they love them all the same and pray for their souls.

The kindness standard righteous leaders are expected to emulate has been set very high. Our leader role model, Jesus Christ, was mocked, spat on, whipped, given a crown of thorns, smote on his head with a reed, given vinegar with gall to drink, and then crucified; yet hanging on the cross He asked, "Father, forgive them; for they know not what they do" (Luke 23:34).

DO NOT SEEK REVENGE

The commandments of the Lord are difficult enough when someone offends you in church or cuts you off on the highway, but how can you love someone who has harmed or killed a family member? The instinct of the natural man is to pick up a gun and get revenge. However, this is not the Lord's way. The prophet and general Mormon understood this principle and refused to lead the Nephites once they sought vengeance against the Lamanites:

And in the three hundred and sixty and second year they [the Lamanites] did come down again to battle. And we did beat them again, and did slay a great number of them, and their dead were cast into the sea.

And now, because of this great thing which my people, the Nephites, had done, they began to boast in their own strength, and began to swear before the heavens that they would avenge themselves of the blood of their brethren who had been slain by their enemies.

And they did swear by the heavens, and also by the throne of God, that they would go up to battle against their enemies, and would cut them off from the face of the land.

And it came to pass that I, Mormon, did utterly refuse from this time forth to be a commander and a leader of this people, because of their wickedness and abomination.

And when they had sworn by all that had been forbidden them by the Lord and Savior Jesus Christ, that they would go up unto their enemies to battle, and avenge themselves of the blood of their brethren, behold the voice of the Lord came unto me saying:

Vengeance is mine, and I will repay; and because this people [the Nephites] repented not after I had delivered them, behold, they shall be cut off from the face of the earth. (Mormon 3:8–11, 14–15)

Sadly, the Nephites did not listen to their general. Instead, they marched off to seek revenge on the Lamanites and were sorely defeated (Mormon 4:1–5). The Doctrine and Covenants provides rather specific guidelines on how to treat those who have wronged you and your family:

Now, I speak unto you concerning your families—if men will smite you, or your families, once, and ye bear it patiently and revile not against them, neither seek revenge, ye shall be rewarded;

But if ye bear it not patiently, it shall be accounted unto you as being meted out as a just measure unto you.

And again, if your enemy shall smite you the second time, and you revile not against your enemy, and bear it patiently, your reward shall be an hundred-fold.

And again, if he shall smite you the third time, and ye bear it patiently, your reward shall be doubled unto you four-fold;

And these three testimonies shall stand against your enemy if he repent not, and shall not be blotted out.

And now, verily I say unto you, if that enemy shall escape my vengeance, that he be not brought into judgment before me, then ye shall see to it that ye warn him in my name, that he come no more upon you, neither upon your family, even your children's children unto the third and fourth generation.

And then, if he shall come upon you or your children, or your children's children unto the third and fourth generation, I have delivered thine enemy into thine hands;

And then if thou wilt spare him, thou shalt be rewarded for they righteousness; and also thy children and thy children's children unto the third and fourth generation.

Nevertheless, thine enemy is in thine hands; and if thou rewardest him according to his works thou are justified; if he has sought thy life, and thy life is endangered by him, thine enemy is in thine hands and thou art justified. (D&C 98:23–31)

A righteous leader needs to focus on present needs of his or her followers, not on doing harm to their enemies. The Lord will quickly deal with the wicked during the dark days leading up to His Second Coming:

Behold, vengeance cometh speedily upon the inhabitants of the earth, a day of wrath, a day of burning, a day of desolation, of weeping, of mourning, and of lamentation; and as a whirlwind it shall come upon all the face of the earth, saith the Lord. (D&C 112:24)

Perhaps the bad news is that He will start by cleansing His own house first:

And upon my house shall it begin, and from my house shall it go forth, saith the Lord;

First among those among you, saith the Lord, who have professed to know my name and have not known me, and have blasphemed against me in the midst of my house, saith the Lord. (D&C 112:25–26)

FORGIVE YOUR ENEMIES

Turning the other cheek is difficult enough; however, forgiving those who harmed our families will be much more difficult and will require the Lord's help. As challenging as it will be, we must forgive even those who do not acknowledge that they have harmed us. If not, keeping the pain of holding a bitter grudge will physically, emotionally, and spiritually weaken us and impair our ability to lead others. President Nelson has counseled us: "[T]he Savior will grant you the ability to forgive anyone who has mistreated you in any way. Then their hurtful acts can no longer canker your soul."[2]

The Rwanda genocide survivor Immaculée Ilibagiza found it nearly impossible to forgive the Hutu killing gangs who slaughtered her parents, grandparents, and two of her three brothers along with a million other innocent Tutsis. She provides this account of her struggle to forgive the murderers and the divine help she needed to start the healing process:

Why do You expect the impossible from me? I asked God. *How can I forgive people who are trying to kill me, people who may have already slaughtered my family and friends? It isn't logical for me to forgive these killers. Let me pray for their victims instead, for those who've been raped and murdered and mutilated. Let me pray for the orphans and widows . . . let me pray for justice. God, I will ask You to punish those wicked men, but I cannot forgive them—I just can't.*

---

2. Russell M. Nelson, "The Savior's Four Gifts of Joy," *New Era*, December 2019.

. . . It was no use—my prayers felt hollow. A war had started in my soul, and I could no longer pray to a God of love with a heart full of hatred.

. . . One night I heard screaming not far from the house, and then a baby crying. The killers must have slain the mother and left her infant to die in the road. The child wailed all night; by morning, its cries were feeble and sporadic, and by nightfall, it was silent. I heard dogs snarling nearby and shivered as I thought about how that baby's life had ended. I prayed for God to receive the child's innocent soul, and then asked Him, *How can I forgive people who would do such a thing to an infant?*

I heard His answer as clearly as if we'd been sitting in the same room chatting: *You are all my children . . . and the baby is with Me now.*

It was such a simple sentence, but it was the answer to the prayers I'd been lost in for days.

The killers were like children. Yes, they were barbaric creatures who would have to be punished severely for their actions, but they were still children. They were cruel, vicious, and dangerous, as kids sometimes can be, but nevertheless, they were children. They saw, but didn't understand the terrible harm they'd inflicted. They'd blindly hurt others without thinking, they'd hurt their Tutsi brothers and sisters, they'd hurt God—and they didn't understand how badly they were hurting themselves. Their minds had been infected with the evil that had spread across the country, but their souls weren't evil. Despite their atrocities, they were children of God, and I could forgive a child, although it would not be easy . . . especially when that child was trying to kill me.

In God's eyes, the killers were part of His family, deserving of love and forgiveness. I knew that I couldn't ask God to love me if I were unwilling to love His children. At that moment, I prayed for the killers, for their sins to be forgiven.[3]

---

3. Immaculée Ilibagiza, *Left to Tell: Discovering God Amidst the Rwandan Holocaust*, (Carlsbad, California: Hay House Inc., 2006), 92–94.

Forgiving your enemy is a fundamental element of righteous leadership. The most amazing, profound, and beyond human comprehension is the tortuous suffering that the Savior endured to atone for our sins; yet He willingly forgives us.

General Moroni was not a blood thirsty warrior, rather he was a caring disciple of Jesus Christ who only fought to preserve his nation's religion, liberty, and homes. He did not seek revenge for the excessive number of Nephites who had been killed defending their religion and homeland (Alma 44:21). We read again from the account of this righteous leader's victory in the war against Zerahemnah:

> Now Moroni, when he saw their terror, commanded his men that they should stop shedding their blood. (Alma 43:54)

> Yea, and this is not all; I command you [Zerahemnah] by all the desires which ye have for life, that ye deliver up your weapons of war unto us, and we will seek not your blood, but we will spare your lives, if ye will go your way and come not again to war against us. (Alma 44:6)

Unfortunately for Zerahemnah and many of his warriors, the Lamanite king rejected Moroni's offer. The battle continued leaving many more dead without reason. Once again, Moroni attempted to forgive the Lamanites:

> Now Zerahemnah, when he saw that they were all about to be destroyed, cried mightily unto Moroni, promising that he would covenant and also his people with them, if they would spare the remainder of their lives, that they never would come to war again against them.

> And it came to pass that Moroni caused that the work of death should cease among the people. And he took the weapons of war from the Lamanites; and after they had entered into a covenant with him of peace they were suffered to depart into the wilderness. (Alma 44:19–20)

MERCY AND JUSTICE

As we can see from General Moroni's example, leading in righteousness requires both the mercy of forgiveness and the wisdom of applied justice. Peace, even if only temporary, will only be achieved by the application of both eternal principles. Law and order requires a firm hand:

> And now it came to pass that when they had taken all the robbers [Gadianton] prisoners, insomuch that none did escape who were not slain, they did cast their prisoners into prison, and did cause the word of God to be preached unto them; and as many as would repent of their sins and enter into a covenant that they would murder no more were set at liberty.
>
> But as many as there were who did not enter into a covenant, and who did still continue to have those secret murders in their hearts, yea, as many as were found breathing out threatenings against their brethren were condemned and punished according to the law.
>
> And thus they did put an end to all those wicked, and secret, and abominable combinations, in the which there was so much wickedness, and so many murders committed. (3 Nephi 5:4–6)

Mercy through forgiveness is the required commandment. However, if the enemy is like King Zerahemnah, who insisted on harming others, justice requires ending the enemy's efforts to harm others. From a young age, Hannibal was taught by his father to hate Rome and to do his all to destroy it. Before the battle of Zama, Hannibal asked for a meeting with Scipio Africanus to plead for a truce. However, the Roman General knew Hannibal's desire to ultimately destroy Rome. Scipio's reply was that he would end the war today—and he did. As a result, Carthage never threaten Rome again.

That said, the Lord has instructed us to forgive seven times seventy. Again, we can see this leadership trait in the humility and humanity of General Ulysses S. Grant. Matt Lively writes of the general who grieved over the death of his own soldiers:

When facing rival generals, Grant never underestimated his opponents or neglected to show them decent common courtesy and compassion. He offered very generous terms to the Confederates upon his capture of Vicksburg, not taking prisoners but allowing the enemy to merely return home. He said "I knew many of them were tired of the war and would get home just as soon as they could." Grant empathized with the enemy, who he never stopped considering his countrymen, throughout the war. He worked with General Lee through correspondence to ensure that both sides could peaceably retrieve their dead after combat. He took no prisoners at a Confederate hospital, noting that "after the battle . . . one is naturally disposed to do as much to alleviate the suffering of an enemy as a friend." He noticed and gave praise when his enemy was able, calling the Confederate General Johnston "very wise" after he was incompetently removed from his command. Most tellingly, Grant was remarkably humble and compassionate in his acceptance of General Lee's final surrender at Appomattox. He received General Lee in a small house. He was wearing ragged and dirty clothes compared to Lee's immaculate uniform. The two generals talked for a little while, and Grant remarked that he knew of Lee's capability and reputation from the Mexican-American War, and that he was sure Lee did not remember him, as he himself didn't do anything to deserve notice. Grant ordered that Lee's men be given large amounts of rations, and that they were to keep most of their personal belongings. Finally, he ordered the Union forces stationed about the town not to cheer upon hearing the news of the surrender. It was not an occasion for celebration, but reconciliation. Grant remarked that he was "depressed" during the surrender, empathizing with the enemy that he never dehumanized or belittled. At the root of all of these actions and attitudes towards the enemy laid Grant's deep-rooted humility. He never placed him above others, even those he fought against. It allowed him to learn, it allowed him to win, and it allowed him to provide an example of human decency that has rarely been matched in history. We should strive to embody his example in our daily lives.[4]

When General Grant became president of the United States, he tried to follow the advice of his mentor Abraham Lincoln who wrote, "Do I not destroy my enemies when I make them my friends?"

TURNING LEMONS INTO LEMONADE

While in the midst of hell, one can still remain righteous and continue to build the Lord's kingdom. What might seem a hopeless situation can still offer faith and salvation to others. Captain Whaley, like many other faithful Latter-day Saints in the Vietnam War, were true heroes in Christ. Richard relates:

There was a young man that I was teaching the Missionary Discussions to who was under charges to be kicked out of the Army on drugs. He was a good guy, got off the drugs and I baptized him in the South China Sea. That was a unique experience: blue ocean, white sands, barbed wire and machine guns behind us on the beach and the two of us dressed in white participating in a Gospel Ordinance. It was quite a juxtaposition of all that is good against all that is evil.

He was discharged from the Army even though I intervened but couldn't stop the process as it was too far along and he got an Administrative Discharge. Later, he wrote me from England and in the same mission I had served in: British South. That was a success story.

Attending Church was the highlight of the week for us guys. We always arranged for some sort of meal: steak, chicken, etc. after the service—anything to create a sense of brotherhood and maintaining commitment. Sometimes we were able to drive over to the DaNang Air Base and see a

---

4. Matt Lively, "To Lead, Be Humble—Ulysses S. Grant," *Medium: Start it up,* 19 August 2019, https://medium.com/swlh/to-lead-be-humble-ulysses-s-grant-b3374233a99f#:~:text=Grant%20was%20always%20humble.,and%20won%20the%20Civil%20War, accessed 19 June 2020.

movie (the Air Force always lives good!) I know that some would criticize us for doing that on the Sabbath, but it was the only time we could relax and we figured it was a worthwhile event.

We had a great home teaching program that was rather unique: we were each assigned only one person, and he was assigned to us. Our goal was to meet each other daily for prayer and a time of socializing. That was really good home teaching and it sure worked. I got closer to Frank than anyone I could think of. Frank was inactive when he came to Vietnam but fortunately, he found our branch and got involved. After Vietnam, he and his wife were sealed in the Ogden Temple and I was there with him.

Towards the end of my tour, I was called to be the District Mission President. That kept me busy. We had a lot of missionary work going on both within the military as well as with the Vietnamese. We had two Vietnamese Sisters attending with us for a while; I don't know what happened to them. My last month in country, we had 30 baptisms so I guess we were doing something worthwhile.[5]

Dark and violent days are sure to come. Wars will prevail, families will be divided, hearts will break, and towns and homes destroyed. Jeffrey R. Holland writes:

Sometimes the events of life can damage our highest hopes and dreams. Some of our sweetest possessions and most cherished ideals end up being bruised, and sometimes they are broken. In the world of items we treasure we may break a lovely piece of china or a pocket watch handed down from an ancestor. Sometimes even bones break, and even more painfully, marriages or family ties are broken. In severed circumstances we truly feel "like a broken vessel"; we are certain that, as with Humpty Dumpty, all the king's horses and all the king's men will never be able to put us together again.

5. Richard, Whaley, "Vietnam Experiences 1971–1972, " email to author, May 29, 2020.

But someone wrote once that God apparently loves—and turns to our benefit—broken things. It takes broken clouds to nourish the earth, it takes broken earth to grow grain, it takes broken grain to make bread, it takes broken bread to nourish us, and so are the cycles of life. This divine sequence is akin to the Savior's parable that no kernel of corn can grow to fruition until it is first thrown away and in effect, lost in the earth before its bounty can come back to us.[6]

FOLLOW THE LEADERSHIP OF THE PROPHET AND APOSTLES

In the Lord's "preface to the doctrine, covenants, and command-ments given in this dispensation" (D&C 1 heading), He states:

And the arm of the Lord shall be revealed; and the day cometh that they who will not hear the voice of the Lord, neither the voice of his servants, neither give heed to the words of the prophets and apostles, shall be cut off from among the people;

For they have strayed from mine ordinances, and have broken mine everlasting covenant. (D&C 1:14–15)

The message of listening to and following the guidance from the Lord's anointed prophets and apostles is an eternal command-ment and a sure way for leaders to keep their followers safe. Still some people seem to causally brush off this commandment as witnessed by apostate nut jobs who think we should listen to their counsel. Again, the Lord's warning is not new to this dispensation and remains vitally important for anyone seeking safety and salvation in the last days. The Apostle Paul gave the Ephesians the same counsel:

For through him we both have access by one Spirit unto the Father.

Now therefore ye are no more strangers and foreigners, but fellowcitizens with the saints, and of the household of God;

---

6. Jeffrey R. Holland, *For Times of Trouble* (Salt Lake City: Deseret Book, 2012), 69–70.

And are built upon the foundation of the apostles and prophets, Jesus Christ himself being the chief corner stone;

In whom all the building fitly framed together *groweth* unto an holy temple in the Lord. (Ephesians 2:18–21, emphasis added)

Rejecting the guidance of the Lord's prophets and apostles is the worst thing a leader could do if they intend to survive the last days and to earn eternal life. Nephite dissenters were more often than not the reason the Lamanites rose up against the Nephites, which caused bloodshed and destruction to both civilizations. In turn, the dissenters themselves were usually killed.

You might feel at times justified in disagreeing with a position of a Church leader on a certain issue, judging his or her motives without knowledge of them. But true safety comes from obeying and sustaining our Church leaders whether or not we fully agree with their counsel or we believe we have observed their personal weaknesses. Elder Jeffrey R. Holland teaches:

> We have anointed prophets, apostles, and leaders in our day. They have never claimed to be perfect, as indeed only one human being in all of history has been. But imperfect as they are, they represent the One who *was* perfect—a staggering responsibility indeed. Trying to be the best they can be, these leaders have been called to perform certain functions and carry out certain duties in the name of God. No one is more conscious of that responsibility than these priesthood bearers themselves. No one feels the weight of it more, no one is more mindful of his limitations, no one worries more that however good he is, he needs to be even better. We who observe them know this and love them for their service. We see so few limitations. And while we strive to sustain them, to join in holding them up in their service, we also can at the very least not harm them, not detract or decry or destroy them in word or in deed.[7]

---

7. Jeffrey R. Holland, *For Times of Trouble* (Salt Lake City: Deseret Book, 2012), 117–118.

Good leadership starts with good fellowship. From my mission journal, I provide a personal example of the need to follow the counsel of our leaders. One evening, a former branch president in Cusco, Peru came to visit my companion and I. We loved this young pioneer of the Church in Cusco. Indeed, everyone we knew, members and non-members alike admired this young man. Unfortunately, the member had become less active. For over an hour the former branch president begged us to loan him the small amount he needed to buy a plane ticket to Lima for a job interview. He explained that he had already been promised the job, but only needed to have a final interview before starting. He assured us that it was a guaranteed job from a European government. He pleaded with us that the job would help him get back on his feet and back in the Church. Christian-like justification for loaning him the money, as well as his promise to repay the money in a week, tempted us to give him the money he needed. Still, we had to explain to him that we could not loan him the money because it was against mission rules. I recorded in my mission journal the next day:

August 10, 1970

This afternoon we were giving a missionary discussion in an apartment building with a view toward the southern end of the Cusco valley. During the discussion we noticed a Lanza Airplane making a very low ascent out of the valley as it took off from the Cusco Airport. We finished the discussion and as we left we noticed a large cloud of black smoke coming from the southern end of the valley. We went to the Church for the Branch President's meeting where we were told that the smoke we saw was from the crash of the Lanza airliner. Worse of all, the inactive ex-branch president was on the plane. We went to the city officials to check the list of passengers. All 99 had died, including our friend. My memory of him is that he was once an amazing example of a Nephi-like member – handsome, strong and tall, and with a strong testimony. I believe the Lord took him before he could slip further into inactivity.

August 11, 1970

We were asked by the family to try to identify the body of the former branch president. The plane had crashed just minutes after take-off and was full of jet fuel. 48 of the passengers on the plane were high school students from the United States – beautiful young boys and girls, some of whom we had chatted with on the streets of Cusco. Because of the fire, when we got to the site of the wreckage the scene was far worse than any horror movie. The bodies were burned out and the skeletons distorted, most arms and legs were missing, the chest cavity remaining as only charred ribs, and the faces with mouths wide open as if screaming to the very end. The bodies were impossible to identify. We were told that many of the bodies had already been taken to a temporary morgue at a school. We went to the school and saw many more bodies chard beyond recognition. We found the former branch president's cousin there who told us that his body was identified and taken away. He said that the former branch president's body was in perfect condition except for a cut in his forehead. He related an inspiring story. A farmer had been working in the field where the plane crashed, and that to his amazement, a tall and handsome man, walked out of the wreckage apparently going for help. The farmer said that then there was an explosion and a large fireball consumed the entire plane. The man who walked from the wreckage then turned around and said, "My brothers and sisters, I am coming to help you." It was the former branch president who hearing the cries for help walked into the fireball, another explosion occurred and he was struck by a piece of metal and died. Thus his body was not burned and he died performing an act of charity. That was the true nature of the former branch president.

Decades later, I still remember the images of the victims of the plane crash and wonder how I would have felt all these years if I had disobeyed the mission rules and had been the one who gave the former Branch President the money he needed to board the doomed flight.

My faith in our living prophets has been confirmed over and over again. I was living in Switzerland and doing business in Germany when the Iron Curtain came down and the Eastern Block of nations were opened for missionary work. At the time, I could not begin to have envisioned the fall of communism in those countries. The sudden end to communism in Eastern Europe humbled me and made me recall the prophetic words of President Spencer W. Kimball just a few years before the Iron Curtain fell, "Our brothers and sisters in Russia must hear the gospel; and if we are attentive and prayerful, the Lord will open the way."[8] Many years later I witnessed again the divine guidance and promises the Lord can bestow upon us through the president of the Church. In 2018 while living in Saudi Arabia, the members there were instructed that the Church wanted the members living on the Arabian Peninsula to pray for a temple to be built in the land. The very notion seemed impossible at the time. Two years later President Russell M. Nelson announced that the government of the United Arabia Emirates invited the Church to build a temple in Dubai, the first in Muslim Arabia.[9]

General Moroni was given the command of the Nephite armies when he was only twenty-five years old (Alma 43:17). Though very young, he showed wisdom in one of the first actions he took. When the Lamanite armies retreated into the wilderness:

> . . . Moroni, also, knowing of the prophecies of Alma, sent certain men unto him, desiring him that he should inquire of the Lord whither the armies of the Nephites should go to defend themselves against the Lamanites.
>
> And it came to pass that the word of the Lord came unto Alma, and Alma informed the messengers of Moroni, that the armies of the Lamanites were marching round about in the wilderness, that they might come over into the land of Manti . . . (Alma 43:23–24)

---

8. Spencer W. Kimball, address at the Regional Representatives seminar, 29 September 1978.
9. Russell M. Nelson, "Go Forward in Faith," April 2020 general conference.

Moroni's reliance on the prophet resulted in a victory for the Nephite army. Today, our prophets and apostles are constantly counseling us on where the armies of Satan are attacking us. General conference talks are rich in warnings that can lead us and our families to victory over the forces of the adversary.

As a sure leadership principle, commit today to follow our Church leaders regardless of your knowledge or lack thereof as to why they ask us to do something. You might not agree with the idea, but it just might save you and your family from being cast out in this world and more importantly in the world to come. Dissenters from the Church commonly rationalize their behavior by criticizing one or more members of the First Presidency or the Quorum of the Twelve Apostles, who are all prophets representing the Savior. When the Lord appeared in the Americas, His message could not have been clearer:

> Wo, wo, wo unto this people; wo unto the inhabitants of the whole earth except they shall repent; for the devil laugheth, and his angels rejoice, because of the slain of the fair sons and daughters of my people; and it is because of their iniquity and abominations that they are fallen! (3 Nephi 9:2)

> And it was the more righteous part of the people who were saved, and *it was they who received the prophets* and stoned them not; and it was they who had not the blood of the saints, who were spared— (3 Nephi 10:12, emphasis added)

No one is perfect, not even for a short season. To enjoy the supreme gift of the Atonement, leaders must be on guard and consistently repent when they stumble. Even the great prophet of the last dispensation, Joseph Smith, Jr. was warned:

> Verily, I say unto my servant Joseph Smith, Jun., or in other words, I will call you friends, for you are my friends, and ye shall have an inheritance with me—
>
> I call you servants for the world's sake, and ye are their servants for my sake—

And now, verily I say unto Joseph Smith, Jun.—You have not kept the commandments, and must needs stand rebuked before the Lord;

Your family must needs repent and forsake some things, and give more earnest heed unto your sayings, or be removed out of their place. (D&C 93:45-48)

While perilous times are coming our way, if leaders repent and have faith in the Lord, their families will not be removed out of their place. Why? The answer is simple; we have the most loving and powerful ally, even the Lord Jesus Christ. He is our ultimate leader and guide through troubled waters. Through the commandments he gives us through his prophets and apostles, we will be safe.

> *"When the Lord commands, do it."*
>
> *—Joseph Smith's motto*[10]

---

10. *Teachings of Presidents of the Church: Joseph Smith*, (Salt Lake City: The Church of Jesus Christ of Latter-day Saints, 2007), 160.

Nevertheless, the Lord God showeth us our weakness that we may know that it is by his grace, and his great condescensions unto the children of men, that we have power to do these things.

—Jacob 4:7

Conclusion

Despite the heartbreak and bloodshed surrounding you in the Great Tribulation, continue to love and serve the Lord with all your heart, might, mind, and strength (D&C 4:2). Let us collectively follow the Lord's anointed prophet and apostles, and let God prevail. Together and individually, we can "Hear Him" who has already atoned for us. President Russell M. Nelson has asked the world.

The Book of Mormon chronicles the classic rise and fall of two major civilizations. Their history demonstrates how easy it is for a majority of the people to forget God, reject warnings of the Lord's prophets, and seek power, popularity, and pleasures of the flesh. Repeatedly, past prophets have declared "great and marvelous things unto the people, which they did not believe."

It is no different in our day. Through the years, great and marvelous things have been heard from dedicated pulpits across the earth. Yet most people do not embrace these truths—either because they do not know where to look for them or because they are listening to those who do not have the whole truth or because they have rejected truth in favor of worldly pursuits.

The adversary is clever. For millennia he has been making good look evil and evil look good. His messages tend to be loud, bold, and boastful.

However, messages from our Heavenly Father are strikingly different. He communicates simply, quietly, and with such stunning plainness that we cannot misunderstand Him.

For example, whenever He has introduced His Only Begotten Son to mortals upon the earth, He has done so with remarkably few words. On the Mount of Transfiguration to Peter, James, and John, God said, "This is my beloved Son: hear him." His words to the Nephites in ancient Bountiful were "Behold my Beloved Son, in whom I am well pleased, in whom I have glorified my name—hear ye him." And to Joseph Smith, in that profound declaration that opened this dispensation, God simply said, "*This is My Beloved Son. Hear Him!*"

Now, my dear brothers and sisters, consider the fact that in these three instances just mentioned, just before the Father introduced the Son, the people involved were in a state of fear and, to some degree, desperation.

The Apostles were afraid when they saw Jesus Christ encircled by a cloud on the Mount of Transfiguration.

The Nephites were afraid because they had been through destruction and darkness for several days.

Joseph Smith was in the grips of a force of darkness just before the heavens opened.

Our Father knows that when we are surrounded by uncertainty and fear, what will help us the very most is to hear His Son.

Because when we seek to hear—truly hear—His Son, we will be guided to know what to do in any circumstance.[1]

Leaders in the dark years ahead must need to remember that the Lord, Jesus Christ, will comfort us, shield us, and guide us through

---

1. Russell M. Nelson, "Hear Him," April 2020 general conference.

any situation we might encounter. First and foremost, leaders must be humble children of God and listen to their Father and his Beloved Son. President Nelson has warned:

> Of the time prior to His Second Coming, the Savior predicted days of great tribulation. He said, "There shall be famines, and pestilences, and earthquakes, in divers places" (Joseph Smith—Matthew 1:29).
>
> Compounding such tribulation is the increasing darkness and deception that surround us. As Jesus told His disciples, "Iniquity shall abound" before His return (Joseph Smith—Matthew 1:30).
>
> Satan has marshaled his forces and is raging against the work of the Lord and those of us engaged in it. Because of the increasing dangers we face, our need for divine guidance has never been greater, and our effort to hear the voice of Jesus Christ—our Mediator, Savior, and Redeemer—have never been more urgent.[2]

Leaders should take comfort in the scriptures, realizing that the Lord has already provided us with a divine library full of wisdom and truth, such as, Messianic Psalm 91:

> . . . He is my refuge and my fortress: my God; in him will I trust.
>
> Surely he shall deliver thee from the snare of the fowler, and from the noisome pestilence.
>
> He shall cover thee with his feathers, and under his wings shall thou trust: his truth shall be thy shield and buckler.
>
> Thou shalt not be afraid for the terror by night; nor for the arrow that flieth by day;
>
> Nor for the pestilence that walketh in darkness; nor for the destruction that wasteth at noonday.
>
> A thousand shall fall at thy side, and ten thousand at thy right hand; but it shall not come nigh thee.

---

2. Russel M. Nelson, "Grow into the Principle of Revelation," *Liahona*, January 2020, 8.

Only with thine eyes shalt thou behold and see the reward of the wicked.

Because thou hast made the Lord, which is my refuge, even the most High, thy habitation;

There shall no evil befall thee, neither shall any plague come nigh thy dwelling.

For he shall give his angels charge over thee, to keep thee in all thy ways.

They shall bear thee up in their hands, lest thou dash thy foot against a stone.

Thou shalt tread upon the lion and adder: the young lion and the dragon shalt thou trample under feet.

Because he hath set his love upon me, therefore will I deliver him: I will set him on high, because he hath known my name.

He shall call upon me, and I will answer him: I will be with him in trouble; I will deliver him, and honour him.

With long life will I satisfy him, and shew him my salvation.

During the week I finished this book, I received an email from the First Presidency of the Church of Jesus Christ of Latter-day Saints that started with these words: "Dear Brothers and Sisters: We find ourselves fighting a war against the ravages of COVID-19 and its variants, an unrelenting pandemic."

In the same week, the United States withdrew its forces from Afghanistan after a twenty-year military intervention, instigating the overrunning of the entire nation by Taliban Islamic terrorist in less than a week; causing tens of thousands of innocent people to try to flee for their lives; and allowing Al Qaeda terrorists to reestablish its home base. As I look out my window instead of seeing the blue skies of Utah, I see a dark red sunset fueled by an out-of-control fire in California that has already burned more than a half million acres of land. The western states are in a hundred-year drought while the eastern states are experiencing hundred-year floods. The US National Debt Clock reads US$28.64 trillion dollars while government spending continues to rampage causing the US dollars to fall against even third world currencies. Three volcanos are simultaneously erupting in Alaska, adding toxic gases into a climate that is already been the hottest year ever recorded. A 7.2 magnitude earthquake struck Haiti. Food, gasoline, electronic chips, and even school supplies are experiencing shortages. Police are quitting their jobs in record number. Yes, all this is taking place in just one week!

Certainly, life does not feel the same as it did just eighteen months ago. In reality, it is not the same, nor will it be the same ever again. Whether we like it or not, we need to prepare our families and communities temporally, emotionally, and spiritually for the even harder times that are rapidly approaching. Fortunately, we need not fear, for we are blessed to have the true gospel of Jesus Christ to guide and assure us. We also have the eight leadership principles explored in this book to give us the leadership competencies we will need to save our families and communities. My final advice is to listen carefully to the Lord's prophet and apostles and to lead others in righteousness by living all the commandments. Either you follow the law or there will be no place where the law is followed (D&C 88:35).

May we always remember that regardless of how bad circumstances may appear, our Lord and Savior is always in command. He is our ultimate leader role model. He is the light "which shinneth, which giveth you light, is through him who enlighteneth your eyes, which is the same light that quickenth your understanding. The light which is in all things, which giveth life to all things, which is the law by which all things are governed, even the power of God who sitteth upon his throne, who is in the bosom of eternity, who is in the midst of all things" (D&C 88:13).

Notes

Notes

Notes

Notes

Notes

About the Author

FOR TWENTY-SEVEN YEARS, GEORGE POTTER WAS A FULL-TIME executive leadership consultant for one of the largest companies in the world. Prior to his consultancy, he held the positions of senior vice president, vice president for finance, and managing director for a multinational corporation. He has lectured in leadership and management at universities in the United States, Canada, Europe, and the Middle East.

George received a bachelor's degree with high honors from the University of California–San Diego and an MBA from the University of California–Berkeley. He also completed doctoral studies (abd) at Nova Southwest University before being assigned to offices in Zurich, Switzerland.

Besides his upbringing in the United States, George has lived in Bolivia, Peru, Spain, Switzerland, and Saudi Arabia. He has traveled to over seventy countries. He served a mission in Peru and now serves as a ward mission leader. He is retired and lives with his wife in Utah.

George Potter's career has allowed him the opportunity to explore Book of Mormon lands. His discoveries can only be described as groundbreaking and remarkable. Like no one before, he has thoroughly documented the historicity of the Book of Mormon. His books on his discoveries include *Lehi's Trail, Nephi in the Promised Land, The Voyages of the Book of Mormon,* and *Discovering the Amazing Jaredites.* He has produced thirteen films on Book of Mormon archaeology that provide even more documented evidence that the Book of Mormon is true history.

You've dreamed of accomplishing your publishing goal for ages—holding *that* book in your hands. We want to partner with you in bringing this dream to light.

Whether you're an aspiring author looking to publish your first book or a seasoned author who's been published before, we want to hear from you. Please submit your manuscript to

CEDARFORT.SUBMITTABLE.COM/SUBMIT

CEDAR FORT HAS PUBLISHED BOOKS IN THE FOLLOWING GENRES

- LDS Nonfiction
- Fiction
- Juvenile & YA
- Biographies
- Regency Romances
- Cozy Mysteries
- General Nonfiction
- Cookbooks
- Children's Books
- Self-Help
- Comic & Activity books

- Children's books with customizable character illustrations